ZEN BUDDHISM

ZEN BUDDHISM

Selected Writings of D. T. Suzuki

EDITED BY WILLIAM BARRETT

IMAGE BOOKS
DOUBLEDAY
New York   London   Toronto   Sydney   Auckland

AN IMAGE BOOK
PUBLISHED BY DOUBLEDAY
a division of Bantam Doubleday Dell Publishing Group, Inc.
1540 Broadway, New York, New York 10036

IMAGE, DOUBLEDAY, and the portrayal of a deer drinking
from a stream are trademarks of Doubleday,
a division of Bantam Doubleday Dell Publishing Group, Inc.

Originally published by Anchor Books in 1956.
This Image Edition published August 1996.
The selections from the following books by D. T. Suzuki are reprinted
here by arrangement with Rider & Co., London: *Essays in Zen Buddhism,
First Series* (1949); *The Zen Doctrine of No-Mind* (1949); *Essays in Zen
Buddhism, Second Series* (1950); *Essays in Zen Buddhism, Third Series*
(1953); and *Studies in Zen* (1955). *Studies in Zen* is published in the United
States by Philosophical Library.

Library of Congress Catalog Number 56-9406
ISBN 0-385-48349-x
Copyright © 1956 by William Barrett
All Rights Reserved.
Printed in the United States of America

3   5   7   9   10   8   6   4   2

Contents

Zen[1] for the West

I

Zen Buddhism presents a surface so bizarre and irrational, yet so colorful and striking, that some Westerners who approach it for the first time fail to make sense of it, while others, attracted by this surface, take it up in a purely frivolous and superficial spirit. Either response would be unfortunate. The fact is that Zen, as Dr. Suzuki demonstrates, is an essential expression of Buddhism, and Buddhism is one of the most tremendous spiritual achievements in human history—an achievement which we Westerners probably have not yet fully grasped. We have to remember how recent it is that we have sought out any knowledge of the East. Only a century separates us from Schopenhauer, the first Western philosopher who attempted a sympathetic interpretation of Buddhism, a brilliant and sensational misunderstanding on the basis of meagre translations. Since then great strides have been made in Oriental studies, but a curiously paradoxical provincialism still haunts the West: the civilization which has battered its way into every corner of the globe has been very tardy in examining its own prejudices by the wisdom of the non-Western peoples. Even today when the slogan "One World!" is an incessant

[1] Zen from Japanese *zazen*, to sit and meditate, a translation of the Chinese *ch'an*, which in turn was the translation of the Indian *Dhyana* (meditation). Thus Zen begins as a particular sect of Buddhism, an essentially meditative one, but in its development it radically transforms the traditional Buddhist discipline of meditation: the dualism between meditation and activity is abolished. For this, see Suzuki, particularly in Chapter 7. For a detailed account of the origin and development of Zen Buddhism and its difference from other forms of Buddhism, see Chapters 2 and 3.

theme of Sunday journalism and television, we tend to interpret it in a purely Western sense to mean merely that the whole planet is now bound together in the net of modern technology and communications. That the phrase may imply a necessity for coming to terms with our Eastern opposite and brother, seems to pass publicly unnoticed. There are many signs, however, that this tide must turn.

I consider it a great stroke of personal good fortune to have stumbled (and quite by chance) upon the writings of D. T. Suzuki years ago. I emphasize the word "personal" here because I am not a professional Orientalist and my interest in Suzuki's writings has been what it is simply because these writings shed light upon problems in my own life—one proof that Zen does have a much needed message for Westerners. There are now a good many books available on Buddhism, but what makes Suzuki unique—and unique not only among writers on Buddhism but among contemporary religious writers generally—is that he starts from the assumption that Buddhism is a living thing that began some 2500 years ago with Gotama's experience of enlightenment, has been developing ever since, and is still alive and growing. Hence the extraordinary freshness and vitality of his writings, so that if you go on from them to other books on Buddhism you will find that these latter take on a life from him that they themselves would never have initially for the Westerner. Suzuki has steeped himself thoroughly in Chinese Buddhism, and the practical and concrete Chinese spirit probably provides an introduction to Buddhism more congenial to the Westerner than the soaring metaphysical imagination of the Indians. One picture is worth a thousand words, as the old Chinese saying has it, and this Chinese genius for the concrete may never have been better realized than in the anecdotes, paradoxes, poems of the Zen masters. Westerners usually think that the religious and philosophic thought of China is summed up in the two names of Lao-tsu and Confucius; Suzuki shows us that some of the great figures of Chinese Buddhism were at least the equal of these two. And if his writings did nothing else, they would still be important for giving us knowledge of this great chapter of

Buddhist history that had been virtually unknown to us hitherto.

But do these ancient Oriental masters have anything to say to us who belong to the present-day West? Very much so, I think; and the reason is that we Westerners have only recently come to face certain realities of life with which the Oriental has been living for centuries. This is a large claim, and requires some itemized documentation.

What we call the Western tradition is formed by two major influences, Hebraic and Greek, and both these influences are profoundly dualistic in spirit. That is, they divide reality into two parts and set one part off against the other. The Hebrew makes his division on religious and moral grounds: God absolutely transcends the world, is absolutely separate from it; hence there follow the dualisms of God and creature, the Law and the erring members, spirit and flesh. The Greek, on the other hand, divides reality along intellectual lines. Plato, who virtually founded Western philosophy single-handed—Whitehead has remarked that 2500 years of Western philosophy is but a series of footnotes to Plato—absolutely cleaves reality into the world of the intellect and the world of the senses. The great achievement of the Greeks was to define the ideal of rationality for man; but in doing so, Plato and Aristotle not only made reason the highest and most valued function, they also went so far as to make it the very center of our personal identity. The Orientals never succumbed to this latter error; favoring intuition over reason, they grasped intuitively a center of the personality which held in unity the warring opposites of reason and unreason, intellect and senses, morality and nature. So far as we are Westerners, we inherit these dualisms, they are part of us: an irrationally nagging conscience from the Hebrews, an excessively dividing rational mind from the Greeks. Yet the experience of modern culture, in the most diverse fields, makes them less and less acceptable.

Medieval Christianity still lives in the rational world of the Greeks. The universe of St. Thomas Aquinas is the same bandbox universe of Aristotle, a tight tiny tidy rational whole, where all is in apple-pie order, and everything occupies its logical and meaningful place in the absolute hierarchy of Being. When we turn from such humanized universes to Indian thought, we are at first staggered by the vision of vast spaces, endless aeons of time, universe upon universe, against which man looks very small and meaningless; then we realize these are the spaces and times of modern astronomy, and the Indian idea is therefore closer to us. The distinguished Protestant theologian Paul Tillich has described the essential experience of modern man as an encounter with "meaninglessness": lost in the vastness of the universe, man begins to think that his own existence and that of the universe are "meaningless". The God of Theism, says Tillich echoing Nietzsche, is dead, and Western man must find a God beyond the God of Theism: the God offered us by rational theology is no longer acceptable. From the point of view of the medieval Catholic (and many still survive) the very premises of Buddhist thinking would look "meaningless"; they are also more difficult and grim, but they look much closer to what we moderns may have to swallow.

In science itself, modern developments have combined to make our inherited rationalism more shaky. Physics and mathematics, the two most advanced of Western sciences, have in our time become paradoxical: that is, arrived at the state where they breed paradoxes for reason itself. One hundred fifty years ago the philosopher Kant attempted to show that there were ineluctable limits to reason, but the Western mind, positivistic to the core, could be expected to take such a conclusion seriously only when it showed up in science itself. Well, science in this century has at last caught up with Kant: almost simultaneously Heisenberg in physics, and Godel in mathematics, have shown ineluctable limits to human reason. Heisenberg's Principle of Indeterminacy shows essential limits to our ability to know and predict physical states of affairs, and opens up to us the glimpse of a nature irrational and chaotic at bottom. Godel's results would seem to have even more far-reaching consequences when one reflects that in the Western tradition, from the Pythagoreans and Plato onward, mathematics has inspired the most absolute claims of rationalism. Now it turns out that even in his most precise science—in the province where his reason had seemed omnipotent—man cannot escape his essential finitude: every system of mathematics that he constructs is doomed to incompleteness. Mathematics is like a ship in mid-ocean that has sprung leaks (paradoxes) which have been temporarily plugged, but our reason can never guarantee that the ship will not spring other leaks. That this human insecurity should manifest itself in what had hitherto been the very citadel of reason, mathematics, marks a new turn in Western thinking. The next step would be to recognize the essentially paradoxical nature of reason itself.

This step has been taken by some modern philosophers. The most original and influential philosopher now alive on the European continent is the German Existentialist Martin Heidegger. A German friend of Heidegger told me that one day when he visited Heidegger he found him reading one of Suzuki's books; "If I understand this man correctly," Heidegger remarked, "this is what I have been trying to say in all my writings." This remark may be the slightly exaggerated enthusiasm of a man under the impact of a book in which he recognizes some of his own thoughts; certainly Heidegger's philosophy in its tone and temper and sources is Western to its core, and there is much in him that is not in Zen, but also very much more in Zen that is not in Heidegger; and yet the points of correspondence between the two, despite their disparate sources, are startling enough. For what, after all, is Heidegger's final message but that Western philosophy is a great error, the result of the dichotomizing intellect that has cut man off from unity with Being itself and from his own Being. This error begins (in Plato) with locating truth in the intellect; the world of nature thereby becomes a realm of objects set over against the mind, eventually objects to be manipulated by scientific and practical calculation. Twenty-five hundred years of Western metaphysics move from Plato's intellectualism to Nietzsche's Will to Power, and concurrently man does become in fact the technological master of the whole planet; but the conquest of nature merely estranges him from Being itself and from his own Being and delivers him over to an ever ascending, ever more frantic will to power. "Divide and conquer" might thus be said to be the motto which Western man has adopted toward Being itself; but this of course is the counsel of power not of wisdom. Heidegger repeatedly tells us that this tradition of the West has come to the end of its cycle; and as he says this, one can only gather that he himself has already stepped beyond that tradition. Into the tradition of the Orient? I should say at least that he has come pretty close to Zen.

If these happenings in science and philosophy indicate changed ways of thinking in the West, our modern art would seem to indicate very new ways of feeling. Whatever may be said on the thorny subject of modern art, the one fact that is clear is that to the artistic conservative it represents a scandal and a break with the tradition. Our modern art presents a surface so irrational, bizarre, and shocking that it must be considered a break with the older more rational canons of Western art. That Western painters and sculptors in this century have gone outside their tradition to nourish themselves with the art of the rest of the world—Oriental, African, Melanesian—signifies that what we knew as *the* tradition is no longer able to nourish its most creative members; its confining mould has broken, under pressures from within. Our painting has detached itself from three-dimensional space, the arena of Western man's power and mobility; detached itself from the object, the supreme fixation of Western man's extroversion; and it has become subjective, contrary to the whole tenor of our Western life. Is all this merely malaise and revolt, or prophecy of a different spirit to come? In the past, new styles in painting have often been thus prophetic. In the art of literature, of course, the writer can be vocal about the new and revolutionary thing, and we find a novelist like D. H. Lawrence preaching against the bloodless rationalism of his culture. Lawrence urged the necessity of something he called "mindlessness", of becoming "mindless", if the meddlesome and self-conscious intellect were not in the end to cut off Western man irreparably from nature and even the possibility of real sexual union. Oddly enough, this "mindlessness" of Lawrence is a groping intuition after the doctrine of "no-mind" which Zen Buddhism had elaborated a thousand years before. (See Chapter 7.) Unlike Lawrence, however, the Zen masters developed this doctrine without falling into primitivism and the worship of the blood. In Lawrence's behalf it must be remembered that his culture gave him no help at all on these matters, and he had to grope in the dark pretty much on his own. And to change to one final literary example that involves no preaching or thesis whatsoever: the most considerable work of prose in English in this century is probably James Joyce's *Ulysses,* and this is so profoundly Oriental a book that the psychologist C. G. Jung recommended it as a long-needed bible for the white-skinned peoples. Joyce shattered the aesthetic of the Georgians that would divide reality into a compartment of the Beautiful forever separate from the opposite compartments of the Ugly or Sordid. *Ulysses,* like the Oriental mind, succeeds in holding the opposites together: light and dark, beautiful and ugly, sublime and banal. The spiritual premise of this work is an acceptance of life that no dualism—whether puritanical or aesthetic—could ever possibly embrace.

Admittedly, all these happenings I have cited—from science, philosophy, art—make up a very selective list; this list could be expanded greatly; nevertheless even as it stands, these instances make up a body of "coincidence" so formidable that they must make us pause. When events run parallel this way, when they occur so densely together in time and in such diverse fields, they can no longer be considered as mere meaningless "coincidence" but as very meaningful symptoms; in this case symptoms that the West in its own depths begins to experience new things, begins in fact to experience its own opposite. In this new climate a concern with something like Zen Buddhism can no longer be taxed as idle exoticism, for it has to do with the practical daily bread of the spirit.

The really somber paradox about all these changes is that they have happened in the deep and high parts of our culture, while in the areas in between everything goes on as usual. Despite the discoveries of its artists, philosophers, theoretical scientists, the West, in its public and external life at any rate, is just as Western as ever, if not more so. Gadgets and traffic accumulate, the American way of life (or else the Russian) spreads all over the globe, the techniques for externalizing life become year by year more slick and clever. All of which may only show what a creature of contradictions Western man has become. And now that at last his technology has put in his hands the hydrogen bomb, this fragmented creature has the power to blow himself and his planet to bits. Plain common sense would seem to advise that he turn to look inward a little.

II

None of the above considerations has to do with Zen itself. Or rather—to put it abruptly as Zen likes to do—Zen has nothing at all to do with them. They deal with the complicated abstractions of the intellect—philosophy, culture, science, and the rest—and what Zen seeks above all is the concrete and the simple that lie beyond the snarled tangles of intellectualization. Zen *is* the concrete itself. Zen eschews abstractions, or uses them only to get beyond them. Even when Zen declares against abstractions, it has to put the matter concretely: thus when the great Master Tokusan has his enlightenment, he does not merely say in pallid fashion that concepts are not enough; no, he burns all his philosophic texts, declaring, "All our understanding of the abstractions of philosophy is like a single hair in the vastness of space." Let the Western reader fasten upon this image and he will find it harder to miss the point. Or when another Master remarks on the difficulty of solving one of the Zen questions—which is equivalent to answering the riddle of existence itself—he does not merely say that it is difficult or so very very difficult that it is well-nigh impossible, but this: "It is like a mosquito trying to bite into an iron bull." The image lives because the image suggests the meaning beyond conceptualization.

Now it is just this concreteness of expression, this extraordinary profusion of images and examples, that can make Zen most helpful to the Westerner, who in fact derives from a more highly abstract culture. But it would be a mistake for the Western reader to imagine that these are merely so many literary devices or adornments adopted by the Zen masters. On the contrary, the language of Zen is of the essence, the manner of expression is one with the matter. Zen expresses itself concretely because Zen is above all interested in facts not theories, in realities and not those pallid counters for reality which we know as concepts. "Fact" may suggest to the Western mind something merely quantitative or statistical—therefore also a lifeless and abstract thing. Zen wants, rather, the facts as living and concrete. In this sense, Zen might be described as Radical Intuitionism—if the Westerner wishes a handle by which to lay hold of it. This does not mean that it is merely a philosophy of intuition like Bergson's, though it agrees with Bergson that the conceptualizing intellect does not reach reality; rather, it is radical intuition in the act itself. Radical Intuitionism means that Zen holds that thinking and sensing live, move, and have their being within the vital medium of intuition. We see with the two eyes only insofar as we are also seeing (though we may not know it) with the third eye—the eye of intuition. Hence, any sensory facts will do for Zen provided they serve to awaken the third eye, and we encounter in the Zen writings the most extraordinary incidents of illumination in connection with the most humble objects. In the end all language is pointing: we use language to point beyond language, beyond concepts to the concrete. The monk asks the Master, "How may I enter in the Way?", and the Master, pointing to the mountain spring, responds, "Do you hear the sound of that torrent? There you may enter." Another time Master and monk are walking upon the mountain, and the Master asks, "Do you smell the mountain laurel?" "Yes." "There, I have held nothing back from you."

In its emphasis upon the living fact over the mere idea, Zen is true to the essential teaching of Buddha. Buddha cared very little for the philosophers; there were said to be already some 63 schools in existence in his time, and he had occasion to observe from their wrangling how imprisoned in the labyrinths of the intellect the human spirit can become. Thus Zen itself is not a philosophy (the Western reader must be warned here), though there lie behind it some of the great philosophies of

Mahayana Buddhism. Though Buddha began by opposing the philosophers, nevertheless in the course of its history Buddhism evolved one of the greatest and most profound philosophies ever created. Is this a contradiction of the original spirit of the founder? No; for Buddhist philosophy is activated by an altogether different purpose from that of Western philosophy: Buddhism takes up philosophy only as a device to save the philosopher from his conceptual prison; its philosophy is, as it were, a non-philosophy, a philosophy to undo philosophy. A comparison of the mind of Buddha and Plato—probably the greatest intellects of East and West—may make us understand how sharply East and West diverge on this crucial point. For Plato philosophy is a discipline that leads us from the lower to the higher world, from the world of the senses to the world of ideas, to leave us abiding in this latter world as much as is humanly possible; for the Buddhist, philosophy should lead us beyond the intellect back into the one real world that was always there in its undivided wholeness. Zen presupposes this view of philosophy, but goes beyond the mere restatement of it to make actual use of it in its practical and concrete Chinese fashion.

This passion for the living fact accounts for that quality in the Zen masters which must seem most amazing to the Westerner: their supreme matter-of-factness. "What is the Tao (the way, the truth)?" asks the disciple. "Your everyday mind," replies the Master; and he goes on to amplify: "When I am hungry, I eat; when tired, I sleep." The disciple is puzzled, and asks whether this is not what everybody else does too. No, the Master replies; most people are never wholly in what they are doing; when eating, they may be absent-mindedly preoccupied with a thousand different fantasies; when sleeping, they are not sleeping. The supreme mark of the thoroughly integrated man is to be without a divided mind. This matter-of-fact spirit of Zen is expressed in another paradoxical statement: "Before you have studied Zen, mountains are mountains and rivers are rivers; while you are studying it, mountains are no longer mountains and rivers no longer rivers; but once you have had Enlightenment, mountains are once again mountains and rivers are rivers." The stories of their arduous struggles for Enlightenment teach us that this matter-of-fact spirit of the Zen masters is not a thing easily come by: they are indeed awesome figures who have crossed the mountains and rivers, floods and fires of the spirit in order to come back sole and whole to the most banal things of daily life. The nearest thing to this, so far as I know, that the West has produced is Kierkegaard's wonderful comparison of the Knight of Resignation and the Knight of Faith: the former all fidgets and romanticism, aspiring after the infinite but never at home with the finite, while the Knight of Faith sits so solidly in his existence that from without he looks as prosaic and matter-of-fact as a tax-collector. But this ideal of being in direct and unmediated relation to ordinary reality was something that poor Kierkegaard, who waged a feverish lifelong struggle against the mediating and devouring power of his intelligence, could only aspire after but never realize.

In this striving for an unmediated relation to reality, as well as in its doctrine of an enlightenment (satori) that goes beyond reason, Zen would seem to be a form of Mysticism. But Zen is not mysticism as the West understands mysticism. The mystic, as defined by William James in *Varieties of Religious Experience* (James did not know about Zen), is one who pierces the veil of the natural or sensuous world in order to experience direct union with the higher reality. This formula holds for most of the great Western mystics from Plotinus onward, but it would not hold of Zen, which would reject this kind of mysticism as dualistic through and through, since it divides reality into lower and higher worlds. For Zen, higher and lower are one world; and in the records of Zen enlightenment which Suzuki sets before us there does not seem to occur anywhere the blurring of consciousness, the trancelike or semi-hallucinated state, which you will find among Western mystics. Even where it seems to move closest to mysticism, Zen remains supremely matter-of-fact. Nor is Zen to be confused with anything like pantheism, even though the Zen writings abound in statements that the Buddha-nature is to be found everywhere, in the dried up dirt-scraper, the cypress tree in the courtyard, etc. etc. Pantheism involves a division between the God who penetrates nature and nature itself as the phenomenal garment of God. But this too is a dualism that Zen leaves behind.

Neither a philosophy, then, in the Western sense, nor a mysticism, not Pantheism and not Theism, Zen might seem to the reader at this point so much a matter of subtlety and nuance as to be devoid of all practical value. On the contrary; for the greatest contemporary tribute to the practicality of Zen comes not from philosophers or artists, but from two prominent *practicing* psychiatrists, C. G. Jung and Karen Horney, who became passionately interested in Zen for its therapeutic possibilities. Jung has written about Zen, and before her death Karen Horney visited Japan to observe the life of a Zen monastery at first hand. What attracted Jung to Zen was its remarkable pursuit of psychological wholeness. Horney saw something similar, but in terms of her own psychology: namely, the search for self-realization without either the false image of an idealized self ("We are saved such as we are," says the Zen master), or without the resigned and dependent clinging to external props like family, social group, or church (after his enlightenment the disciple slaps the Master Obaku's face, remarking "There is not, after all, very much in the Buddhism of Obaku", and the master is pleased, for the disciple shows he can now stand on his own two feet). Certainly the Zen masters, as we read of them in Suzuki's pages give us the powerful impression of fully individuated individuals, carved out of one whole and solid block. What is most incredible to the Westerner is that this demand for the individuation of the disciple should be made by a *religion!* Western religions have always been willing to settle for less, very much less, from the believer—his filial obedience or docility, let him be a miserable psychological fragment otherwise. The reason is that Western religion has always placed the weight of emphasis upon the religious object outside the individual—God beyond the world, the Mosaic Law, the Church, the divine personality of Jesus. One can hardly imagine a Western religion producing a saying like the Zen Master's to his monks, "When you utter the name of Buddha, wash your mouth out". Zen is individualistic, and so iconoclastic and antinomian in its individualism that it will seem irreverent to many Westerners; but this is only because Zen wishes to strip the individual naked in order to return him to himself: in the end he cannot lean even upon the image of Buddha. Here precisely is the aspect of Zen Buddhism which is the greatest challenge to Western religions, and which needs to be studied most by us Westerners; for the march of our own history, as the great world of medieval religious images recedes ever further from our grasp and an increasingly secularized society engulfs us, has stripped Western man naked and left no rocklike security anywhere to lean upon. Here there looms before the frightened eyes of the Westerner what Buddhism calls the Great Emptiness; but if he does not run away in fear, this great void may bloom with all manner of miracles, and heaven and earth, in consort once again, engender effortlessly all their ancient marvels.

As to what Zen is, I leave the reader to discover in Suzuki's own pages that follow; what I have provided have been but a few negative warnings, signposts not to stray off the road, which come out of my own earlier failures of understanding. But there is one final misgiving I imagine taking shape in the reader's mind, because it has been taking shape in mine as I write, which needs to be faced before we are done; and it is this: Must not Buddhism forever remain an alien form to the Westerner? something he cannot appropriate and make his own? Are not the conditions that make ourselves and our lives what they are such that something like Zen could never be lived here? The question cannot be shirked; Zen itself would insist upon it, since Zen holds that it is not the abstract or bookish truth but the lived truth that counts. Indeed, the question looms so intensely before my mind that it seems almost to take on the imaginary body of some Zen master shaking his stick, threatening thirty blows and crying, "Speak quick, quick!" Well then, quickly: I would agree with Suzuki when he holds that Zen is the living fact in all religions East or West; or, a little more modestly, that Zen touches what is the living fact in all religions. For the readers of this book the question will hardly arise of becoming a Buddhist, but that does not lessen the importance of Zen to them: for however small the fragment of Zen that makes live contact with the Westerner, its influence is bound to work through, and he will never be quite the same again. In the beautiful words of the Master Hoyen: *When water is scooped up in the hands, the moon is reflected in them; when flowers are handled, the scent soaks into the robe.*

William Barrett

I. THE MEANING OF ZEN BUDDHISM

CHAPTER 1

The Sense of Zen

Zen in its essence is the art of seeing into the nature of one's own being, and it points the way from bondage to freedom. By making us drink right from the fountain of life, it liberates us from all the yokes under which we finite beings are usually suffering in this world. We can say that Zen liberates all the energies properly and naturally stored in each of us, which are in ordinary circumstances cramped and distorted so that they find no adequate channel for activity.

This body of ours is something like an electric battery in which a mysterious power latently lies. When this power is not properly brought into operation, it either grows mouldy and withers away or is warped and expresses itself abnormally. It is the object of Zen, therefore, to save us from going crazy or being crippled. This is what I mean by freedom, giving free play to all the creative and benevolent impulses inherently lying in our hearts. Generally, we are blind to this fact, that we are in possession of all the necessary faculties that will make us happy and loving towards one another. All the struggles that we see around us come from this ignorance. Zen, therefore, wants us to open a "third eye", as Buddhists call it, to the hitherto undreamed-of region shut away from us through our own ignorance. When the cloud of ignorance disappears, the infinity of the heavens is manifested, where we see for the first time into the nature of our own being. We now know the signification of life, we know that it is not blind striving, nor is it a mere display of brutal forces, but that while we know not definitely what the ultimate purport of life is, there is some-

[1] From *Essays in Zen Buddhism*, 1st. Series, pp. 11–34.

thing in it that makes us feel infinitely blessed in the living of it and remain quite contented with it in all its evolution, without raising questions or entertaining pessimistic doubts.

When we are full of vitality and not yet awakened to the knowledge of life, we cannot comprehend the seriousness of all the conflicts involved in it which are apparently for the moment in a state of quiescence. But sooner or later the time will come when we have to face life squarely and solve its most perplexing and most pressing riddles. Says Confucius, "At fifteen my mind was directed to study, and at thirty I knew where to stand." This is one of the wisest sayings of the Chinese sage. Psychologists will all agree to this statement of his; for, generally speaking, fifteen is about the age youth begins to look around seriously and inquire into the meaning of life. All the spiritual powers until now securely hidden in the subconscious part of the mind break out almost simultaneously. And when this breaking out is too precipitous and violent, the mind may lose its balance more or less permanently; in fact, so many cases of nervous prostration reported during adolescence are chiefly due to this loss of the mental equilibrium. In most cases the effect is not very grave and the crisis may pass without leaving deep marks. But in some characters, either through their inherent tendencies or on account of the influence of environment upon their plastic constitution, the spiritual awakening stirs them up to the very depths of their personality. This is the time you will be asked to choose between the "Everlasting No" and the "Everlasting Yea". This choosing is what Confucius means by "study"; it is not studying the classics, but deeply delving into the mysteries of life.

Normally, the outcome of the struggle is the "Everlasting Yea", or "Let thy will be done"; for life is after all a form of affirmation, however negatively it might be conceived by the pessimists. But we cannot deny the fact that there are many things in this world which will turn our too sensitive minds towards the other direction and make us exclaim with Andreyev in "The Life of Man": "I curse everything that you have given. I curse the day on which I was born. I curse the day on which I shall die. I curse the whole of my life. I fling everything back at your cruel face, senseless Fate! Be accursed, be forever accursed! With my curses I conquer you. What else can you do to me? . . . With my last thought I will shout into your asinine ears: Be accursed, be accursed!" This is a terrible indictment of life, it is a complete negation of life, it is a most dismal picture of the destiny of man on earth. "Leaving no trace" is quite true, for we know nothing of our future except that we all pass away, including the very earth from which we have come. There are certainly things justifying pessimism.

Life, as most of us live it, is suffering. There is no denying the fact. As long as life is a form of struggle, it cannot be anything but pain. Does not a struggle mean the impact of two conflicting forces, each trying to get the upper hand of the other? If the battle is lost, the outcome is death, and death is the fearsomest thing in the world. Even when death is conquered, one is left alone, and the loneliness is sometimes more unbearable than the struggle itself. One may not be conscious of all this, and may go on indulging in those momentary pleasures that are afforded by the senses. But this being unconscious does not in the least alter the facts of life. However insistently the blind may deny the existence of the sun, they cannot annihilate it. The tropical heat will mercilessly scorch them, and if they do not take proper care they will all be wiped away from the surface of the earth.

The Buddha was perfectly right when he propounded his "Fourfold Noble Truth", the first of which is that life is pain. Did not everyone of us come to this world screaming and in a way protesting? To come out into cold and prohibitive surroundings after a soft, warm motherly womb was surely a painful incident, to say the least. Growth is always attended with pain. Teething is more or less a painful process. Puberty is usually accompanied by a mental as well as a physical disturbance. The growth of the organism called society is also marked with painful cataclysms, and we are at present witnessing one of its birth-throes. We may calmly reason and say that this is all inevitable, that inasmuch as every reconstruction means the destruction of the old regime, we cannot help going through a painful operation. But this cold intellectual analysis does not alleviate whatever harrowing feelings we have to undergo. The pain heartlessly inflicted on our nerves is ineradicable. Life is, after all arguing, a painful struggle.

This, however, is providential. For the more you suffer the deeper grows your character, and with the deepening of your character you read the more penetratingly into the secrets of life. All great artists, all great religious leaders, and all great social reformers have come out of the intensest struggles which they fought bravely, quite frequently in tears and with bleeding hearts. Unless you eat your bread in sorrow, you cannot taste of real life. Mencius is right when he says that when Heaven wants to perfect a great man it tries him in every possible way until he comes out triumphantly from all his painful experiences.

To me Oscar Wilde seems always posing or striving for an effect; he may be a great artist, but there is something in him that turns me away from him. Yet he exclaims in his *De Profundis*: "During the last few months I have, after terrible difficulties and struggles, been able to comprehend some of the lessons hidden in the heart of pain. Clergymen and people who use phrases without wisdom sometimes talk of suffering as a mystery. It is really a revelation. One discerns things one never discerned before. One approaches the whole of history from a different standpoint." You will observe here what sanctifying effects his prison life produced on his character. If he had had to go through a similar trial in the beginning of his career, he might have been able to produce far greater works than those we have of him at present.

We are too ego-centred. The ego-shell in which we live is the hardest thing to outgrow. We seem to carry it all the time from childhood up to the time we finally pass away. We are, however, given many chances to break through this shell, and the first and greatest of them is when we reach adolescence. This is the first time the ego really comes to recognize the "other". I mean the awakening of sexual love. An ego, entire and undivided, now begins to feel a sort of split in itself. Love hitherto dormant deep in his heart lifts its head and causes a great commotion in it. For the love now stirred demands at once the assertion of the ego and its annihilation. Love makes the ego lose itself in the object it loves, and yet at the same time it wants to have the object as its own. This is a contradiction, and a great tragedy of life. This elemental feeling must be one of the divine agencies whereby man is urged to advance in his upward walk. God gives tragedies to perfect man. The greatest bulk of literature ever produced in this world is but the harping on the same string of love, and we never seem to grow weary of it. But this is not the topic we are concerned with here. What I want to emphasize in this connection is this: that through the awakening of love we get a glimpse into the infinity of things, and that this glimpse urges youth to Romanticism or to Rationalism according to his temperament and environment and education.

When the ego-shell is broken and the "other" is taken into its own body, we can say that the ego has denied itself or that the ego has taken its first steps towards the infinite. Religiously, here ensues an intense struggle between the finite and the infinite, between the intellect and a higher power, or, more plainly, between the flesh and the spirit. This is the problem of problems that has driven many a youth into the hands of Satan. When a grown-up man looks back to these youthful days he cannot but feel a sort of shudder going through his entire frame. The struggle to be fought in sincerity may go on up to the age of thirty, when Confucius states that he knew where to stand. The religious consciousness is now fully awakened, and all the possible ways of escaping from the struggle or bringing it to an end are most earnestly sought in every direction. Books are read, lectures are attended, sermons are greedily taken in, and various religious exercises or disciplines are tried. And naturally Zen too comes to be inquired into.

How does Zen solve the problem of problems?

In the first place, Zen proposes its solution by directly appealing to facts of personal experience and not to book-knowledge. The nature of one's own being where apparently rages the struggle between the finite and the infinite is to be grasped by a higher faculty than the intellect. For Zen says it is the

latter that first made us raise the question which it could not
answer by itself, and that therefore it is to be put aside to
make room for something higher and more enlightening. For
the intellect has a peculiarly disquieting quality in it. Though
it raises questions enough to disturb the serenity of the mind, it
is too frequently unable to give satisfactory answers to them.
It upsets the blissful peace of ignorance and yet it does not
restore the former state of things by offering something else.
Because it points out ignorance, it is often considered illuminating, whereas the fact is that it disturbs, not necessarily always bringing light on its path. It is not final, it waits for
something higher than itself for the solution of all the questions
it will raise regardless of consequences. If it were able to bring
a new order into the disturbance and settle it once for all, there
would have been no need for philosophy after it had been first
systematized by a great thinker, by an Aristotle or by a Hegel.
But the history of thought proves that each new structure
raised by a man of extraordinary intellect is sure to be pulled
down by the succeeding ones. This constant pulling down and
building up is all right as far as philosophy itself is concerned;
for the inherent nature of the intellect, as I take it, demands
it and we cannot put a stop to the progress of philosophical
inquiries any more than to our breathing. But when it comes
to the question of life itself we cannot wait for the ultimate
solution to be offered by the intellect, even if it could do so.
We cannot suspend even for a moment our life-activity for
philosophy to unravel its mysteries. Let the mysteries remain
as they are, but live we must. The hungry cannot wait until a
complete analysis of food is obtained and the nourishing value
of each element is determined. For the dead the scientific
knowledge of food will be of no use whatever. Zen therefore
does not rely on the intellect for the solution of its deepest
problems.

By personal experience it is meant to get at the fact at first
hand and not through any intermediary, whatever this may be.
Its favourite analogy is: to point at the moon a finger is needed,
but woe to those who take the finger for the moon; a basket
is welcome to carry our fish home, but when the fish are safely

on the table why should we eternally bother ourselves with the basket? Here stands the fact, and let us grasp it with the naked hands lest it should slip away—this is what Zen proposes to do. As nature abhors a vacuum, Zen abhors anything coming between the fact and ourselves. According to Zen there is no struggle in the fact itself such as between the finite and the infinite, between the flesh and the spirit. These are idle distinctions fictitiously designed by the intellect for its own interest. Those who take them too seriously or those who try to read them into the very fact of life are those who take the finger for the moon. When we are hungry we eat; when we are sleepy we lay ourselves down; and where does the infinite or the finite come in here? Are not we complete in ourselves and each in himself? Life as it is lived suffices. It is only when the disquieting intellect steps in and tries to murder it that we stop to live and imagine ourselves to be short of or in something. Let the intellect alone, it has its usefulness in its proper sphere, but let it not interfere with the flowing of the life-stream. If you are at all tempted to look into it, do so while letting it flow. The fact of flowing must under no circumstances be arrested or meddled with; for the moment your hands are dipped into it, its transparency is disturbed, it ceases to reflect your image which you have had from the very beginning and will continue to have to the end of time.

Almost corresponding to the "Four Maxims" of the Nichiren Sect, Zen has its own four statements:

> "A special transmission outside the Scriptures;
> No dependence upon words and letters;
> Direct pointing to the soul of man;
> Seeing into one's nature and the attainment of
> Buddhahood."[2]

This sums up all that is claimed by Zen as religion. Of course we must not forget that there is a historical background to this bold pronunciamento. At the time of the introduction of Zen into China, most of the Buddhists were addicted to the discussion of highly metaphysical questions, or satisfied with the

[2] See also Chapter 3, "The History of Zen," p. 59ff.

merely observing of the ethical precepts laid down by the Buddha or with the leading of a lethargic life entirely absorbed in the contemplation of the evanescence of things worldly. They all missed apprehending the great fact of life itself, which flows altogether outside of these vain exercises of the intellect or of the imagination. Bodhi-Dharma and his successors recognized this pitiful state of affairs. Hence their proclamation of "The Four Great Statements" of Zen as above cited. In a word, they mean that Zen has its own way of pointing to the nature of one's own being, and that when this is done one attains to Buddhahood, in which all the contradictions and disturbances caused by the intellect are entirely harmonized in a unity of higher order.

For this reason Zen never explains but indicates, it does not appeal to circumlocution, nor does it generalize. It always deals with facts, concrete and tangible. Logically considered, Zen may be full of contradictions and repetitions. But as it stands above all things, it goes serenely on its own way. As a Zen master aptly puts it, "carrying his home-made cane on the shoulder, he goes right on among the mountains one rising above another". It does not challenge logic, it simply walks its path of facts, leaving all the rest to their own fates. It is only when logic neglecting its proper functions tries to step into the track of Zen that it loudly proclaims its principles and forcibly drives out the intruder. Zen is not an enemy of anything. There is no reason why it should antagonize the intellect which may sometimes be utilized for the cause of Zen itself. To show some examples of Zen's direct dealing with the fundamental facts of existence, the following are selected:

Rinzai[3] (Lin-chi) once delivered a sermon, saying: "Over a mass of reddish flesh there sits a true man who has no title; he is all the time coming in and out from your sense-organs. If you have not yet testified to the fact, Look! Look!" A monk came forward and asked, "Who is this true man of no title?" Rinzai came right down from his straw chair and taking hold of the monk exclaimed: "Speak! Speak!" The monk remained

[3] The founder of the Rinzai School of Zen Buddhism, died 867.

irresolute, not knowing what to say, whereupon the master, letting him go, remarked, "What worthless stuff is this true man of no title!" Rinzai then went straight back to his room.

Rinzai was noted for his "rough" and direct treatment of his disciples. He never liked those roundabout dealings which generally characterized the methods of a lukewarm master. He must have got this directness from his own teacher Obaku (Huang-nieh), by whom he was struck three times for asking what the fundamental principle of Buddhism was. It goes without saying that Zen has nothing to do with mere striking or roughly shaking the questioner. If you take this as constituting the essentials of Zen, you would commit the same gross error as one who took the finger for the moon. As in everything else, but most particularly in Zen, all its outward manifestations or demonstrations must never be regarded as final. They just indicate the way where to look for the facts. Therefore these indicators are important, we cannot do well without them. But once caught in them, which are like entangling meshes, we are doomed; for Zen can never be comprehended. Some may think Zen is always trying to catch you in the net of logic or by the snare of words. If you once slip your steps, you are bound for eternal damnation, you will never get to freedom, for which your hearts are so burning. Therefore, Rinzai grasps with his naked hands what is directly presented to us all. If a third eye of ours is opened undimmed, we shall know in a most unmistakable manner where Rinzai is driving us. We have first of all to get into the very spirit of the master and interview the inner man right there. No amount of wordy explanations will ever lead us into the nature of our own selves. The more you explain, the further it runs away from you. It is like trying to get hold of your own shadow. You run after it and it runs with you at the identical rate of speed. When you realize it, you read deep into the spirit of Rinzai or Obaku, and their real kindheartedness will begin to be appreciated.

Ummon[4] (Yun-men) was another great master of Zen at

[4] The founder of the Ummon School of Zen Buddhism, died 996.

the end of the T'ang dynasty. He had to lose one of his legs in order to get an insight into the life-principle from which the whole universe takes rise, including his own humble existence. He had to visit his teacher Bokuju (Mu-chou), who was a senior disciple of Rinzai under Obaku, three times before he was admitted to see him. The master asked, "Who are you?" "I am Bun-yen (Wen-yen)," answered the monk. (Bun-yen was his name, while Ummon was the name of the monastery where he was settled later.) When the truth-seeking monk was allowed to go inside the gate, the master took hold of him by the chest and demanded: "Speak! Speak!" Ummon hesitated, whereupon the master pushed him out of the gate, saying, "Oh, you good-for-nothing fellow!" While the gate was hastily shut, one of Ummon's legs was caught and broken. The intense pain resulting from this apparently awakened the poor fellow to the greatest fact of life. He was no more a solicitous, pity-begging monk; the realization now gained paid more than enough for the loss of his leg. He was not, however, a solitary instance in this respect, there were many such in the history of Zen who were willing to sacrifice a part of the body for the truth. Says Confucius, "If a man understands the Tao in the morning, it is well with him even when he dies in the evening." Some would feel indeed that truth is of more value than mere living, mere vegetative or animal living. But in the world, alas, there are so many living corpses wallowing in the mud of ignorance and sensuality.

This is where Zen is most difficult to understand. Why this sarcastic vituperation? Why this seeming heartlessness? What fault had Ummon to deserve the loss of his leg? He was a poor truth-seeking monk, earnestly anxious to get enlightenment from the master. Was it really necessary for the latter from his way of understanding Zen to shut him out three times, and when the gate was half opened to close it again so violently, so inhumanly? Was this the truth of Buddhism Ummon was so eager to get? But the outcome of all this singularly was what was desired by both of them. As to the master, he was satisfied to see the disciple attain an insight into the secrets of his being; and as regards the disciple he was most grateful for all that was done to him. Evidently, Zen is the most irrational, inconceivable thing in the world. And this is why I said before that Zen was not subject to logical analysis or to intellectual treatment. It must be directly and personally experienced by each of us in his inner spirit. Just as two stainless mirrors reflect each other, the fact and our own spirits must stand facing each other with no intervening agents. When this is done we are able to seize upon the living, pulsating fact itself.

Freedom is an empty word until then. The first object was to escape the bondage in which all finite beings find themselves, but if we do not cut asunder the very chain of ignorance with which we are bound hands and feet, where shall we look for deliverance? And this chain of ignorance is wrought of nothing else but the intellect and sensuous infatuation, which cling tightly to every thought we may have, to every feeling we may entertain. They are hard to get rid of, they are like wet clothes as is aptly expressed by the Zen masters. "We are born free and equal." Whatever this may mean socially or politically, Zen maintains that it is absolutely true in the spiritual domain, and that all the fetters and manacles we seem to be carrying about ourselves are put on later through ignorance of the true condition of existence. All the treatments, sometimes literary and sometimes physical, which are most liberally and kindheartedly given by the masters to inquiring souls, are intended to get them back to the original state of freedom. And this is never really realized until we once personally experience it through our own efforts, independent of any ideational representation. The ultimate standpoint of Zen, therefore, is that we have been led astray through ignorance to find a split in our own being, that there was from the very beginning no need for a struggle between the finite and the infinite, that the peace we are seeking so eagerly after has been there all the time. Sotoba (Su Tung-p'o), the noted Chinese poet and statesman, expresses the idea in the following verse:

> "Misty rain on Mount Lu,
> And waves surging in Che-chiang;
> When you have not yet been there,
> Many a regret surely you have;

> But once there and homeward you wend,
> How matter-of-fact things look!
> Misty rain on Mount Lu,
> And waves surging in Che-chiang."

This is what is also asserted by Seigen Ishin (Ch'ing-yuan Wei-hsin), according to whom, "Before a man studies Zen, to him mountains are mountains and waters are waters; after he gets an insight into the truth of Zen through the instruction of a good master, mountains to him are not mountains and waters are not waters; but after this when he really attains to the abode of rest, mountains are once more mountains and waters are waters."

Bokuju (Mu-chou), who lived in the latter half of the ninth century, was once asked, "We have to dress and eat every day, and how can we escape from all that?" The master replied, "We dress, we eat." "I do not understand you," said the questioner. "If you don't understand put your dress on and eat your food."

Zen always deals in concrete facts and does not indulge in generalization. And I do not wish to add unnecessary legs to the painted snake, but if I try to waste my philosophical comments on Bokuju, I may say this. We are all finite, we cannot live out of time and space; inasmuch as we are earth-created, there is no way to grasp the infinite, how can we deliver ourselves from the limitations of existence? This is perhaps the idea put in the first question of the monk, to which the master replies: Salvation must be sought in the finite itself, there is nothing infinite apart from finite things; if you seek something transcendental, that will cut you off from this world of relativity, which is the same thing as the annihilation of yourself. You do not want salvation at the cost of your own existence. If so, drink and eat, and find your way of freedom in this drinking and eating. This was too much for the questioner, who, therefore, confessed himself as not understanding the meaning of the master. Therefore, the latter continued: Whether you understand or not, just the same go on living in the finite, with the finite; for you die if you stop eating and keeping yourself warm on account of your aspiration for the infinite. No matter how you struggle, Nirvana is to be sought in the midst of Samsara (birth-and-death). Whether an enlightened Zen master or an ignoramus of the first degree, neither can escape the so-called laws of nature. When the stomach is empty, both are hungry; when it snows, both have to put on an extra flannel. I do not, however, mean that they are both material existences, but they are what they are, regardless of their conditions of spiritual development. As the Buddhist scriptures have it, the darkness of the cave itself turns into enlightenment when a torch of spiritual insight burns. It is not that a thing called darkness is first taken out and another thing known by the name of enlightenment is carried in later, but that enlightenment and darkness are substantially one and the same thing from the very beginning; the change from the one to the other has taken place only inwardly or subjectively. Therefore the finite is the infinite, and *vice versa*. These are not two separate things, though we are compelled to conceive them so, intellectually. This is the idea, logically interpreted, perhaps contained in Bokuju's answer given to the monk. The mistake consists in our splitting into two what is really and absolutely one. Is not life one as we live it, which we cut to pieces by recklessly applying the murderous knife of intellectual surgery?

On being requested by the monks to deliver a sermon, Hyakujo Nehan (Pai-chang Nieh-p'an) told them to work on the farm, after which he would give them a talk on the great subject of Buddhism. They did as they were told, and came to the master for a sermon, when the latter, without saying a word, merely extended his open arms towards the monks. Perhaps there is after all nothing mysterious in Zen. Everything is open to your full view. If you eat your food and keep yourself cleanly dressed and work on the farm to raise your rice or vegetables, you are doing all that is required of you on this earth, and the infinite is realized in you. How realized? When Bokuju was asked what Zen was he recited a Sanskrit phrase from a Sutra, "Mahaprajnaparamita!" The inquirer acknowledged his inability to understand the purport of the strange phrase, and the master put a comment on it, saying:

> "My robe is all worn out after so many years' usage.
> And parts of it in shreds loosely hanging have been
> blown away to the clouds."

Is the infinite after all such a poverty-stricken mendicant?

Whatever this is, there is one thing in this connection which we can never afford to lose sight of—that is, the peace of poverty (for peace is only possible in poverty) is obtained after a fierce battle fought with the entire strength of your personality. A contentment gleaned from idleness or from a *laissez-faire* attitude of mind is a thing most to be abhorred. There is no Zen in this, but sloth and mere vegetation. The battle must rage in its full vigour and masculinity. Without it, whatever peace that obtains is a simulacrum, and it has no deep foundation, the first storm it may encounter will crush it to the ground. Zen is quite emphatic in this. Certainly, the moral virility to be found in Zen, apart from its mystic flight, comes from the fighting of the battle of life courageously and undauntedly.

From the ethical point of view, therefore, Zen may be considered a discipline aiming at the reconstruction of character. Our ordinary life only touches the fringe of personality, it does not cause a commotion in the deepest parts of the soul. Even when the religious consciousness is awakened, most of us lightly pass over it so as to leave no marks of a bitter fighting on the soul. We are thus made to live on the superficiality of things. We may be clever, bright, and all that, but what we produce lacks depth, sincerity, and does not appeal to the inmost feelings. Some are utterly unable to create anything except makeshifts or imitations betraying their shallowness of character and want of spiritual experience. While Zen is primarily religious, it also moulds our moral character. It may be better to say that a deep spiritual experience is bound to effect a change in the moral structure of one's personality.

How is this so?

The truth of Zen is such that when we want to comprehend it penetratingly we have to go through with a great struggle, sometimes very long and exacting constant vigilance. To be disciplined in Zen is no easy task. A Zen master once remarked that the life of a monk can be attained only by a man of great moral strength, and that even a minister of the state cannot expect to become a successful monk. (Let us remark here that in China to be a minister of the state was considered to be the greatest achievement a man could ever hope for in this world.) Not that a monkish life requires the austere practice of asceticism, but that it implies the elevation of one's spiritual powers to their highest notch. All the utterances or activities of the great Zen masters have come from this elevation. They are not intended to be enigmatic or driving us to confusion. They are the overflowing of a soul filled with deep experiences. Therefore, unless we are ourselves elevated to the same height as the masters, we cannot gain the same commanding views of life. Says Ruskin: "And be sure also, if the author is worth anything, that you will not get at his meaning all at once— nay, that at his whole meaning you will not for a long time arrive in any wise. Not that he does not say what he means, and in strong words, too; but he cannot say it all and what is more strange, will not, but in a hidden way and in parable, in order that he may be sure you want it. I cannot see quite the reason of this, nor analyse that cruel reticence in the breasts of wise men which makes them always hide their deeper thought. They do not give it you by way of help, but of reward, and will make themselves sure that you deserve it before they allow you to reach it." And this key to the royal treasury of wisdom is given us only after patient and painful moral struggle.

The mind is ordinarily chock full with all kinds of intellectual nonsense and passional rubbish. They are of course useful in their own ways in our daily life. There is no denying that. But it is chiefly because of these accumulations that we are made miserable and groan under the feeling of bondage. Each time we want to make a movement, they fetter us, they choke us, and cast a heavy veil over our spiritual horizon. We feel as if we are constantly living under restraint. We long for naturalness and freedom, yet we do not seem to attain them. The Zen masters know this, for they have gone through with the same experiences once. They want to have us get rid of all these wearisome burdens which we really do not have to carry in order to live a life of truth and enlightenment. Thus they utter a few words and demonstrate with action that, when rightly comprehended, will deliver us from the oppression and tyranny of these intellectual accumulations. But the comprehension does not come to us so easily. Being so long accustomed to the oppression, the mental inertia becomes hard to remove. In fact it has gone down deep into the roots of our own being, and the whole structure of personality is to be overturned. The process of reconstruction is stained with tears and blood. But the height the great masters have climbed cannot otherwise be reached; the truth of Zen can never be attained unless it is attacked with the full force of personality. The passage is strewn with thistles and brambles, and the climb is slippery in the extreme. It is no pastime but the most serious task in life; no idlers will ever dare attempt it. It is indeed a moral anvil on which your character is hammered and hammered. To the question, "What is Zen?" a master gave this answer, "Boiling oil over a blazing fire." This scorching experience we have to go through with before Zen smiles on us and says, "Here is your home."

One of these utterances by the Zen masters that will stir a revolution in our minds is this: Hokoji (P'ang-yun), formerly a Confucian, asked Baso (Ma-tsu, –788), "What kind of man is he who does not keep company with any thing?" Replied the master, "I will tell you when you have swallowed up in one draught all the waters in the West River." What an irrelevant reply to the most serious question one can ever raise in the history of thought! It sounds almost sacrilegious when we know how many souls there are who go down under the weight of this question. But Baso's earnestness leaves no room for doubt, as is quite well known to all the students of Zen. In fact, the rise of Zen after the sixth patriarch, Hui-neng, was due to the brilliant career of Baso, under whom there arose more than eighty fully qualified masters, and Hokoji, who was one of the foremost lay disciples of Zen, earned a well-deserved reputation as the Vimalakirti of Chinese Buddhism.

A talk between two such veteran Zen masters could not be an idle sport. However easy and even careless it may appear, there is hidden in it a most precious gem in the literature of Zen. We do not know how many students of Zen were made to sweat and cry in tears because of the inscrutability of this statement of Baso's.

To give another instance: a monk asked the master Shin of Chosa (Chang-sha Ching-ch'en), "Where has Nansen (Nan-ch'uan) gone after his death?" Replied the master, "When Sekito (Shih-tou) was still in the order of young novitiates, he saw the sixth patriarch." "I am not asking about the young novitiate. What I wish to know is, where is Nansen gone after his death?" "As to that," said the master, "it makes one think."

The immortality of the soul is another big question. The history of religion is built upon this one question, one may almost say. Everybody wants to know about life after death. Where do we go when we pass away from this earth? Is there really another life? or is the end of this the end of all? While there may be many who do not worry themselves as to the ultimate significance of the solitary, "companionless" One, there are none perhaps who have not once at least in their lives asked themselves concerning their destiny after death. Whether Sekito when young saw the sixth patriarch or not does not seem to have any inherent connection with the departure of Nansen. The latter was the teacher of Chosa, and naturally the monk asked him whither the teacher finally passed. Chosa's answer is no answer, judged by the ordinary rules of logic. Hence the second question, but still a sort of equivocation from the lips of the master. What does this "making one think" explain? From this it is apparent that Zen is one thing and logic another. When we fail to make this distinction and expect of Zen to give us something logically consistent and intellectually illuminating, we altogether misinterpret the signification of Zen. Did I not state in the beginning that Zen deals with facts and not with generalizations? And this is the very point where Zen goes straight down to the foundations of personality. The intellect ordinarily does not lead us there, for we do not live in the intellect, but in the will. Brother Lawrence speaks the truth when he says (*The Practice of the Presence of God*), "that we ought to make a great difference between the acts of the understanding and those of the will: that the first were comparatively of little value, and the others, all".

Zen literature is all brim full of such statements, which seem to have been uttered so casually, so innocently, but those who actually know what Zen is will testify to the fact that all these utterances dropped so naturally from the lips of the masters are like deadly poisons, that when they are once taken in they cause such a violent pain as to make one's intestines wriggle nine times and more, as the Chinese would express it. But it is only after such pain and turbulence that all the internal impurities are purged and one is born with quite a new outlook on life. It is strange that Zen grows intelligible when these mental struggles are gone through. But the fact is that Zen is an experience actual and personal, and not a knowledge to be gained by analysis or comparison. "Do not talk poetry except to a poet; only the sick know how to sympathize with the sick." This explains the whole situation. Our minds are to be so matured as to be in tune with those of the masters. Let this be accomplished, and when one string is struck, the other will inevitably respond. Harmonious notes always result from the sympathetic resonance of two or more chords. And what Zen does for us is to prepare our minds to be yielding and appreciative recipients of old masters. In other words, psychologically Zen releases whatever energies we may have in store, of which we are not conscious in ordinary circumstances.

Some say that Zen is self-suggestion. But this does not explain anything. When the word "Yamato-damashi" is mentioned it seems to awaken in most Japanese a fervent patriotic passion. The children are taught to respect the flag of the rising sun, and when the soldiers come in front of the regimental colours they involuntarily salute. When a boy is reproached for not acting like a little samurai, and with disgracing the name of his ancestor, he at once musters his courage and will resist temptations. All these ideas are energy-releasing ideas for the Japanese, and this release, according to some psychologists, is self-suggestion. Social conventions and imitative instincts may also be regarded as self-suggestions. So is moral discipline. An example is given to the students to follow or imitate it. The idea gradually takes root in them through suggestion, and they finally come to act as if it were their own. Self-suggestion is a barren theory, it does not explain anything. When they say that Zen is self-suggestion, do we get any clearer idea of Zen? Some think it scientific to call certain phenomena by a term newly come into fashion, and rest satisfied with it as if they disposed of them in an illuminating way. The study of Zen must be taken up by the profounder psychologists.

Some think that there is still an unknown region in our consciousness which has not yet been thoroughly and systematically explored. It is sometimes called the Unconscious or the Subconscious. This is a territory filled with dark images, and naturally most scientists are afraid of treading upon it. But this must not be taken as denying the fact of its existence. Just as our ordinary field of consciousness is filled with all possible kinds of images, beneficial and harmful, systematic and confusing, clear and obscure, forcefully assertive and weakly fading; so is the Subconscious a storehouse of every form of occultism or mysticism, understanding by the term all that is known as latent or abnormal or psychic or spiritualistic. The power to see into the nature of one's own being may lie also hidden there, and what Zen awakens in our consciousness may be that. At any rate the masters speak figuratively of the opening of a third eye. "Satori" is the popular name given to this opening or awakening.

How is this to be effected?

By meditating on those utterances or actions that are directly poured out from the inner region undimmed by the intellect or the imagination, and that are calculated successfully to exterminate all the turmoils arising from ignorance and confusion.[5]

It may be interesting to readers in this connection to get

[5] Zen has its own way of practising meditation. Zen has nothing to do with mere quietism or losing oneself in trance.

acquainted with some of the methods[6] used by the masters in order to open the spiritual eye of the disciple. It is natural that they frequently make use of the various religious insignia which they carry when going out to the Hall of the Dharma. Such are generally the "hossu",[7] "shippe",[8] "nyoi",[9] or "shujvo" (a staff). The last-mentioned seems to have been the most favourite instrument used in the demonstration of the truth of Zen. Let me cite some examples of its use.

According to Ye-ryo (Hui-leng), of Chokei (Chang-ch'ing), "when one knows what that staff is, one's life study of Zen comes to an end". This reminds us of Tennyson's flower in the crannied wall. For when we understand the reason of the staff, we know "what God and man is"; that is to say, we get an insight into the nature of our own being, and this insight finally puts a stop to all the doubts and hankerings that have upset our mental tranquillity. The significance of the staff in Zen can thus readily be comprehended.

Ye-sei (Hui-ch'ing), of Basho (Pa-chiao), probably of the tenth century, once made the following declaration: "When you have a staff, I will give you one; when you have none, I will take it away from you." This is one of the most characteristic statements of Zen, but later Bokitsu (Mu-chi), of Daiyi (Ta-wei), was bold enough to challenge this by saying what directly contradicts it, viz.: "As to myself, I differ from him. When you have a staff, I will take it away from you; and when you have none, I will give you one. This is my statement. Can you make use of the staff? or can you not? If you can, Tokusan (Te-shan) will be your vanguard and Rinzai (Lin-chi) your rearguard. But if you cannot, let it be restored to its original master."

A monk approached Bokuju and said, "What is the state-

[6] See also Chapter 5, "Practical Methods of Zen Instruction," p. 111ff.

[7] Originally a mosquito driver in India.

[8] A bamboo stick a few feet long.

[9] Also a stick or baton fancifully shaped and made of all kinds of material. It means literally "as one wishes or thinks" (*cinta*, in Sanskrit).

ment surpassing [the wisdom of] all Buddhas and Patriarchs?" The master instantly held forth his staff before the congregation, and said, "I call this a staff, and what do you call it?" The monk who asked the question uttered not a word. The master holding it out again said, "A statement surpassing [the wisdom of] all Buddhas and Patriarchs—was that not your question, O monk?"

Those who carelessly go over such remarks as Bokuju's may regard them as quite nonsensical. Whether the stick is called a staff or not it does not seem to matter very much, as far as the divine wisdom surpassing the limits of our knowledge is concerned. But the one made by Ummon, another great master of Zen, is perhaps more accessible. He also once lifted his staff before a congregation and remarked, "In the scriptures we read that the ignorant take this for a real thing, the Hinayanists resolve it into a nonentity, the Pratyekabuddhas regard it as a hallucination, while the Bodhisattvas admit its apparent reality, which is, however, essentially empty." "But," continued the master, "monks, you simply call it a staff when you see one. Walk or sit as you will, but do not stand irresolute."

The same old insignificant staff and yet more mystical statements from Ummon. One day his announcement was, "My staff has turned into a dragon, and it has swallowed up the whole universe; where would the great earth with its mountains and rivers be?" On another occasion, Ummon, quoting an ancient Buddhist philosopher who said "Knock at the emptiness of space and you hear a voice; strike a piece of wood and there is no sound," took out his staff and, striking space, cried, "Oh, how it hurts!" Then tapping at the board, he asked, "Any noise?" A monk responded, "Yes, there is a noise." Thereupon the master exclaimed, "Oh you ignoramus!"

If I go on like this there will be no end. So I stop, but expect some of you to ask me the following questions: "Have these utterances anything to do with one's seeing into the nature of one's being? Is there any relationship possible between those apparently nonsensical talks about the staff and the all-important problem of the reality of life?"

In answer I append these two passages, one from Jimyo (Tz'u-ming) and the other from Yengo (Yuan-wu): In one of his sermons, Jimyo said: "As soon as one particle of dust is raised, the great earth manifests itself there in its entirety. In one lion are revealed millions of lions, and in millions of lions is revealed one lion. Thousands and thousands of them there are indeed, but know ye just one, one only." So saying he lifted up his staff, and continued, "Here is my own staff, and where is that one lion?" He set the staff down, and left the pulpit.

In the *Hekigan* (Pi-yen-lu), Yengo expresses the same idea in his introductory remark to the "one-finger Zen" of Gutei (*Chuh-chih i chih t'ou ch'an*):

"One particle of dust is raised and the great earth lies therein; one flower blooms and the universe rises with it. But where should our eye be fixed when the dust is not yet stirred and the flower has not yet bloomed? Therefore, it is said that, like cutting a bundle of thread, one cut cuts all asunder; again, like dyeing a bundle of thread, one dyeing dyes all in the same colour. Now yourself get out of all the entangling relations and rip them up to pieces, but do not lose track of your inner treasure; for it is through this that the high and the low universally responding and the advanced and the backward making no distinction, each manifests itself in full perfection."

II. THE HISTORICAL BACKGROUND
OF ZEN BUDDHISM

CHAPTER 2

Zen in Relation to Buddhism Generally

I

Superficially, indeed, there is something in Zen so bizarre and even irrational as to frighten the pious literary followers of the so-called primitive Buddhism and to make them declare that Zen is not Buddhism but a Chinese anomaly of it. What, for instance, would they really make out of such statements as follows: In the *Sayings of Nan-ch'uan*[1] we read that, when T'sui, governor of Ch'i District, asked the fifth patriarch of the Zen sect—that is, Hung-jen—how it was that while he had five hundred followers, Hui-neng, in preference to all others, was singled out to be given the orthodox robe of transmission as the sixth patriarch, the fifth patriarch replied: "Four hundred and ninety-nine out of my disciples understand well what Buddhism is, except one Hui-neng. He is a man not to be measured by an ordinary standard. Hence the robe of faith was handed over to him." On this comments Nan-ch'uan: "In

---

[1] Compare this with the statement made by the sixth patriarch himself when he was asked how it was that he came to succeed the fifth patriarch, "Because I do not understand Buddhism." Let me also cite a passage from the *Kena-Upanishad,* in which the readers may find a singular coincidence between the Brahman seer and those Zen masters, not only in thought but in the way it is expressed:

"It is conceived of by him by whom it is not conceived of;
He by whom It is conceived of, knows It not.
It is not understood by those who understand It;
It is understood by those who understand It not."

Lao-tsu, founder of Taoist mysticism, breathes the same spirit when he says: "He who knows it speaks not, he who speaks knows not."

the age of Void there are no words whatever; as soon as the Buddha appears on earth, words come into existence, hence our clinging to signs. . . . And thus as we now so firmly take hold of words, we limit ourselves in various ways, while in the Great Way there are absolutely no such things as ignorance or holiness. Everything that has a name thereby limits itself. Therefore, the old master of Chiang-hsi declared that 'it is neither mind, nor Buddha, nor a thing'. It was in this way that he wished to guide his followers, while these days they vainly endeavour to experience the Great Way by hypostasizing such an entity as mind. If the Way could be mastered in this manner, it would be well for them to wait until the appearance of Maitreya Buddha [which is said to be at the end of the world] and then to awaken the enlightenment-thought. How could such ones ever hope for spiritual freedom? Under the fifth patriarch, all of his five hundred disciples, except one Hui-neng, understood Buddhism well. The lay-disciple, Neng, was quite unique in this respect, for *he did not at all understand Buddhism.*[2] He understood the Way only and no other thing."

These are not very extraordinary statements in Zen, but to most of the Zen critics they must spell abomination. Buddhism is flatly denied, and its knowledge is regarded not to be indispensable to the mastery of Zen, the Great Way, which on the contrary is more or less identified with the negation of Buddhism. How is this? In the following pages an attempt is made to answer this question.

II. THE LIFE AND SPIRIT OF BUDDHISM

To make this point clear and to justify the claim for Zen that it transmits the essence of Buddhism and not its formulated articles of faith as are recorded in letters, it is necessary to strip the spirit of Buddhism of all its outer casings and appendages, which, hindering the working of its original life-force, are apt to make us take the unessential for the essential. We know that the acorn is so different from the oak, but as long as there is a continuation of growth their identity is a

[2] Ibid.

logical conclusion. To see really into the nature of the acorn is to trace an uninterrupted development through its various historical stages. When the seed remains a seed and means nothing more, there is no life in it; it is a finished piece of work and, except as an object of historical curiosity, it has no value whatever in our religious experience. In like manner, to determine the nature of Buddhism we must go along its whole line of development and see what are the healthiest and most vital germs in it which have brought it to the present state of maturity. When this is done we shall see in what manner Zen is to be recognized as one of the various phases of Buddhism and, in fact, as the most essential factor in it.

To comprehend fully, therefore, the constitution of any existent religion that has a long history, it is advisable to separate its founder from his teaching, as a most powerful determinant in the development of the latter. By this I mean, in the first place, that the founder so called had in the beginning no idea of being the founder of any religious system which would later grow up in his name; in the second that to his disciples, while he was yet alive, his personality was not regarded as independent of his teaching, at least as far as they were conscious of the fact; in the third that what was unconsciously working in their minds as regards the nature of their master's personality came out in the foreground after his passing with all the possible intensity that had been latently gaining strength within them, and lastly that the personality of the founder grew up in his disciples' minds so powerful as to make itself the very nucleus of his teaching; that is to say, the latter was made to serve as explanation of the meaning of the former.

It is a great mistake to think that any existent religious system was handed down to posterity by its founder as the fully matured product of his mind, and, therefore, that what the followers had to do with their religious founder and his teaching was to embrace both the founder and his teaching as sacred heritage—a treasure not to be profaned by the content of their individual spiritual experience. For this view fails to take into consideration what our spiritual life is and petrifies religion to

its very core. This static conservatism, however, is always opposed by a progressive party which looks at a religious system from a dynamic point of view. And these two forces which
are seen conflicting against each other in every field of human
activity weave out the history of religion as in other cases. In
fact, history is the record of these struggles everywhere. But
the very fact that there are such struggles in religion shows
that they are here to some purpose and that religion is a living
force; for they gradually bring to light the hidden implications of the original faith and enrich it in a manner undreamed
of in the beginning. This takes place not only with regard to
the personality of the founder but with regard to his teaching,
and the result is an astounding complexity or rather confusion
which sometimes prevents us from properly seeing into the
constitution of a living religious system.

While the founder was still walking among his followers and
disciples, the latter did not distinguish between the person of
their leader and his teaching; for the teaching was realized
in the person and the person was livingly explained in the
teaching. To embrace the teaching was to follow his steps—
that is, to believe in him. His presence among them was
enough to inspire them and convince them of the truth of his
teaching. They might not have comprehended it thoroughly,
but his authoritative way of presenting it left in their hearts
no shadow of doubt as to its truth and eternal value. So long
as he lived among them and spoke to them his teaching and
his person appealed to them as an individual unity. Even when
they retired into a solitary place and meditated on the truth of
his teaching, which they did as a form of spiritual discipline,
the image of his person was always before their mental eyes.
But things went differently when his stately and inspiring
personality was no more seen in the flesh. His teaching was
still there, his followers could recite it perfectly from memory,
but its personal connection with the author was lost, the living
chain which solidly united him and his doctrine as one was for
ever broken. When they reflected on the truth of the doctrine,
they could not help thinking of their teacher as a soul far

deeper and nobler than themselves. The similarities that were, either consciously or unconsciously, recognized as existing in various forms between leader and disciple gradually vanished, and as they vanished, the other side—that is, that which made him so distinctly different from his followers—came to assert itself all the more emphatically and irresistibly. The result was the conviction that he must have come from quite a unique spiritual source. The process of deification thus constantly went on until, some centuries after the death of the Master, he became a direct manifestation of the Supreme Being himself—in fact, he was the Highest One in the flesh, in him there was a divine humanity in perfect realization. He was Son of God or the Buddha and the Redeemer of the world. He will then be considered by himself independently of his teaching; he will occupy the centre of interest in the eyes of his followers. The teaching is of course important, but mainly as having come from the mouth of such an exalted spirit, and not necessarily as containing the truth of love or Enlightenment. Indeed, the teaching is to be interpreted in the light of the teacher's divine personality. The latter now predominates over the whole system; he is the centre whence radiate the rays of Enlightenment, salvation is only possible in believing in him as saviour.

Around this personality or this divine nature there will now grow various systems of philosophy essentially based on his own teaching, but more or less modified according to the spiritual experiences of the disciples. This would perhaps never have taken place if the personality of the founder were not such as to stir up the deep religious feelings in the hearts of his followers; which is to say, what most attracted the latter to the teaching was not primarily the teaching itself but that which gave life to it, and without which it would never have been what it was. We are not always convinced of the truth of a statement because it is so logically advanced, but mainly because there is an inspiring life-impulse running through it. We are first struck with it and later try to verify its truth. The understanding is needed, but this alone will never move us to risk the fate of our souls.

One of the greatest religious souls in Japan once confessed, "I do not care whether I go to hell or elsewhere, but because my old master taught me to invoke the name of the Buddha, I practise the teaching." This was not a blind acceptance of the master, in whom there was something deeply appealing to one's soul, and the disciple embraced this something with his whole being. Mere logic never moves us; there must be something transcending the intellect. When Paul insisted that "if Christ be not raised, your faith is vain; ye are yet in your sins", he was not appealing to our logical idea of things, but to our spiritual yearnings. It did not matter whether things existed as facts of chronological history or not, the vital concern of ours was the fulfilment of our inmost inspirations; even so-called objective facts could be so moulded as to yield the best result to the requirements of our spiritual life. The personality of the founder of any religious system that has survived through centuries of growth must have had all the qualities that fully meet such spiritual requirements. As soon as the person and his teaching are separated after his own passing in the religious consciousness of his followers, if he was sufficiently great, he will at once occupy the centre of their spiritual interest and all his teachings will be made to explain this fact in various ways.

To state it more concretely, how much Christianity, for instance, as we have it today is the teaching of Christ himself? and how much of it is the contribution of Paul, John, Peter, Augustine, and even Aristotle? The magnificent structure of Christian dogmatics is the work of Christian faith as has been experienced successively by its leaders; it is not the work of one person, even of Christ. For dogmatics is not necessarily always concerned with historical facts which are rather secondary in importance compared with the religious truth of Christianity: the latter is what ought to be rather than what is or what was. It aims at the establishment of what is universally valid, which is not to be jeopardized by the fact or non-fact of historical elements, as is maintained by some of the modern exponents of Christian dogmatics. Whether Christ really claimed to be the Messiah or not is a great historical discussion still unsettled among Christian theologians. Some say that it does not make any difference as far as Christian faith is concerned whether or not Christ claimed to be the Messiah. In spite of all such theological difficulties, Christ is the centre of Christianity. The Christian edifice is built around the person of Jesus. Buddhists may accept some of his teachings and sympathize with the content of his religious experience, but so long as they do not cherish any faith in Jesus as "Christ" or Lord, they are not Christians.

Christianity is therefore constituted not only with the teaching of Jesus himself but with all the dogmatical and speculative interpretations concerning the personality of Jesus and his doctrine that have accumulated ever since the death of the founder. In other words, Christ did not found the religious system known by his name, but he was made its founder by his followers. If he were still among them, it is highly improbable that he would sanction all the theories, beliefs, and practices which are now imposed upon self-styled Christians. If he were asked whether their learned dogmatics were his religion, he might not know how to answer. He would in all likelihood profess complete ignorance of all the philosophical subtleties of Christian theology of the present day. But from the modern Christians' point of view they will most definitely assure us that their religion is to be referred to "a unitary starting point and to an original basic character", which is Jesus as Christ, and that whatever manifold constructions and transformations that were experienced in the body of their religion did not interfere with their specific Christ-faith. They are Christians just as much as the brethren of their primitive community were; for there is an historical continuation of the same faith all along its growth and development which is its inner necessity. To regard the form of culture of a particular time as something sacred, and to be transmitted for ever as such is to suppress our spiritual yearnings after eternal validity. This I believe is the position taken up by progressive modern Christians.

How about progressive modern Buddhists then in regard to their attitude towards Buddhist faith constituting the essence of Buddhism? How is the Buddha conceived by his disciples? What is the nature and value of Buddhahood? When Buddhism is defined merely as the teaching of the Buddha, does it explain the life of Buddhism as it moves on through the course of history? Is not the life of Buddhism the unfolding of the inner spiritual life of the Buddha himself rather than his exposition of it, which is recorded as the Dharma in Buddhist literature? Is there not something in the wordy teaching of the Buddha, which gives life to it and which lieth underneath all the arguments and controversies characterizing the history of Buddhism throughout Asia? This life is what progressive Buddhists endeavour to lay hands on.

It is therefore not quite in accordance with the life and teaching of the Buddha to regard Buddhism merely as a system of religious doctrines and practices established by the Buddha himself; for it is more than that, and comprises as its most important constituent elements all the experiences and speculations of the Buddha's followers, especially concerning the personality of their master and his relations to his own doctrine. Buddhism did not come out of the Buddha's mind fully armed, as did Minerva from Jupiter. The theory of a perfect Buddhism from the beginning is the static view of it, and cuts it short from its continuous and never-ceasing growth. Our religious experience transcends the limitations of time, and its ever-expanding content requires a more vital form which will grow without doing violence to itself. Inasmuch as Buddhism is a living religion and not an historical mummy stuffed with dead and functionless materials, it must be able to absorb and assimilate all that is helpful to its growth. This is the most natural thing for any organism endowed with life. And this life may be traceable under divergent forms and constructions.

According to scholars of Pali Buddhism and of the Agama literature, all that the Buddha taught, as far as his systematic teaching went, seems to be summed up by the Fourfold Noble Truth, the Twelvefold Chain of Causation, the Eightfold Path of Righteous Living, and the doctrine of Non-ego (*Anatman*) and Nirvana. If this was the case, what we call primitive Buddhism was quite a simple affair when its doctrinal aspect alone is considered. There was nothing very promising in these doctrines that would eventually build up a magnificent structure to be known as Buddhism, comprising both the Hinayana and the Mahayana. When we wish to understand Buddhism thoroughly we must dive deep into its bottom where lies its living spirit. Those that are satisfied with a superficial view of its dogmatical aspect are apt to let go the spirit which will truly explain the inner life of Buddhism. To some of the Buddha's immediate disciples the deeper things in his teachings failed to appeal, or they were not conscious of the real spiritual forces which moved them towards their Master. We must look underneath if we want to come in contact with the ever-growing life-impetus of Buddhism. However great the Buddha was, he could not convert a jackal into a lion, nor could a jackal comprehend the Buddha above his beastly nature. As the later Buddhists state, a Buddha alone understands another Buddha; when our subjective life is not raised to the same level as the Buddha's, many things that go to make up his inner life escape us; we cannot live in any other world than our own.[3] Therefore, if the primitive Buddhists read so much

[3] This was very well understood by the Buddha himself when he first attained Enlightenment; he knew that what he realized in his enlightened state of mind could not be imparted to others, and that if it were imparted they could not understand it. This was the reason why he in the beginning of his religious career expressed the desire to enter into Nirvana without trying to revolve the Wheel of the Dharma. We read in one of the Sutras belonging to the Agama class of Buddhist literature, which is entitled *Sutra on the Cause and Effect in the Past and Present* (fas. II.): "My original vows are fulfilled, the Dharma [or Truth] I have attained is too deep for the understanding. A Buddha alone is able to understand what is in the mind of another Buddha. In this age of the Five Taints (*panca-kashaya*), all beings are enveloped in greed, anger, folly, falsehood, arrogance, and flattery; they have few blessings and are stupid and have no understanding to comprehend the Dharma I have attained. Even if I make the Dharma-Wheel revolve, they would surely be confused and incapable of accepting it. They may on the contrary indulge in defamation, and, thereby falling into the evil paths, suffer all kinds of pain. It is best for me to remain quiet and enter into

in the life of their Master as is recorded in their writings, and no more, this does not prove that everything belonging to the Buddha has thereby been exhausted. There were probably other Buddhists who penetrated deeper into his life, as their own inner consciousness had a richer content. The history of religion thus becomes the history of our own spiritual unfolding. Buddhism must be conceived biologically, so to speak, and not mechanically. When we take this attitude, even the doctrine of the Fourfold Noble Truth becomes pregnant with yet deeper truths.

The Buddha was not a metaphysician and naturally avoided discussing such subjects as were strictly theoretical and had no practical bearing on the attainment of Nirvana. He might have had his own views on those philosophical problems that at the time engaged Indian minds. But like other religious leaders his chief interest was in the practical result of speculation and not in speculation as such. He was too busy in trying to get rid of the poisonous arrow that had pierced the flesh, he had no desire to inquire into the history, object, and constitution of the arrow; for life was too short for that. He thus took the world as it was; that is, he interpreted it as it appeared to his religious insight and according to his own valuation. He did not intend to go any further. He called his way of looking at the world and life "Dharma", a very comprehensive and flexible term, though it was not a term first used by the Buddha; for it had been in vogue some time prior to him, mainly in the sense of ritual and law, but the Buddha gave it a deeper spiritual signification.

Nirvana." In the *Sutra on the Story of the Discipline*, which is considered an earlier translation of the preceding text and was rendered into Chinese by an Indian Buddhist scholar, Ta-li and a Tibetan, Mangsiang, in A.D. 197, no reference is yet made to the Buddha's resolution to keep silent about his Enlightenment, only that what he attained was all-knowledge which was beyond the understanding and could not be explained, as its height was unscalable and its depth unfathomable, "containing the whole universe in it and yet penetrating into the unpenetrable" . . . Cf. the *Mahapadana Suttanta* (Digha Nikaya, XIV), and the *Ariyapariyesana Suttam* (Majjhima, XXVI).

That the Buddha was practical and not metaphysical may be seen from the criticism which was hurled at him by his opponents: "As Gautama is always found alone sitting in an empty room, he has lost his wisdom . . . Even Sariputra, who is the wisest and best disciple of his, is like a babe, so stupid and without eloquence."[4] Here however lies the seed of a future development. If the Buddha had been given up to theorizing, his teaching never could be expected to grow. Speculation may be deep and subtle, but if it has no spiritual life in it its possibilities are soon exhausted. The Dharma was ever maturing, because it was mysteriously creative.

The Buddha evidently had quite a pragmatic conception of the intellect and left many philosophical problems unsolved as unnecessary for the attainment of the final goal of life. This was quite natural with him. Whilst he was still alive among his disciples, he was the living illustration of all that was implied in his doctrine. The Dharma was manifest in him in all its vital aspects, and there was no need to indulge in idle speculation as to the ultimate meaning of such concepts as Dharma, Nirvana, Atman (ego), Karma, Bodhi (enlightenment), etc. The Buddha's personality was the key to the solution of all these. The disciples were not fully aware of the significance of this fact. When they thought they understood the Dharma, they did not know that this understanding was really taking refuge in the Buddha. His presence somehow had a pacifying and satisfying effect on whatever spiritual anguish they had; they felt as if they were securely embraced in the arms of a loving, consoling mother; to them the Buddha was really such.[5] Therefore, they had no need to press the Buddha

---

[4] Cf. Samyukta Agama (Chinese), Fas. XXXII.

[5] That the personality of the Buddha was an object of admiration and worship as much as, or perhaps more than, his extraordinary intellectual attributes, is gleaned throughout the Agama literature. To quote one or two instances: "When Subha-Manava Todeyyaputta saw the Blessed One sitting in the woods, the Brahman was struck with the beautiful serenity of his personality which most radiantly shone like the moon among the stars; his features were perfect, glowing like a golden mountain; his dignity was majestic with all his senses

very hard to enlighten them on many of the philosophical problems that they might have grown conscious of. They were easily reconciled in this respect to the Buddha's unwillingness to take them into the heart of metaphysics. But at the same time this left much room for the later Buddhists to develop their own theories not only as to the teaching of the Buddha but mainly as to its relation to his personality.

The Buddha's entrance into Nirvana meant to his disciples the loss of the World-Light,[6] through which they had such

---

under perfect control, so tranquil and free from all beclouding passions, and so absolutely calm with his mind subdued and quietly disciplined." (The Middle Agama, fas. XXXVIII.) This admiration of his personality later developed into the deification of his being, and all the evils moral and physical were supposed to be warded off if one thought of him or his virtues. "When those beings who practised evil deeds with their bodies, mouths, or minds, think of the merits of the Tathagata at the moment of their deaths, they would be kept away from the three evil paths and born in the heavens; even the vilest would be born in the heavens." (The Ekottara Agama, fas. XXXII.) "Wherever Sramana Gautama appears, no evil spirits or demons can approach him; therefore let us invite him here and all those evil gods [who have been harassing us] would by themselves take to their heels." (*Loc. cit.*) It was quite natural for the Buddhists that they later made the Buddha the first object of Recollection (*smrti*), which, they thought, would keep their minds from wandering away and help them realize the final aim of the Buddhist life. These statements plainly demonstrate that while on the one hand the teaching of the Buddha was accepted by his followers as the Dharma beautiful in the beginning, beautiful in the middle, and beautiful in the end, his person was on the other hand regarded as filled with miraculous powers and divine virtues, so that his mere presence was enough to create a most auspicious atmosphere not only spiritually but materially.

[6] When the Buddha entered Nirvana, the monks cried, "Too soon has the Tathagata passed away, too soon has the World-honoured One passed away, too soon has the Great Law died out; all beings are for ever left to misery; for the Eye of the World is gone." Their lamentation was beyond description, they lay on the ground like great trees with roots, stems, and branches all torn and broken to pieces, they rolled and wrig-

an illuminating view of things. The Dharma was there, and in it they tried to see the Buddha as they were instructed by him, but it had no enlivening effect on them as before; the moral precepts consisting of many rules were regularly observed in the Brotherhood, but the authoritativeness of these regulations was missed somehow. They retired into a quietude and meditated on the teaching of the Master, but the meditation was not quite so life-giving and satisfying because they were ever assailed by doubts, and, as a natural consequence their intellectual activities were resumed. Everything was now to be explained to the full extent of the reasoning faculty. The metaphysician began to assert himself against the simple-hearted devotion of the disciple. What had been accepted as an authoritative injunction from the mouth of the Buddha was now to be examined as a subject of philosophical discussion. Two factions were ready to divide the field with each other, and radicalism was opposed to conservatism, and between the two wings there were arranged schools of various tendencies. The Sthaviras were pitted against the Mahasamghikas, with twenty or more different schools representing various grades of diversity.

We cannot, however, exclude from the body of Buddhism all the divergent views on the Buddha and his teaching as something foreign and not belonging to the constituent elements of Buddhism. For these views are exactly what support the frame of Buddhism, and without them the frame itself will be a non-entity altogether. The error with most critics of any existent religion with a long history of development is to conceive it as a completed system which is to be accepted as such, while the fact is that anything organic and spiritual—and we consider religion such—has no geometrical outline which can be traced on paper by ruler and compass. It refuses to be objectively defined, for this will be setting a limit to the growth

gled like a slain snake. Such excessive expressions of grief were quite natural for those Buddhists whose hearts were directed towards the personality of their master more than towards his sane and rationalistic teachings. Cf. the Pali *Parinibbana-suttanta.*

of its spirit. Thus to know what Buddhism is will be to get into the life of Buddhism and to understand it from the inside as it unfolds itself objectively in history. Therefore, the definition of Buddhism must be that of the life-force which carries forward a spiritual movement called Buddhism. All these doctrines, controversies, constructions, and interpretations that were offered after the Buddha's death as regards his person, life, and teaching were what essentially constituted the life of Indian Buddhism, and without these there could be no spiritual activity to be known as Buddhism.

In a word, what constituted the life and spirit of Buddhism is nothing else than the inner life and spirit of the Buddha himself; Buddhism is the structure erected around the inmost consciousness of its founder. The style and material of the outer structure may vary as history moves forward, but the inner meaning of Buddhahood which supports the whole edifice remains the same and ever living. While on earth the Buddha tried to make it intelligible in accordance with the capacities of his immediate followers; that is to say, the latter did their best to comprehend the deeper significance of the various discourses of their master, in which he pointed the way to final deliverance. As we are told, the Buddha discoursed "with one voice",[7] but this was interpreted and understood by his devotees in as manifold manners as possible. This was inevitable, for we have each our own inner experience which is to be explained in terms of our own creation, naturally varying in depth and breath. In most cases these so-called individual inner experiences, however, may not be so deep and forceful as to demand absolutely original phraseology, but may remain satisfied with new interpretations of the

[7] Cf. *The Sukhavati-vyuha* (edited by Max Muller and B. Nanjio), p. 7, where we have: "Buddhasvaro anantaghoshah"; that is, the Buddha's voice is of infinite sounds. See also the *Saddharma-pundarika* (p. 128), where we read: "Savarena caikena vadami dharmam"—I preach the law with one voice. The parable of the water of one taste (*ekarasam vari*), variously producing herbs, shrubs, and others, is very well known among the Mahayanists.

old terms—once brought into use by an ancient original spiritual leader. And this is the way every great historical religion grows enriched in its contents or ideas. In some cases this enrichment may mean the overgrowth of superstructures ending in a complete burial of the original spirit. This is where critical judgment is needed, but otherwise we must not forget to recognize the living principle still in activity. In the case of Buddhism we must not neglect to read the inner life of the Buddha himself asserting itself in the history of a religious system designated after his name. The claim of the Zen followers that they are transmitting the essence of Buddhism is based on their belief that Zen takes hold of the enlivening spirit of the Buddha, stripped of all its historical and doctrinal garments.

III. THE DOCTRINE OF ENLIGHTENMENT AS ZEN IN CHINA

To understand how the doctrine of Enlightenment or self-realization came to be translated in China as Zen Buddhism, we must first see where the Chinese mind varies from the Indian generally. When this is done, Zen will appear as a most natural product of the Chinese soil, where Buddhism has been successfully transplanted in spite of many adverse conditions. Roughly, then, the Chinese are above all a most practical people, while the Indians are visionary and highly speculative. We cannot perhaps judge the Chinese as unimaginative and lacking in the dramatic sense, but when they are compared with the inhabitants of the Buddha's native land they look so grey, so sombre.

The geographical features of each country are singularly reflected in the people. The tropical luxuriance of imagination so strikingly contrasts with the wintry dreariness of common practicalness. The Indians are subtle in analysis and dazzling in poetic flight; the Chinese are children of earthly life, they plod, they never soar away in the air. Their daily life consists in tilling the soil, gathering dry leaves, drawing water, buying and selling, being filial, observing social duties, and developing the most elaborate system of etiquette. Being practical means in a sense being historical, observing the progress of time and recording its traces as they are left behind. The Chinese can very well boast of their being great recorders —such a contrast to the Indian lack of sense of time. Not satisfied with books printed on paper and with ink, the Chinese would engrave their deeds deep in stone, and have developed a special art of stone-cutting. This habit of recording events has developed their literature, and they are quite literary and not at all warlike; they love a peaceful life of culture. Their weakness is that they are willing to sacrifice facts for literary effects, for they are not very exact and scientific. Love of fine rhetoric and beautiful expressions has frequently drowned their practical sense, but here is also their art. Well restrained even in this, their soberness never reaches that form of fantasy which we encounter in most of the Mahayana texts.

The Chinese are in many ways great, their architecture is great indeed, their literary achievements deserve the world's thanks, but logic is not one of their strong points; nor are their philosophy and imagination. When Buddhism with all its characteristically Indian dialectics and imageries was first introduced into China, it must have staggered the Chinese mind. Look at its gods with many heads and arms—something that has never entered into their heads, in fact into no other nation's than the Indian's. Think of the wealth of symbolism with which every being in Buddhist literature seems to be endowed. The mathematical conception of infinities, the Bodhisattva's plan of world-salvation, the wonderful stage-setting before the Buddha begins his sermons, not only in their general outlines but in their details—bold, yet accurate, soaring in flight, yet sure of every step—these and many other features must have been things of wonderment to the practical and earth-plodding people of China.

One quotation from a Mahayana Sutra will convince readers of the difference between Indian and Chinese minds, in regard to their imaginative powers. In the *Saddharma-pundarika* the Buddha wishes to impress his disciples as to the length of time passed since his attainment of Supreme Enlightenment;

he does not merely state that it is a mistake to think that his Enlightenment took place some countable number of years ago under the Bodhi-tree near the town of Gaya; nor does he say in a general way that it happened ages ago, which is very likely the way with the Chinese, but he describes in a most analytical way in how remote an age it was that he came to Enlightenment.

"But, young men of good family, the truth is that many hundred thousand myriads of kotis of æons ago I have arrived at Supreme, Perfect Enlightenment. By way of example, young men of good family, let there be the atoms of earth of fifty hundred thousand myriads of kotis of worlds; let there exist some man who takes one of these atoms of dust and then goes in an eastern direction fifty hundred thousand myriads of kotis of worlds further on, there to deposit that atom of dust; let the man in this manner carry away from all those worlds the whole mass of earth, and in the same manner, and by the same act as supposed, deposit all those atoms in an eastern direction. Now would you think, young men of good family, that anyone should be able to weigh, imagine, count, or determine the number of these worlds? The Lord having thus spoken, the Bodhisattva Mahasattva Maitreya and the entire host of Bodhisattvas replied: They are incalculable, O Lord, those worlds, countless, beyond the range of thought. Not even all the Sravakas and Pratyekabuddhas, O Lord, with their Arya-knowledge, will be able to imagine, count, or determine them. For us also, O Lord, who are Bodhisattvas standing on the place from whence there is no turning back, this point lies beyond the sphere of our comprehension; so innumerable, O Lord, are those worlds.

"This said, the Buddha spoke to those Bodhisattvas Mahasattvas as follows: I announce to you, young men of good family, I declare to you: However numerous be those worlds where that man deposits those atoms of dust and where he does not, there are not, young men of good family, in all those hundred thousands of myriads of kotis of worlds, so many dust atoms as there are hundred thousands of myriads of kotis of

æons since I have arrived at Supreme, Perfect Enlightenment."[8]

Such a conception of number and such a method of description would never have entered the Chinese mind. They are, of
course, capable of conceiving long duration, and great achievements, in which they are not behind any nation; but to express
their idea of vastness in the manner of the Indian philosophers
would be beyond their understanding.

When things are not within the reach of conceptual description and yet when they are to be communicated to others, the
ways open to most people will be either to remain silent, or
to declare them simply to be beyond words, or to resort to
negation saying, "not this", "not that", or if one were a philosopher, to write a book explaining how logically impossible it
was to discourse on such subjects; but the Indians found quite
a novel way of illustrating philosophical truths that cannot be
applied to analytical reasoning. They resorted to miracles or
supernatural phenomena for their illustration. Thus they made
the Buddha a great magician; not only the Buddha but almost
all the chief characters appearing in the Mahayana scriptures
became magicians. And in my view this is one of the most
charming features of the Mahayana texts—this description of
supernatural phenomena in connection with the teaching of
abstruse doctrine. Some may think it altogether childish and
injuring the dignity of the Buddha as teacher of solemn religious truths. But this is a superficial interpretation of the
matter. The Indian idealists knew far better; they had a more
penetrating imagination which was always effectively employed by them whenever the intellect was put to a task beyond its power.

We must understand that the motive of the Mahayanists
who made the Buddha perform all these magical feats was to
illustrate through imageries what in the very nature of things
could not be done in an ordinary method open to human in-

[8] Kern's translation, *Sacred Books of the East*, Vol. XXI, pp.
299–300.

tellect. When the intellect failed to analyse the essence of Buddhahood, their rich imagination came in to help them out by
visualizing it. When we try to explain Enlightenment logically
we always find ourselves involved in contradictions. But when
an appeal is made to our symbolical imagination—especially
if one is liberally endowed with this faculty—the matter is more
readily comprehended. At least this seems to have been the
Indian way of conceiving the signification of supernaturalism.

When Vimalakirti was asked by Sariputra how such a small
room as his with just one seat for himself could accommodate
all the hosts of Bodhisattvas and Arhats and Devas numbering
many thousands, who were coming there with Manjusri to visit
the sick philosopher, replied Vimalakirti, "Are you here to seek
chairs or the Dharma? . . . One who seeks the Dharma finds
it in seeking it in nothing." Then learning from Manjusri where
to obtain seats, he asks a Buddha called Sumerudiparaja to
supply him with 32,000 lion-seats. majestically decorated and
as high as 84,000 yojanas. When they were brought in, his
room, formerly large enough for one seat, now miraculously
accommodated all the retinue of Manjusri, each one of whom
was comfortably seated in a celestial chair, and yet the whole
town of Vaisali and the rest of the world did not appear on
this account crammed to overflowing. Sariputra was surprised
beyond measure to witness this supernatural event, but
Vimalakirti explained that for those who understand the doctrine of spiritual emancipation, even the Mount of Sumeru
could be sealed up in a seed of mustard, and the waves of the
four great oceans could be made to flow into one pore of the
skin (*romakupa*), without even giving any sense of inconven-
ience to any of the fishes, crocodiles, tortoises, and other living
beings in them; the spiritual kingdom was not bound in space
and time.

To quote another instance from the first chapter of the
Lankavatarasutra, which does not appear in the oldest Chinese translation. When King Ravana was requesting the Buddha through the Bodhisattva Mahamati to disclose the content
of his inner experience, the king unexpectedly noticed his
mountain-residence turned into numberless mountains of pre-

cious stones and most ornately decorated with celestial grandeur, and on each of these mountains he saw the Buddha
manifested. And before each Buddha there stood King Ravana
himself with all his assemblage as well as all the countries in
the ten quarters of the world, and in each of those countries
there appeared the Tathagata, before whom again there were
King Ravana, his families, his palaces, his gardens, all decorated exactly in the same style as his own. There was also the
Bodhisattva Mahamati in each of these innumerable assem-
blies asking the Buddha to declare the content of his inner
spiritual experience; and when the Buddha finished his discourse on the subject with hundreds of thousands of exquisite
voices, the whole scene suddenly vanished, and the Buddha
with all his Bodhisattvas and his followers were no more; then
King Ravana found himself all alone in his old palace. He now
reflected: "Who was he that asked the question? Who was he
that listened? What were those objects that appeared before
me? Was it a dream? or a magical phenomenon?" He again
reflected: "Things are all like this, they are all creations of
one's own mind. When mind discriminates there is manifold-
ness of things; but when it does not it looks into the true state
of things." When he thus reflected he heard voices in the air
and in his own palace, saying: "Well you have reflected, O
King! You should conduct yourself according to this view."

The Mahayana literature is not the only recorder of the
miraculous power of the Buddha, which transcends all the
relative conditions of space and time as well as of human activities, mental and physical. The Pali scriptures are by no means
behind the Mahayana in this respect. Not to speak of the Buddha's threefold knowledge, which consists in the knowledge of
the past, the future, and of his own emancipation, he can also
practise what is known as the three wonders, which are the
mystic wonder, the wonder of education, and the wonder of
manifestation. But when we carefully examine the miracles described in the Nikayas, we see that they have no other objects
in view than the magnification and deification of the personality of the Buddha.

The recorders of these miracles must have thought that they

could thus make their master greater and far above ordinary mortals in the estimate of their rivals. From our modern point of view it was quite childish for them to imagine that any unusual deeds performed by their master would attract, as we read in the *Kevaddha Sutta,* people's attention to Buddhism and recognize its superior value on that very account; but in those ancient days in India, the masses, nay even learned scholars, thought a great deal of supernaturalism, and naturally the Buddhists made the best possible use of this belief. But when we come to the Mahayana Sutras we at once perceive that the miracles described here on a much grander scale have nothing to do with supernaturalism as such or with any ulterior motives such as propagandism or self-aggrandizement, but that they are essentially and intimately connected with the doctrine itself which is expounded in the texts. For instance, in the *Prajna-paramita Sutra* every part of the body of the Buddha simultaneously emits innumerable rays illuminating at once the furthest ends of the worlds, whereas in the *Avatamsaka Sutra* the different parts of his body shoot out beams of light on different occasions. In the *Saddharma-pundarika Sutra* a ray of light issues from within the circle of hair between the eyebrows of the Buddha which illuminates over eighteen hundred thousand Buddha-countries in the eastern quarter, revealing every being in them, even the inhabitants of the deepest hell called Avici. It is evident that the Mahayana writers of these Sutras had in their minds something much different from the Hinayana compilers of the Nikayas in their narratives of the miraculous power of the Buddha. What that something was I have here pointed out in a most general way. A systematic study in detail of the Mahayana supernaturalism will no doubt be an interesting one.

At all events the above references will suffice, I believe, to establish my thesis that the reason for the introduction of supernaturalism into the Mahayana literature of Buddhism was to demonstrate the intellectual impossibility of comprehending spiritual facts. While philosophy exhausted its resources logically to explain them, Vimalakirti like Bahva, a Vedic mystic, remained silent; not satisfied with this, the Indian Mahayana writers further introduced supernaturalistic symbolism, but it remained with the Chinese Zen Buddhists to invent their own methods to cope, according to their own needs and insight, with the difficulties of communicating one's highest and deepest spiritual experience known as Enlightenment in Buddhism.

The Chinese have no aptitude like the Indians for hiding themselves in the clouds of mystery and supernaturalism. Chwang-tzu and Lieh-tzu were the nearest to the Indian type of mind in ancient China, but their mysticism does not begin to approach that of the Indian Mahayanists in grandeur, in elaborateness, and in the height of soaring imagination. Chwang-tzu did his best when he rode up in the air on the back of the Tai-p'eng, whose wings soared like overhanging clouds; and Lieh-tzu when he could command winds and clouds as his charioteers. The later Taoists dreamed of ascending to the heavens after so many years of ascetic discipline and by taking an elixir of life concocted from various rare herbs. Thus in China we have so many Taoist hermits living in the mountains far away from human habitations. No Chinese saints or philosophers are, however, recorded in history who have been capable of equalling Vimalakirti or Manjusri or even any of the Arhats. The Confucian verdict that superior man never talks about miracles, wonders, and supernaturalism, is the true expression of Chinese psychology. The Chinese are thoroughly practical. They must have their own way of interpreting the doctrine of Enlightenment as applied to their daily life, and they could not help creating Zen as an expression of their inmost spiritual experience.

If the imagery of supernaturalism did not appeal to sober Chinese character, how did the Chinese followers of Enlightenment contrive to express themselves? Did they adopt the intellectual method of the Sunyata philosophy? No; this, too, was not after their taste, nor was it quite within the reach of their mental calibre. The *Prajna-Paramita* was an Indian creation and not the Chinese. They could have produced a Chwang-tzu or those Taoist dreamers of the Six Dynasties, but not a Nagarjuna or a Sankara.

The Chinese genius was to demonstrate itself in some other way. When they began inwardly to assimilate Buddhism as the doctrine of Enlightenment, the only course that opened to their concrete practical minds was to produce Zen. When we come to Zen after seeing all the wonderful miracles displayed by the Indian Mahayana writers, and after the highly abstracted speculations of the Madhyamika thinkers, what a change of scenery do we have here? No rays are issuing from the Buddha's forehead, no retinues of Boddhisattvas reveal themselves before you, there is indeed nothing that would particularly strike your senses as odd or extraordinary, or as beyond intelligence, beyond the ken of logical reasoning. The people you associate with are all ordinary mortals like yourselves, no abstract ideas, no dialectical subtleties confront you. Mountains tower high towards the sky, rivers all pour into the ocean. Plants sprout in the spring and flowers bloom in red. When the moon shines serenely, poets grow mildly drunk and sing a song of eternal peace. How prosaic, how ordinary, we may say! but here was the Chinese soul, and Buddhism came to grow in it.

When a monk asks who is the Buddha, the master points at his image in the Buddha Hall; no explanations are given, no arguments are suggested. When the mind is the subject of discourse, asks a monk, "What is mind, anyway?" "Mind," says the master. "I do not understand, Sir." "Neither do I," quickly comes from the master. On another occasion, a monk is worried over the question of immortality. "How can I escape the bondage of birth and death?" Answers the master, "Where are you?" The Zen adepts as a rule never waste time in responding to questions, nor are they at all argumentative. Their answers are always curt and final, which follow the questions with the rapidity of lightning. Someone asked, "What is the fundamental teaching of the Buddha?" Said the master, "There is enough breeze in this fan to keep me cool." What a most matter-of-fact answer this! That inevitable formula of Buddhism, the Fourfold Noble Truth, apparently has no place in the scheme of Zen teaching, nor does that persistently enigmatic statement in the *Prajna-Paramita,* "taccittam yaccittam acittam", threaten us here.

Ummon (Yun-men) once appeared in the pulpit, and said, "In this school of Zen no words are needed; what, then, is the ultimate essence of Zen teaching?" Thus himself proposing the question, he extended both his arms, and without further re-marks came down from the pulpit. This was the way the Chi-nese Buddhists interpreted the doctrine of Enlightenment, this was the way they expounded the *Pratyatmajnanagocara* of the *Lankavatara.* And for the Chinese Buddhists this was the only way, if the inner experience of the Buddha were to be dem-onstrated, not intellectually or analytically, nor in supernatural manners, but directly in our practical life. For life, as far as it is lived *in concreto,* is above concepts as well as images. To understand it we have to dive into it and to come in touch with it personally; to pick up or cut out a piece of it for in-spection murders it; when you think you have got into the essence of it, it is no more, for it has ceased to live but lies immobile and all dried up. For this reason Chinese minds, ever since the coming of Bodhi-Dharma, worked on the problem how best to present the doctrine of Enlightenment in their native garment cut to suit their modes of feeling and thinking, and it was not until after Hui-neng (Yeno) that they satisfac-torily solved the problem and the great task of building up a school to be known thenceforward as Zen was accomplished.

That Zen was the thing Chinese minds wanted to have when they thoroughly comprehended the teaching of Buddhism is proved by the two incontestable historical facts: first, after the establishment of Zen, it was this teaching that ruled China while all the other schools of Buddhism, except the Pure Land sect, failed to survive; and secondly, before Buddhism was translated into Zen it never came into an intimate relation with the native thought of China, by which I mean Confucianism.

Let us see first how Zen came to rule the spiritual life of China. The inner sense of Enlightenment was not understood in China, except intellectually, in the earlier days of Buddhism. This was natural, seeing that it was in this respect that the

Chinese mind was excelled by the Indian. As I said before, the boldness and subtlety of Mahayana philosophy must have fairly stunned the Chinese, who had, before the introduction of Buddhism, practically no system of thought worthy of the name, except moral science. In this latter they were conscious of their own strength; even such devout Buddhists as I-ching (Gijo) and Hs'uan-chuang (Genjo) acknowledged it, with all their ardour for the Yogacara psychology and the Avatamsaka metaphysics; they thought that their country, as far as moral culture was concerned, was ahead of the land of their faith or at least had nothing to learn from the latter.

As the Mahayana Sutras and Shastras were translated in rapid succession by able, learned, devout scholars, both native and Indian, the Chinese mind was led to explore a region where they had not ventured very far before. In the early Chinese biographical histories of Buddhism, we notice commentators, expounders, and philosophers far outnumbering translators and adepts in dhyana so called. The Buddhist scholars were at first quite busily engaged in assimilating intellectually the various doctrines propounded in Mahayana literature. Not only were these doctrines deep and complicated but they were also contradicting one another, at least on the surface. If the scholars were to enter into the depths of Buddhist thought, they had to dispose of these entanglements somehow. But if they were sufficiently critical, they could do that with comparative ease, which was, however, something we could never expect of those earlier Buddhists; for even in these modern days critical Buddhist scholars will, in some quarters, be regarded as not quite devout and orthodox. They all had not a shadow of doubt as to the genuineness of the Mahayanist texts as faithfully and literally recording the very words of the Buddha, and therefore they had to plan out some systems of reconciliation between diverse doctrines taught in the Scriptures. This meant to find out what was the primary object of the Buddha's appearance in the world ignorant, corrupted, and given up to the karma of eternal transmigration. Such efforts on the part of Buddhist philosophers developed what is to be distinctly designated as Chinese Buddhism.

While this intellectual assimilation was going on on the one hand, the practical side of Buddhism was also assiduously studied. Some were followers of the Vinaya texts, and others devoted themselves to the mastery of dhyana. But what was here known as dhyana was not the dhyana of Zen Buddhism; it was a meditation, concentrating one's thought on some ideas such as impermanence, egolessness of things, chain of causation, or the attributes of the Buddha. Even Bodhi-Dharma, the founder of Zen Buddhism, was regarded by historians as belonging to this class of dhyana-adepts, his peculiar merits as teacher of an entirely novel school of Buddhism were not fully appreciated. This was inevitable, the people of China were not yet quite ready to accept the new form; for they had only inadequately grasped the doctrine of Enlightenment in all its bearings.

The importance of Enlightenment in its practical aspects, however, was not altogether overlooked in the maze of doctrinal intricacies. Chih-i (Chigi, 531–597), one of the founders of the T'ien Tai school and the greatest Buddhist philosopher in China, was fully awake to the significance of dhyana as the means of attaining Enlightenment. With all his analytical powers, his speculation had room enough for the practice of dhyana. His work on "Tranquillization and Contemplation" is explicit on this point. His idea was to carry out intellectual and spiritual exercises in perfect harmony, and not partially to emphasize either one of the two, Samadhi or Prajna, at the expense of the other. Unfortunately, his followers grew more and more onesided until they neglected the dhyana practice for the sake of intellection. Hence their antagonistic attitude later towards advocates of Zen Buddhism, for which however the latter were to a certain extent to be responsible, too.

It was due to Bodhi-Dharma (died 528)[9] that Zen came to be the Buddhism of China. It was he that started this movement which proved so fruitful among a people given up to the practical affairs of life. When he declared his message, it was

[9] For this and the following, see Chapter 3, "The History of Zen," p. 59ff.

still tinged with Indian colours, he could not be entirely independent of the traditional Buddhist metaphysics of the times. His allusion to the *Vajra-samadhi* and the *Lankavatara* was natural, but the seeds of Zen were sown by his hands. It now remained with his native disciples to see to it that these seeds grew up in harmony with the soil and climate. It took about two hundred years for the Zen seeds to bear fruit, rich and vigorous in life, and fully naturalized while retaining intact the essence of what makes up Buddhism.

Hui-neng (637–713), who was the sixth patriarch after Bodhi-Dharma, was the real Chinese founder of Zen; for it was through him and his direct followers that Zen could cast off the garment borrowed from India and began to put on one cut and sewn by the native hands. The spirit of Zen was of course the same as the one that came to China transmitted without interruption from the Buddha, but the form of expression was thoroughly Chinese, for it was their own creation. The rise of Zen after this was phenomenal. The latent energy that had been stored up during the time of naturalization suddenly broke out in active work, and Zen had almost a triumphal march through the whole land of Cathay. During the T'ang dynasty (618–906), when Chinese culture reached its consummation, great Zen masters succeeded one after another in building up monasteries and educating monks as well as lay-disciples who were learned not only in the Confucian classics but in the Mahayana lore of Buddhism. The emperors too were not behind them in paying respects to these Zen seers, who were invited to come to the court in order to give sermons to these august personages. When for political reasons Buddhism was persecuted, which caused the loss of many valuable documents, works of art, and the decline of some schools, Zen was always the first to recover itself and to renew its activities with redoubled energy and enthusiasm. Throughout the Five Dynasties, in the first half of the tenth century, when China was torn up into minor kingdoms again, and general political situations seemed to be unfavourable to the thriving of religious sentiments, Zen prospered as before and the masters kept up their monastic centres undisturbed.

With the rise of the Sung dynasty (960–1279) Zen reached the height of its development and influence, while the other sects of Buddhism showed signs of rapid decline. When history opens on the pages of the Yuan (1280–1367) and the Ming (1368–1661) dynasties, Buddhism is found identified with Zen. The Kegon (Avatamsaka), Tendai (T'ien-tai), Sanron (San-lun), Kusha (Abhidharma-kosa), Hosso (Yogacara) and Shingon (Mantra), if they were not completely wiped out through persecution, suffered tremendously from the lack of fresh blood. Perhaps they were to die out anyway on account of their not having been completely assimilated by Chinese thought and feeling; there was too much of an Indian element which prevented them from being fully acclimatized. In any event Zen as the essence of the Buddha's mind continued to flourish so that any Chinese minds at all inclined towards Buddhism came to study Zen and neglected the rest of the Buddhist schools still in existence though at the last stage of their productive activity. The only form of Buddhism that retains its vitality to a certain extent even to this day is Zen, more or less modified to accommodate the Pure Land tendency, that had been growing soon after the introduction of Buddhism into China.

There was reason for this state of things in the religious history of China, and it was thus that Zen dispensed with the images and concepts and modes of thinking that were imported from India along with Buddhist thought; and out of its own consciousness Zen created an original literature best adapted to the exposition of the truth of Enlightenment. This literature was unique in many senses, but it was in perfect accordance with the Chinese mental *modus operandi* and naturally powerfully moved them to the core. Bodhi-Dharma taught his disciples to look directly into the essence of the teaching of the Buddha, discarding the outward manners of presentation; he told them not to follow the conceptual and analytical interpretation of the doctrine of Enlightenment. Literary adherents of the Sutras objected to this and did all they could to prevent the growth of the teaching of Dharma. But it grew on in spite of oppositions.

The disciples mastered the art of grasping the central fact of Buddhism. When this was accomplished, they proceeded to demonstrate it according to their own methods, using their own terminology, regardless of the traditional or rather imported way of expression. They did not entirely abandon the old manner of speaking; for they refer to Buddha, Tathagata, Nirvana, Bodhi, Trikaya, Karma, transmigration, emancipation, and many other ideas making up the body of Buddhism; but they make no mention of the Twelvefold Chain of Origination, the Fourfold Noble Truth, or the Eightfold Righteous Path. When we read Zen literature without being told of its relation to Buddhism, we may almost fail to recognize in it such things as are generally regarded as specifically Buddhist. When Yakusan (Yuehshan, 751–834) saw a monk, he asked, "Where do you come from?" "I come from south of the Lake." "Is the Lake overflowing with water?" "No, sir, it is not yet overflowing." "Strange," said the master, "after so much rain why does it not overflow?" To this last query the monk failed to give a satisfactory answer, whereupon Ungan (Yun-yen), one of Yakusan's disciples, said, "Overflowing, indeed!" while Dosan (Tung-shan), another of his disciples, exclaimed, "In what kalpa did it ever fail to overflow?" In these dialogues do we detect any trace of Buddhism? Do they not look as if they were talking about an affair of most ordinary occurrence? But, according to the masters, their talks are brim-full of Zen, and Zen literature is indeed abounding in such apparent trivialities. In fact, so far as its phraseology and manner of demonstration are concerned, Zen looks as if it had nothing to do with Buddhism, and some critics are almost justified in designating Zen as a Chinese anomaly of Buddhism as was referred to at the beginning of this chapter.

In the history of Chinese literature, Zen writings known as *Yu-lu* (Goroku) form a class by themselves, and it is due to them that the Chinese colloquialism of the T'ang and the early Sung dynasties has been preserved. Men of letters in China despised to write except in classical style, deliberately choosing such words, phrases, and expressions as enhanced the grace of the composition. All the literature we have of those early days of Chinese culture therefore is the model of such a cultivated style. The Zen masters were not necessarily despisers of classicism, they took to fine literature as much as their contemporaries, they were well educated and learned too; but they found colloquialism a better and more powerful medium for the utterance of their inner experiences. This is generally the case with spiritual reformers, who want to express themselves through the medium most intimate to their feelings and best suited for their original ways of viewing things. They avoid wherever possible such nomenclature as has been in use and filled with old associations which are apt to lack in living purposes and therefore in vivifying effects. Living experiences ought to be told in a living language and not in worn-out images and concepts. The Zen masters therefore did what they could not help doing and made free use of the living words and phrases of the day. Does this not prove that in China Buddhism through Zen ceased to be a foreign importation and was transformed into an original creation of the native mind? And just because Zen could turn itself into a native product, it survived all the other schools of Buddhism. In other words, Zen was the only form in which the Chinese mind could accommodate, appreciate, and assimilate the Buddhist doctrine of Enlightenment.

We may conclude now that Zen, in spite of the uncouthness and extraordinariness of its outward features, belongs to the general system of Buddhism. And by Buddhism we mean not only the teaching of the Buddha himself as recorded in the earliest Agamas, but the later speculations, philosophical and religious, concerning the person and life of the Buddha. His personal greatness was such as occasionally made his disciples advance theories somewhat contrary to the advice supposed to have been given by their Master. This was inevitable. The world with all its contents, individually as well as as a whole, is subject to our subjective interpretation, not a capricious interpretation indeed, but growing out of our inner necessity, our religious yearnings. Even the Buddha as an object of one's religious experience could not escape this, his personality was

so constituted as to awaken in us every feeling and thought
that goes under the name of Buddhism now. The most significant and fruitful ideas that were provoked by him were concerned with his Enlightenment and Nirvana. These two facts
stood out most prominently in his long peaceful life of seventy-
nine years, and all the theories and beliefs that are bound up
with the Buddha are attempts to understand these facts in
terms of our own religious experience. Thus Buddhism has
grown to have a much wider meaning than is understood by
most scholars.

The Buddha's Enlightenment and Nirvana were two separate ideas in his life as it unfolded in history so many centuries
ago, but from the religious point of view they are to be regarded as one idea. That is to say, to understand the content
and the value of Enlightenment is the same as realizing the
signification of Nirvana. Taking a stand on this, the Mahayanists developed two currents of thought: the one was to rely on
our intellectual efforts to the furthest extent they could reach,
and the other, pursuing the practical method adopted by the
Buddha himself, indeed by all Indian truth-seekers, endeavoured to find in the practice of dhyana something directly
leading to Enlightenment. It goes without saying that in both
of these efforts the original impulse lies in the inmost religious
consciousness of pious Buddhists.

The Mahayana texts compiled during a few centuries after
the Buddha testify to the view here presented. Of these, the
one expressly composed to propagate the teaching of the Zen
school is the *Lankavatara,* in which the content of Enlightenment is, so far as words admit, presented from a psychological,
philosophical, and practical point of view. When this was introduced into China and thoroughly assimilated according to
the Chinese methods of thinking and feeling, the main thesis
of the Sutra came to be demonstrated in such a way as is now
considered characteristically Zen. The truth has many avenues
of approach through which it makes itself known to the human
mind. But the choice it makes depends on certain limitations
under which it works. The superabundance of Indian imagination issued in supernaturalism and wonderful symbolism, and

the Chinese sense of practicalness and its love for the solid everyday facts of life, resulted in Zen Buddhism. We may now be able to understand, though only tentatively by most readers at present, the following definitions of Zen offered by its masters:

When Joshu was asked what Zen was, he answered, "It is cloudy today and I won't answer."

To the same question, Ummon's reply was: "That's it." On another occasion the master was not at all affirmative, for he said, "Not a word to be predicated."

These being some of the definitions given to Zen by the masters, in what relationship did they conceive of Zen as standing to the doctrine of Enlightenment taught in the Sutras? Did they conceive it after the manner of the *Lankavatara* or after that of the *Prajna-paramita?* No, Zen had to have its own way; the Chinese mind refused blindly to follow the Indian models. If this is still to be contested, read the following:

A monk asked Kan (Chien), who lived in Haryo (Pa-ling), "Is there any difference between the teaching of the Patriarch and that of the Sutras, or not?" Said the master, "When the cold weather comes, the fowl flies up in the trees while the wild duck goes down into water." Ho-yen (Fa-yen) of Gosozan (Wu-tsu-shan) commented on this, saying: "The great teacher of Pa-ling has expressed only a half of the truth. I would not have it so. Mine is: When water is scooped in the hands, the moon is reflected in them; when the flowers are handled, the scent soaks into the robe."

Chapter 3

The History of Zen

I

The legendary story of the origin of Zen in India runs as follows: Sakyamuni was once engaged at the Mount of the Holy Vulture in preaching to a congregation of his disciples. He did not resort to any lengthy verbal discourse to explain his point, but simply lifted a bouquet of flowers before the assemblage, which was presented to him by one of his lay-disciples. Not a word came out of his mouth. Nobody understood the meaning of this except the old venerable Mahakasyapa, who quietly smiled at the Master, as if he fully comprehended the purport of this silent but eloquent teaching on the part of the Enlightened One. The latter perceiving this opened his golden-tongued mouth and proclaimed solemnly, "I have the most precious treasure, spiritual and transcendental, which this moment I hand over to you, O venerable Mahakasyapa!"

Orthodox Zen followers generally blindly take this incident to be the origin of their doctrine, in which, according to them, is disclosed the inmost mind of the Buddha as well as the secret of the religion. As Zen claims to be the inmost essence of Buddhism and to have been directly transmitted by the Buddha to his greatest disciple, Mahakasyapa, its followers naturally look for the particular occasion when this transmission took place between the master and the disciple. We know in a general way that Mahakasyapa succeeded the Buddha as the leader of the Faith, but as to his special transmission of Zen, we have no historical records in the Indian Buddhist writings at present in our possession.

From the modern critical point of view it did not matter very much whether Zen originated with Bodhi-Dharma in

China or with the Buddha in India, inasmuch as Zen is true and has an enduring value. And again from the historian's point of view, which tries scientifically to ascertain the source of development resulting in Zen Buddhism, it is only important to find a logical connection between the Mahayana Doctrine of Enlightenment in India and its practical application by the Chinese to the actualities of life; and as to any special line of transmission in India before Bodhi-Dharma as was established by the Zen devotees, it is not a matter of much concern nor of great importance. But as soon as Zen is formulated into an independent system, not only with its characteristic features but with its historically ascertainable facts, it will be necessary for the historians to trace its line of transmission complete and not interrupted; for in Zen, as we shall see later, it is of the utmost importance for its followers to be duly certified or approved (*abbhanumodana*) by the master as to the genuineness or orthodox character of their realization. Therefore, as long as Zen is the product of the Chinese soil from the Indian seed of Enlightenment as I take it, no special line of transmission need be established in India unless it is in a general logical manner such as was attempted in my previous chapters.

The twenty-eight patriarchs of Zen regarded by its followers as the orthodox line of transmission are as follows:

1. Sakyamuni.	15. Kanadeva.
2. Mahakasyapa.	16. Arya Rahulata.
3. Ananda.	17. Samghanandi.
4. Sanavasa.	18. Samghayasas.
5. Upagupta.	19. Kumarata.
6. Dhritaka.	20. Jayata.
7. Micchaka.	21. Vasubandhu.
8. Buddhanandi.	22. Manura.
9. Buddhamitra.	23. Haklenayasas.
10. Bhikshu Parsva.	24. Bhikshu Simha.
11. Punyayasas.	25. Vasasita.
12. Asvaghosha.	26. Punyamitra.
13. Bhikshu Kapimala.	27. Prajnatara.
14. Nagarjuna.	28. Bodhi-Dharma.

The history of Zen dates with the coming of Bodhi-Dharma (Bodai-Daruma) from the west, A.D. 520. He came to China with a special message which is summed up in the following lines:

"A special transmission outside the scriptures;
  No dependence upon words and letters;
  Direct pointing at the soul of man;
  Seeing into one's nature and the attainment of Buddhahood."

These four lines as describing the principles of Zen teaching as distinguished from other schools of Buddhism already in existence in China were formulated later and not by Dharma himself. We cannot exactly tell who was the real author, as we have no definite information on this subject. One historian, Tsung-chien, who compiled from the Tien-tai point of view a Buddhist history entitled *The Rightful Lineage of the Sakya Doctrine* in 1237, ascribes it to Nansen Fu-gwan; probably the formula originated in those days when Baso (Ma-tsu), Hyakjo (Pai-chang), Obaku (Huang-po), Sekito (Shih-tou), and Yakusan (Yueh-shan) were flourishing in the "West of the River" and in the "South of the Lake". Since then they have been regarded as characteristically Zen, and it was Dharma that breathed this spirit into the minds of the Chinese Buddhists. The latter had more or less been given up, on the one hand, to philosophizing, and, on the other hand, to practising contemplation. They were not acquainted with the direct method of Zen which was to see straightway into the truth of Enlightenment and attain Buddhahood without going through so many stages of preparation prescribed by the scholars.

Our knowledge of the life of Bodhi-Dharma comes from two sources. One, which is the earliest record we have of him is by Tao-hsuan in his *Biographies of the High Priests* which was compiled early in the T'ang dynasty, A.D. 645. The author was the founder of a Vinaya sect in China and a learned scholar, who, however, was living before the movement of the new school to be known as Zen came into maturity under Hui-neng, the sixth patriarch, who was nine years old when Tao-hsuan wrote his *Biographies.* The other source is the *Records of the Transmission of the Lamp,* A.D. 1004, compiled by Tao-yuan early in the Sung dynasty. This was written by a Zen monk after Zen had received full recognition as a special branch of Buddhism, and contains sayings and doings of its masters. The author often refers to some earlier Zen histories as his authorities, which are, however, lost now, being known by the titles only.

It is quite natural that these two accounts of the life of Bodhi-Dharma should vary at several points. The first was written when Zen was not yet fully established as a school, and the second by one of the Zen masters. In the first, Dharma, the founder of Zen, is treated as one of the many other Buddhist priests eminent in various fields as translators, commentators, scholars, Vinaya-followers, masters of meditation, possessors of miraculous virtues, etc., and Dharma could not naturally occupy in such a history any very prominent position distinguishing himself from the other "high priests". He is described merely as one of those "masters of meditation" whose conception of dhyana did not differ from the old traditional one as was practised by the Hinayana followers.

Tao-hsuan, the author of the *Biographies,* refers to Dharma's *tai ch'eng pi kuan,* Mahayanistic wall-contemplation, in his commentary notes to Zen, as the most meritorious work Dharma achieved in China. For this reason he is often spoken of as the *pi-kuan* Brahman—that is, wall-contemplating Brahman—and in Japan the monks belonging to the Soto school of Zen are supposed to follow the example of the founder of their religion when they keep up the practice of sitting facing the wall while meditating. But this is evidently a superficial interpretation of the phrase *pi-kuan;* for how could mere wall-gazing start a revolutionary movement in the Buddhist world as is implied in Fao-hsuan's life of Dharma? How could such an innocent practice provoke a terrible opposition among scholars of those days? To my view, *pi-kuan* has a far deeper meaning, and must be understood in the light of the following passage in the *Records,* which is quoted from a work known as the *Pieh Chi,* meaning some special document of prior existence:

"The master first stayed in the Shorinji (Shao-linszu) monastery for nine years, and when he taught the second patriarch, it was only in the following way: 'Externally keep yourself away from all relationships, and, internally, have no pantings (or hankerings, *ch'uan*) in your heart;[1] when your mind is like unto a straight-standing wall you may enter into the Path.' Hui-k'e tried variously to explain [or to discourse on] the reason of mind, but failed to realize the truth itself. The master simply said, 'No! No!' and never proposed to explain to his disciple what was the mind-essence in its thought-less state [that is, in its pure being]. [Later] said Hui-k'e, 'I know now how to keep myself away from all relationships.' 'You make it a total annihilation, do you not?' queried the master. 'No, master,' replied Hui-k'e, 'I do not make it a total annihilation.' 'How do you testify your statement?' 'For I know it always in a most intelligible manner, but to express it in words—that is impossible.' Thereupon, said the master, 'That is the mind-essence itself transmitted by all the Buddhas. Harbour no doubts about it.'"

The earlier part of Bodhi-Dharma's life while in India as narrated in the *Records* may be discredited as containing a large dose of fiction, but the latter part of it cannot so easily be disposed of. This is where it supplements the story in Tao-hsuan's *Biographies,* which was written by a good historian

---

[1] Is it possible that this passage has some reference to the *Vajrasamadhi* where Bodhisattva Mahabala speaks of a "flaccid mind" and a "strong mind"? The former which is possessed by most common people "pants" (or gasps or hankers) very much, and prevents them from successfully attaining to the Tathagata-dhyana, while the "strong mind" is characteristic of one who can enter upon the realm of reality (*bhutakoti*). So long as there are "pantings" (or gaspings) in the mind, it is not free, it is not liberated, and cannot identify itself with the suchness of reason. The mind must be "strong" or firm and steady, self-possessed and concentrating, before it is ready for the realization of Tathagatadhyana—a dhyana going far beyond the reach of the so-called four dhyanas and eight samadhis.

however, who did not know, anything about the future development of Zen. According to the *Records* then, the first great personage Dharma had an interview with when he came to China was the king of Liang, the greatest Buddhist patron of the time. And the interview took place in the following manner:

The Emperor Wu of Liang asked Dharma:

"Ever since the beginning of my reign I have built so many temples, copied so many sacred books, and supported so many monks and nuns; what do you think my merit might be?"

"No merit whatever, sire!" Dharma bluntly replied.

"Why?" demanded the Emperor astonished.

"All these are inferior deeds," thus began Dharma's significant reply, "which would cause their author to be born in the heavens or on this earth again. They still show the traces of worldliness, they are like shadows following objects. Though they appear actually existing, they are no more than mere nonentities. As to a true meritorious deed, it is full of pure wisdom and is perfect and mysterious, and its real nature is beyond the grasp of human intelligence. Such as this is not to be sought after by any worldly achievement."

The Emperor Wu thereupon asked Bodhi-Dharma again, "What is the first principle of the holy doctrine?"

"Vast emptiness, and there is nothing in it to be called holy, sire!" answered Dharma.

"Who is it then that is now confronting me?"

"I know not, sire!"

The answer was simple enough, and clear enough too, but the pious and learned Buddhist Emperor failed to grasp the spirit prevading the whole attitude of Dharma.

Seeing that there was no further help to be given to the Emperor, Dharma left his dominion and retired into a monastery in the state of Wei, where he sat quietly practising the "wall-contemplation", it is said, for nine long years, until he came to be known as the *pi-kuan* Brahman.

One day a monk Shen-kuang visited him and most earnestly implored him to be enlightened in the truth of Zen, but Dharma paid no attention. Shen-kuang was not to be disap-

pointed, for he knew that all the great spiritual leaders of the
past had gone through with many a heart-rending trial in order
to attain the final object of their aspiration. One evening he
stood in the midst of the snow waiting for Dharma to notice
him when at last the fast-falling snow buried him almost to
his knees.

Finally, the master turned back and said, "What do you
wish me to do for you?" Said Kuang, "I am come to receive
your invaluable instructions; pray open your gate of mercy,
and extend your hand of salvation to this poor suffering
mortal." "The incomparable doctrine of Buddhism," replied
Dharma, "can be comprehended only after a long hard discipline and by enduring what is most difficult to endure, and by
practising what is most difficult to practise. Men of inferior
virtue and wisdom are not allowed to understand anything
about it. All the labours of such ones will come to naught."

Kuang at last cut off his left arm with the sword he was
carrying, and presented it before the teacher as a token of his
sincerity in the desire to be instructed in the doctrine of all the
Buddhas. Said Dharma, "This is not to be sought through
another."

"My soul is not yet pacified. Pray, master, pacify it."

"Bring your soul here, and I will have it pacified."

Kuang hesitated for a moment but finally said, "I have
sought it these many years and am still unable to get hold of
it!"

"There! it is pacified once for all." This was Dharma's sentence.[2]

---

[2] As one can readily see, this story is more or less fictitious.
I mean Kuang's standing in the snow and cutting off his arm
in order to demonstrate his earnestness and sincerity. Some
think that the snow story and that of self-mutilation do not
belong to that of Kuang, but are borrowed from some other
sources, as Tao-hsuan makes no reference to them in his book.
The loss of the arm was due to a party of robbers who attacked
Kuang after his interview with Dharma. We have no way to
verify these stories either way. The whole setting however is
highly dramatic, and there must have been once in the history
of Zen some necessity to interweave imagination with facts.

Dharma then told him to change his name into Hui-k'e.

Nine years passed, and Dharma wished to return to his native country. He called in all his disciples before him, and said, "The time is come for me to depart, and I want to see what your attainments are."

"According to my view," said Tao-fu, "the truth is above affirmation and negation, for this is the way it moveth."

Dharma said, "You have got my skin."

Next came in the nun, Tsung-ch'ih, and said, "As I understand it, it is like Ananda's viewing the Buddhaland of Akshobhya: it is seen once and never again."

Dharma said, "You have got my flesh."

Tao-yu was another disciple who presented his view, saying: "Empty are the four elements and non-existent the five skandhas. According to my view, there is not a thing to be grasped as real."

Dharma said, "You have got my bone."

Finally, Hui-k'e—that is, Shen-kuang—reverently bowing to the master, kept standing in his seat and said nothing.

Dharma then announced, "You have my marrow."

Mystery envelops the end of Bodhi-Dharma's life in China; we do not know how, when, and where he passed away from this earth. Some say that he was poisoned by his rivals, others say that he went back to India, crossing the desert, and still others report that he came over to Japan. In one thing they all agree, which is this: he was quite old, being, according to Tao-hsuan, over one hundred and fifty years at his death.

II. HUI-NENG, THE CHINESE FOUNDER

Hui-neng (638–713) came from Hsin-chou in the southern parts of China. His father died when he was yet young. He supported his mother by selling wood in town. When one day he came out of a house where he sold some fuel, he heard a man reciting a Buddhist Sutra. The words deeply touched his heart. Finding what Sutra it was and where it was possible to get it, a longing came over him to study it with the master. The Sutra was the *Diamond Sutra* (*Vajracchedika-sutra*) and the master was the fifth patriarch residing at Yellow Plum in Chin-chou. Hui-neng somehow managed to get money enough for the support of his aged mother while he was gone.

It took him about a month to reach Yellow Plum, where he at once proceeded to see Hung-jen at the head of five hundred monks (sometimes said to be seven or even ten hundred). At the first interview asked the patriarch:

"Where do you come from? and what do you want here?"

"I am a farmer from Hsin-chou and wish to become a Buddha."

"So you are a Southerner," said the patriarch, "but the Southerners have no Buddha-nature; how could you expect to attain Buddhahood?"

This, however, did not discourage the bold seeker after the truth, for he at once responded: "There may be Southerners and Northerners, but as far as Buddha-nature goes, how could you make such a distinction in it?"

This pleased the master very much. Hui-neng was given an office as rice-pounder for the Brotherhood. More than eight months, it is said, he was employed in this menial labour, when the fifth patriarch wished to select his spiritual successor from among his many disciples. One day he made an announcement that any one who could prove his thorough comprehension of the religion would be given the patriarchal mantle and proclaimed as his legitimate heir. Shen-hsiu (died 706), who was the most learned of all the disciples and thoroughly versed in the lore of his religion, and who was therefore considered by his brethren in the faith to be in possession of an unqualified right to the honour, composed a stanza expressing his view, and posted it on the outside wall of the meditation hall, which read:

> "This body is the Bodhi-tree,
> The soul is like a mirror bright;
> Take heed to keep it always clean,
> And let not dust collect on it."

All those who read these lines were greatly impressed, and secretly cherished the idea that the author of this gatha would surely be awarded the prize. But when they awoke the next morning they were surprised to see another written alongside of it, which ran as follows:

> "The Bodhi is not like the tree,
> The mirror bright is nowhere shining;
> As there is nothing from the first,
> Where can the dust itself collect?"

The writer of these lines was an insignificant layman in the service of the monastery, who spent most of his time in pounding rice and splitting wood for the Brotherhood. He had such an unassuming air that nobody ever thought much of him, and therefore the entire community was now set astir to see this challenge made upon its recognized authority. But the fifth patriarch saw in this unpretentious monk a future leader of mankind, and decided to transfer to him the robe of his office. He had, however, some misgivings concerning the matter; for the majority of his disciples were not enlightened enough to see anything of deep religious intuition in the lines by the rice-pounder, Hui-neng: and if he were publicly awarded the honour they might do him harm. So the fifth patriarch gave a secret sign to Hui-neng to come to his room at midnight, when the rest of the Brotherhood was fast asleep. Then he gave him the robe as insignia of his authority and in acknowledgment of his unsurpassed spiritual attainment, and with the assurance that the future of their faith would be brighter than ever. The patriarch then advised him that it would be wise for him to hide his own light under a bushel until the proper time arrived for his public appearance and active propaganda, and also that the robe which was handed down from Bodhi-Dharma as the sign of faith should no more be given up to Hui-neng's successors, because Zen was now fully recognized by the outside world in general and there was no more necessity to symbolize the faith by the transference of the robe. That night Hui-neng left the monastery.

This narrative is taken from the literature left by the followers of the sixth patriarch and is naturally partial in his favour. If we had another record left by Shen-hsiu and his school, the account here reproduced may materially differ. In fact, we have at least one document telling Shen-hsiu's relation to Hung-jen. It is the memorial inscription on his gravestone written by Chang-shuo, one of his lay-disciples. In this inscription Shen-hsiu is referred to as the one to whom the Dharma has been transmitted from his master, Hung-jen. Judging from this, the patriarchal authority of Hui-neng was not an undisputed one at the time, or the orthodox order of succession was not settled until some time later, when the school of Hui-neng had been well established in authority over all the other schools of Zen that might have been existing then. Unfortunately, this memorial inscription does not give any further information concerning Hui-neng's relation to Hung-jen, but even from the above narrative we can gather certain facts of importance which will shed light on the history of Zen.

First, what necessity was there to make Hui-neng an unlearned rustic in contrast with the erudition and wide information ascribed to Shen-hsiu? Or was Hui-neng really such an ignoramus as could not read anything written? But the *Fa-pao-t'an-ching*, a collection of his sermons, contains passages quoted from such Sutras as the *Nirvana, Vajracchedika, Lankavatara, Saddharma-pundarika, Vimalakirti, Amitabha,* and *Bodhisattva-sila-sutra*. Does this not evince the fact that the author was not altogether unacquainted with Mahayana literature? Probably he was not a learned scholar as compared with Shen-hsiu, but in the narratives of his life we can trace some systematic effort to make him more unlettered than he actually was. What, let me ask, do we read in this attempt at the hand of the editors? In my opinion this emphasizing of the contrast between the two most eminent disciples of the fifth patriarch was at the same time the emphasizing of the real character of Zen as independent of learning and intellectuality. If Zen is, as its followers claim, a "special transmission outside the scriptural teaching", the understanding of it must be possible even for the unlettered and unphilosophizing. The greatness of Hui-neng as Zen master is all the more enhanced. This was in all likelihood the reason why the sixth patriarch was unreasonably and sometimes even dramatically made unlettered.

Secondly, why was not the patriarchal robe transferred beyond Hui-neng? If Hung-jen advised him to keep it with him, what does the advice really imply? That the life of the possessor of the robe would be threatened points to the fact that there was a dispute among the disciples of Hung-jen. Did they regard the robe as the symbol of patriarchal authority? But what advantages, material or spiritual, accrued from the ownership of it? Did the teaching of Bodhi-Dharma come now to be believed as the genuine transmission of the Buddha? And for that reason did the robe really cease to signify anything relative to the truth of Zen? If so, when Bodhi-Dharma first declared his special mission as teacher of Zen, was he looked upon as a heretic and persecuted accordingly? The legend that he was poisoned by his rival teachers from India seems to corroborate this. At all events, the question of the robe is deeply connected with the status of Zen teaching among the various schools of Buddhism at the time, and also with its firmer hold on the popular minds than ever before.

Thirdly, the secrecy observed in all the transactions between Hung-jen and Hui-neng concerning the transmission of the Dharma naturally arrests our attention. To raise the rice-pounder, who is not even an ordained monk, to the rank of a patriarch, though only in name, to succeed a great master who stands at the head of several hundred disciples, seems to be a real cause for envy and jealousy and even for hatred. But if one were really enlightened enough to take charge of the important position of spiritual leadership, could not a combined effort of master and pupil withstand all the opposition? Perhaps even enlightenment could not stand against human passions so irrational and elemental. I cannot, however, help imagining an attempt on the part of the biographers of Hui-neng at the dramatization of the whole scene. I am very likely mistaken, and there might have been some historical conditions of which we are now ignorant due to the lack of documents.

Three days after the flight of Hui-neng from the Yellow Plum Mountain, the news of what had happened in secret became noised abroad throughout the monastery, and a party of indignant monks, headed by one named Ming, pursued the fugitive, Hui-neng, who, in accordance with his master's instructions, was silently leaving the Brotherhood. When he was overtaken by the pursuers while crossing a mountain-pass far from the monastery, he laid down his robe on a rock near by and said to the monk, Ming: "This robe symbolizes our patriarchal faith and is not to be carried away by force. Take this along with thee, however, if thou so desirest."

Ming tried to lift it, but it was as heavy as a mountain. He halted, hesitated, and trembled with awe. At last he said: "I come here to obtain the faith and not the robe. O my brother monk, pray dispel my ignorance."

Said the sixth patriarch: "If thou comest for the faith, stop all thy hankerings. Think not of good, think not of evil, but see what at this moment thy own original face doth look like, which thou hadst even prior to thy own birth."

Being thus demanded, Ming at once perceived the fundamental truth of things, which hitherto he had sought in things without. He now understood everything, as if he had taken a cupful of cold water and tasted it to his own satisfaction. Out of the immensity of his feeling he was literally bathed in tears and perspirations, and most reverently approaching the patriarch he saluted him and asked, "Besides this hidden sense as is embodied in these significant words, is there anything which is secret?"

The patriarch answered: "In what I have shown to thee there is nothing hidden. If thou reflectest within thyself and recognizest thy own face, which was before the world, secrecy is in thyself."

Whatever historical circumstances surrounded Hui-neng in those remote days, it is certain that in this statement, "to see one's own face even before one was born", we find the first proclamation of the new message, which was destined to unroll a long history of Zen and to make Hui-neng really worthy of the patriarchal robe. We can see here what a new outlook Hui-neng has succeeded in opening to the traditional Indian Zen. In him we do not recognize anything of Buddhism as far

as phraseology goes, which means that he opened up his own
way of presenting the truth of Zen after his original and creative experience. Prior to him the Zen experience had some bor-
rowings, either in wording or in method, to express itself. To
say "You are the Buddha", or "You and the Buddha are one",
or "The Buddha is living in you", is too stale, too flat, because
too abstract and too conceptual. They contain deep truth but
are not concrete nor vivifying enough to rouse our dormant
souls from insensibility. They are filled up too much with abstractions and learned phraseology. Hui-neng's simple-minded-
ness, not spoiled by learning and philosophizing, could grasp
the truth at first hand. Hence his unusual freshness in the way
he handled the problem. We may come to this again later.

Hung-jen died, A.D. 675, four years[3] after the Dharma was
transmitted to Hui-neng. He was seventy-four years old. But
Hui-neng never started his mission work until some years later,
for in accordance with the advice of his master he lived a secluded life in the mountains. One day he thought that it was
time for him to go out in the world. He was now thirty-nine
years old, and it was in the first year of I-feng (A.D. 676) during the T'ang dynasty. He came to Fa-hsing temple in the
province of Kuang, where a learned priest, Yin-tsung, was discoursing on the *Nirvana Sutra*. He saw some monks arguing
on the fluttering pennant; one of them said, "The pennant is
an inanimate object and it is the wind that makes it flap."
Against this it was remarked by another monk that "Both wind
and pennant are inanimate things, and the flapping is an impossibility." A third one protested, "The flapping is due to a
certain combination of cause and condition"; while a fourth
one proposed a theory, saying, "After all there is no flapping
pennant, but it is the wind that is moving by itself." The discussion grew quite animated when Hui-neng interrupted with
the remark, "It is neither wind nor pennant but your own mind
that flaps." This at once put a stop to the heated argument.

[3] There is, however, a variation from five years to fifteen
years according to different authorities.

The priest-scholar, Yin-tsung, was greatly struck by the statement of Hui-neng, so conclusive and authoritative. Finding out very soon who this Hui-neng was, Yin-tsung asked him to enlighten him on the teaching of the master of Yellow Plum Mountain. The gist of Hui-neng's reply was as follows:

"My master had no special instruction to give; he simply insisted upon the need of our seeing into our own Nature through our own efforts; he had nothing to do with meditation, or with deliverance. For whatever can be named leads to dualism, and Buddhism is not dualistic. To take hold of this non-duality of truth is the aim of Zen. The Buddha-Nature of which we are all in possession, and the seeing into which constitutes Zen, is indivisible into such oppositions as good and evil, eternal and temporal, material and spiritual. To see dualism in life is due to confusion of thought; the wise, the enlightened, see into the reality of things unhampered by erroneous ideas."

This was the beginning of Hui-neng's career as Zen master. His influence seems to have been immediate and far-reaching. He had many disciples numbering thousands. He did not, however, go around preaching and proselytizing. His activities were confined in his own province in the south, and the Pao-lin monastery at T'sao-ch'i was his headquarters.

When the Emperor Kao-tsung learned that Hui-neng succeeded Hung-jen as one of Dharma's spiritual descendants in the faith of Zen, he sent him one of his Court officials with an imperial message, but Hui-neng refused to come up to the capital, preferring to stay in the mountains. The messenger, however, wished to be instructed in the doctrine of Zen, that he might convey it to his august master at Court. Said Hui-neng in the main as follows:

"It is a mistake to think that sitting quietly in contemplation is essential to deliverance. The truth of Zen opens by itself from within and it has nothing to do with the practice of dhyana. For we read in the *Vajracchedika* that those who try to see the Tathagata in one of his special attitudes, as sitting or lying, do not understand his spirit, and that the Tathagata is designated as Tathagata because he comes from nowhere and departs nowhere, and for that reason he is the Tathagata. His appearance has no whence, and his disappearance no whither, and this is Zen. In Zen, therefore, there is nothing to gain, nothing to understand; what shall we then do with sitting cross-legged and practising dhyana? Some may think that understanding is needed to enlighten the darkness of ignorance, but the truth of Zen is absolute in which there is no dualism, no conditionality. To speak of ignorance and enlightenment, or of Bodhi and Klesa (wisdom and passions), as if they were two separate objects which cannot be merged in one, is not Mahayanistic. In the Mahayana every possible form of dualism is condemned as not expressing the ultimate truth. Everything is a manifestation of the Buddha-Nature, which is not defiled in passions, nor purified in enlightenment. It is above all categories. If you want to see what is the nature of your being, free your mind from thought of relativity and you will see by yourself how serene it is and yet how full of life it is."

The principal ideas of Hui-neng, which make him the real Chinese founder of Zen Buddhism, may be summed up as follows:

1. We can say that Zen has come to its own consciousness by Hui-neng. While Bodhi-Dharma brought it from India and successfully transplanted it in China, it did not fully realize its special message at the time. More than two centuries were needed before it grew aware of itself and knew how to express itself in the way native to the Chinese mind; the Indian mode in which its original teaching had been expressed, as was the case with Bodhi-Dharma and his immediate disciples, had to give way as it were to become truly Chinese. As soon as this transformation or transplantation was accomplished in the hands of Hui-neng his disciples proceeded at once to work out all its implications. The result was what we have as the Zen school of Buddhism. How then did Hui-neng understand Zen?

According to him Zen was the "seeing into one's own Nature". This is the most significant phrase ever coined in the development of Zen Buddhism. Around this Zen is now crystallized, and we know where to direct our efforts and how to represent it in our consciousness. After this the progress of Zen

Buddhism was rapid. It is true that this phrase occurs in the life of Bodhi-Dharma in the *Records of the Transmission of the Lamp,* but it is in the part of his life on which we cannot put much reliance. Even when the phrase was actually used by Dharma it was not necessarily considered by him the essence of Zen as distinguishing itself from other schools of Buddhism. Hui-neng, however, was fully aware of its signification, and impressed the idea unequivocally upon the minds of his audience. When he made his first declaration of Zen for the benefit of Yin-tsung, the statement was quite unmistakable: "We talk of seeing into our own Nature, and not of practising dhyana or obtaining liberation." Here we have the gist of Zen, and all his later sermons are amplifications of this idea.

2. The inevitable result of it was the "abrupt" teaching of the Southern school. The seeing is an instant act as far as the mental eye takes in the whole truth at one glance—the truth which transcends dualism in all form; it is abrupt as far as it knows no gradations, no continuous unfolding. Read the following passage from the *Platform Sutra,* in which the essentials of the abrupt doctrine are given:

"When the abrupt doctrine is understood there is no need of disciplining oneself in things external. Only let a man always have a right view within his own mind, no desires, no external objects will ever defile him. This is the seeing into his Nature. O my friends, have no fixed abode inside or outside,[4] and your conduct will be perfectly free and unfettered. Take away your

---

[4] This is a constant refrain in the teaching of the *Prajnaparamita Sutras*—to awaken one's thought where there is no abode whatever (na kvacit pratishtitam cittam utpadayitavyam). When Joshu called on Ungo, the latter asked, "O you, old wanderer! how is it that you do not seek an abiding place for yourself?" "Where is my abiding place?" "There is an old temple ruin at the foot of this mountain." "That is a fitting place for your old self," responded Joshu. Later, he came to Shuyusan, who asked him the same question, saying, "O you, old wanderer! why don't you get settled?" "Where is the place for me to get settled?" "Why, this old wanderer doesn't know even where to get settled for himself." Said Joshu, "I have been engaged these thirty years in training horses, and today I have been kicked around by a donkey!"

attachment and your walk will know no obstructions whatever. . . . The ignorant will grow wise if they abruptly get
an understanding and open their hearts to the truth.

3. When the seeing into Self-Nature is emphasized and
intuitive understanding is upheld against learning and philosophizing, we know that as one of its logical conclusions the
old view of meditation begins to be looked down on as merely
a discipline in mental tranquillization. And this was exactly the
case with the sixth patriarch.

Hui-neng did not forget that the will was after all the ultimate reality and that enlightenment was to be understood as
more than intellection, more than quietly contemplating the
truth. The Mind or Self-Nature was to be apprehended in the
midst of its working or functioning. The object of dhyana was
thus not to stop the working of Self-Nature but to make us
plunge right into its stream and seize it in the very act. His
intuitionism was dynamic. In the following dialogues both Hui-
neng and his disciples are still using the older terminology,
but the import of this parley is illustrative of the point I want
to specify.

Hsuan-chiao first studied T'ien-tai philosophy and later
while reading the *Vimalakirti* he discovered his Self-Nature.
Being advised to see the sixth patriarch in order to have his
experience certified or testified, he came to Tsao-ch'i. He
walked round the master three times, and erecting his staff
straight stood before him. Said the master, "Monks are supposed to observe three hundred rules of conduct and eighty
thousand minor ones; whence comest thou, so full of pride?"

"Birth-and-death is a matter of grave concern, and time
waits for nobody!" said the T'ien-tai philosopher.

"Why dost thou not grasp that which is birthless and see
into that which is timeless?" the master demanded.

"Birthless is that which grasps, and timeless is that which
sees into."

"That is so, that is so," agreed the master.

When this was over, Hsuan-chiao came to Hui-neng again
in the full attire of the Buddhist monk, and reverently bowing
to the master wished to take leave of him.

Said the master, "Why departest thou so soon?"

"There is from the very beginning no such thing as move-ment, and then why talkest thou of being soon?"

"Who knows that there is no movement?" retorted the mas-ter.

"There," exclaimed Hsuan-chiao, "thou makest a judgment thyself!"

"Thou truly comprehendest the intent of that which is birth-less."

"How could the birthless ever have an intent?" Hsuan-chiao asked.

"If there were no intent, who could ever judge?"

"Judgments are made with no intent whatever." This was the conclusion of Chiao.

The master then expressed his deep appreciation of Hsuan-chiao's view on the subject, saying, "Well thou hast said!"

Chih-huang was an adept in meditation, which he studied under the fifth patriarch. After twenty years' discipline he thought he well understood the purport of meditation or samadhi. Hsuan-t'se, learning his attainment, visited him, and said, "What are you doing there?" "I am entering into a samadhi." "You speak of entering, but how do you enter into samadhi—with a thought-ful mind or with a thought-less mind? If you say with a thought-less mind, all non-sentient beings such as plants or bricks could attain samadhi. If you say with a thought-ful mind, all sentient beings could attain it." "When I enter into samadhi," said Chih-huang, "I am not conscious of either being thought-ful or being thought-less." "If you are conscious of neither, you are right in samadhi all the while; why do you then talk at all of entering into it or coming out of it? If, however, there is really entering or com-ing out, it is not Great Samadhi." Chih-huang did not know how to answer. After a while he asked who was Hsuan-t'se's teacher and what was his understanding of samadhi. Said Hsuan-t'se, "Hui-neng is my teacher, and according to him [the ultimate truth] lies mystically serene and perfectly quiet; substance and function are not to be separated, they are of one Suchness. The five skandhas are empty in their nature, and the six sense-objects have no reality. [The truth knows of] neither entering nor going out, neither being tranquil nor disturbed. Dhyana in essence has no fixed abode. Without attaching yourself to an abode, be serene in dhyana. Dhyana in essence is birthless; without attaching yourself to the thought of birth [-and-death], think in dhyana. Have your mind like unto space and yet have no thought of space." Thus learning of the sixth patriarch's view on samadhi or dhyana, Chih-huang came to the master himself and asked to be further enlightened. Said the patriarch: "What Hsuan-t'se told you is true. Have your mind like unto space and yet entertain in it no thought of emptiness. Then the truth will have its full activity unimpeded. Every movement of yours will come out of an innocent heart, and the ignorant and the wise will have an equal treatment in your hands. Subject and object will lose their distinction, and essence and appearance will be of one suchness. [When a world of absolute oneness is thus realized,] you have attained to eternal samadhi."

To make the position of the sixth patriarch on the subject of meditation still clearer and more definite, let me quote another incident from his *Platform Sutra*. A monk once made reference to a gatha composed by Wo-luan which read as follows:

> "I, Wo-luan, know a device
> Whereby to blot out all my thoughts:
> The objective world no more stirs the mind,
> And daily matures my Enlightenment!"

Hearing this, the sixth patriarch remarked: "That is no enlightenment but leads one into a state of bondage. Listen to my gatha:

> "I, Hui-neng, know no device,
> My thoughts are not suppressed:
> The objective world ever stirs the mind,
> And what is the use of maturing Enlightenment?"

These will be sufficient to show that Hui-neng, the sixth patriarch, was on the one hand no quietist, nor nihilist advocating the doctrine of absolute emptiness, while on the other hand he was no idealist either, in the sense of denying an objective world. His dhyana was full of action, yet above a world of particulars, so long as it was not carried away by it and in it.

4. Hui-neng's method of demonstrating the truth of Zen was purely Chinese and not Indian. He did not resort to abstract terminology nor to romantic mysticism. The method was direct, plain, concrete, and highly practical. When the monk Ming came to him and asked for instruction, he said, "Show me your original face before you were born." Is not the statement quite to the point? No philosophic discourse, no elaborate reasoning, no mystic imagery, but a direct unequivocal dictum. In this the sixth patriarch cut the first turf and his disciples quickly and efficiently followed in his steps. (See Chapter 1.)

Hui-neng died at the age of seventy-six in A.D. 713, while the T'ang dynasty was enjoying its halcyon days and Chinese culture reached the highest point in its history. A little over one hundred years after the passing of the sixth patriarch, Liu Tsung-yuan, one of the most brilliant literati in the history of Chinese literature, wrote a memorial inscription on his tombstone when he was honoured by the Emperor Hsien-tsung with the posthumous title, Great Mirror (*tai-chien*), and in this we read: "In a sixth transmission after Dharma there was Tai-chien. He was first engaged in menial labour and servile work. Just a few words from the master were enough and he at once understood the deepest meaning conveyed in them. The master was greatly impressed, and finally conferred on him an insignia of faith. After that he hid himself in the Southern district; nobody heard of him again for sixteen years, when he thought the time was ripe for him to come out of the seclusion. He was settled at T'sao-ch'i[5] and began to teach. The number of disciples is said once to have reached several thousands.

[5] This is the name of the place where Hui-neng had his Zen headquarters.

"According to his doctrine, non-doing is reality, emptiness is the truth, and the ultimate meaning of things is vast and immovable. He taught that human nature in its beginning as well as in the end is thoroughly good and does not require any artificial weeding-out, for it has its root in that which is serene. The Emperor Chung-tsung heard of him and sent his courtier twice asking him to appear at Court, but failed to get him out. So the Emperor had his words instead which he took for his spiritual guidance. The teaching [of the sixth patriarch] in detail is generally accessible today; all those who talk at all about Zen find their source of information in T'sao-ch'i."

After Hui-neng Zen was split up into several schools, two of which have survived even down to this day, in China as well as in Japan. Though much modified in various aspects, the principle and spirit of Zen Buddhism is still alive as it was in the days of the sixth patriarch, and as one of the great spiritual heritages of the East it is still wielding its unique influence, especially among the cultured people in Japan.

III. THE HEART OF ZEN

CHAPTER 4

Satori, or Enlightenment

I

The essence of Zen Buddhism consists in acquiring a new viewpoint on life and things generally. By this I mean that if we want to get into the inmost life of Zen, we must forgo all our ordinary habits of thinking which control our everyday life, we must try to see if there is any other way of judging things, or rather if our ordinary way is always sufficient to give us the ultimate satisfaction of our spiritual needs. If we feel dissatisfied somehow with this life, if there is something in our ordinary way of living that deprives us of freedom in its most sanctified sense, we must endeavour to find a way somewhere which gives us a sense of finality and contentment. Zen proposes to do this for us and assures us of the acquirement of a new point of view in which life assumes a fresher, deeper, and more satisfying aspect. This acquirement, however, is really and naturally the greatest mental cataclysm one can go through with in life. It is no easy task, it is a kind of fiery baptism, and one has to go through the storm, the earthquake, the overthrowing of the mountains, and the breaking in pieces of the rocks.

This acquiring of a new point of view in our dealings with life and the world is popularly called by Japanese Zen students "satori" (*wu* in Chinese). It is really another name for Enlightenment (*anuttara-samyak-sambodhi*), which is the word used by the Buddha and his Indian followers ever since his realization under the Bodhi-tree by the River Nairanjana. There are several other phrases in Chinese designating this spiritual experience, each of which has a special connotation, showing tentatively how this phenomenon is interpreted. At all events there is no Zen without satori, which is indeed the Alpha and Omega of Zen Buddhism. Zen devoid of satori is like a sun without its light and heat. Zen may lose all its literature, all its monasteries, and all its paraphernalia; but as long as there is satori in it it will survive to eternity. I want to emphasize this most fundamental fact concerning the very life of Zen; for there are some even among the students of Zen themselves who are blind to this central fact and are apt to think when Zen has been explained away logically or psychologically, or as one of the Buddhist philosophies which can be summed up by using highly technical and conceptual Buddhist phrases, Zen is exhausted, and there remains nothing in it that makes it what it is. But my contention is, the life of Zen begins with the opening of satori (*kai wu* in Chinese).

Satori may be defined as an intuitive looking into the nature of things in contradistinction to the analytical or logical understanding of it. Practically, it means the unfolding of a new world hitherto unperceived in the confusion of a dualistically-trained mind. Or we may say that with satori our entire surroundings are viewed from quite an unexpected angle of perception. Whatever this is, the world for those who have gained a satori is no more the old world as it used to be; even with all its flowing streams and burning fires, it is never the same one again. Logically stated, all its opposites and contradictions are united and harmonized into a consistent organic whole. This is a mystery and a miracle, but according to the Zen masters such is being performed every day. Satori can thus be had only through our once personally experiencing it.

Its semblance or analogy in a more or less feeble and fragmentary way is gained when a difficult mathematical problem is solved, or when a great discovery is made, or when a sudden means of escape is realized in the midst of most desperate complications; in short, when one exclaims "Eureka! Eureka!" But this refers only to the intellectual aspect of satori, which is therefore necessarily partial and incomplete and does not touch the very foundations of life considered one indivisible whole. Satori as the Zen experience must be concerned with the entirety of life. For what Zen proposes to do is the revolution, and the revaluation as well, of oneself as a spiritual unity. The solving of a mathematical problem ends with the solution, it does not affect one's whole life. So with all other particular questions, practical or scientific, they do not enter the basic life-tone of the individual concerned. But the opening of satori is the remaking of life itself. When it is genuine—for there are many simulacra of it—its effects on one's moral and spiritual life are revolutionary, and they are so enhancing, purifying, as well as exacting. When a master was asked what constituted Buddhahood, he answered, "The bottom of a pail is broken through." From this we can see what a complete revolution is produced by this spiritual experience. The birth of a new man is really cataclysmic.

In the psychology of religion this spiritual enhancement of one's whole life is called "conversion". But as the term is generally used by Christian converts, it cannot be applied in its strict sense to the Buddhist experience, especially to that of the Zen followers; the term has too affective or emotional a shade to take the place of satori, which is above all noetic. The general tendency of Buddhism is, as we know, more intellectual than emotional, and its doctrine of Enlightenment distinguishes it sharply from the Christian view of salvation; Zen as one of the Mahayana schools naturally shares a large amount of what we may call transcendental intellectualism, which does not issue in logical dualism. When poetically or figuratively expressed, satori is "the opening of the mind-flower", or "the removing of the bar", or "the brightening up of the mind-works".

II

The coming of Bodhi-Dharma (Bodai-daruma in Japanese, P'u-ti Ta-mo in Chinese) to China early in the sixth century was simply to introduce this satori element into the body of Buddhism, whose advocates were then so engrossed in subtleties of philosophical discussion or in the mere literary observance of rituals and disciplinary rules. By the "absolute transmission of the spiritual seal", which was claimed by the first patriarch, is meant the opening of satori, obtaining an eye to see into the spirit of the Buddhist teaching.

The sixth patriarch, Yeno (Hui-neng), was distinguished because of his upholding the satori aspect of dhyana against the mere mental tranquillization of the Northern school of Zen under the leadership of Jinshu (Shen-hsiu). Baso (Ma-tsu), Obaku (Huan-po), Rinzai (Lin-chi), and all the other stars illuminating the early days of Zen in the T'ang dynasty were advocates of satori. Their life-activities were unceasingly directed towards the advancement of this; and as one can readily recognize, they so differed from those merely absorbed in contemplation or the practising of dhyana so called. They were strongly against quietism, declaring its adherents to be purblind and living in the cave of darkness. Before we go on it is advisable, therefore, to have this point clearly understood so that we leave no doubt as to the ultimate purport of Zen, which is by no means wasting one's life away in a trance-inducing practice, but consists in seeing into the life of one's being or opening an eye of satori.

There is in Japan a book going under the title of *Six Essays by Shoshitsu* (that is, by Bodhi-Dharma, the first patriarch of Zen); the book contains no doubt some of the sayings of Dharma, but most of the Essays are not his; they were probably composed during the T'ang dynasty when Zen Buddhism began to make its influence more generally felt among the Chinese Buddhists. The spirit, however, pervading the book is in perfect accord with the principle of Zen. One of the Essays entitled "Kechimyakuron", or "Treatise on the Lineage of Faith", discusses the question of *Chien-hsing*,[1] or satori,

---

[1] *Hsing* means nature, character, essence, soul, or what is innate to one. "Seeing into one's Nature" is one of the set phrases used by the Zen masters, and is in fact the avowed object of all Zen discipline. Satori is its more popular expression. When one gets into the inwardness of things, there is satori. This latter, however, being a broad term, can be used to designate any kind of a thorough understanding, and it is only in Zen that it has a restricted meaning. In this article I have used the term as the most essential thing in the study of Zen; for "seeing into one's Nature" suggests the idea that Zen

which, according to the author, constitutes the essence of Zen Buddhism. The following passages are extracts.

"If you wish to seek the Buddha, you ought to see into your own Nature (*hsing*); for this Nature is the Buddha himself. If you have not seen into your own Nature, what is the use of thinking of the Buddha, reciting the Sutras, observing a fast, or keeping the precepts? By thinking of the Buddha, your cause [i.e. meritorious deed] may bear fruit; by reciting the Sutras your intelligence may grow brighter; by keeping the precepts you may be born in the heavens; by practising charity you may be rewarded abundantly; but as to seeking the Buddha, you are far away from him. If your Self is not yet clearly comprehended, you ought to see a wise teacher and get a thorough understanding as to the root of birth-and-death. One who has not seen into one's own Nature is not to be called a wise teacher.

"When this [seeing into one's own Nature] is not attained, one cannot escape from the transmigration of birth-and-death, however well one may be versed in the study of the sacred scriptures in twelve divisions. No time will ever come to one to get out of the sufferings of the triple world. Anciently there was a Bhikshu Zensho (Shan-hsing[2]) who was capable of reciting all the twelve divisions of scriptures, yet he could not save himself from transmigration, because he had no insight into his own Nature. If this was the case even with Zensho, how about those moderners who, being able to discourse only on a few Sutras and Sastras, regard themselves as exponents

---

has something concrete and substantial which requires being seen into by us. This is misleading, though satori too I admit is a vague and naturally ambiguous word. For ordinary purposes, not too strictly philosophical, satori will answer, and whenever *chien-hsing* is referred to it means this: the opening of the mental eye. As to the sixth patriarch's view on "seeing into one's Nature", see above under *History of Zen Buddhism*.

[2] According to the *Mahaparinirvana-sutra*, translated into Chinese by Dharmaraksha, A.D. 423, Vol. XXXIII, he was one of the three sons of the Buddha while he was still a Bodhisattava. He was most learned in all Buddhist lore, but his views tended to be nihilistic and he finally fell into hell.

of Buddhism? They are truly simple-minded ones. When Mind is not understood it is absolutely of no avail to recite and discourse on idle literature. If you want to seek the Buddha, you ought to see into your own Nature, which is the Buddha himself. The Buddha is a free man—a man who neither works nor achieves.

If, instead of seeing into your own Nature, you turn away and seek the Buddha in external things, you will never get at him.

"The Buddha is your own Mind, make no mistake to bow [to external objects]. 'Buddha' is a Western word, and in this country it means 'enlightened nature'; and by 'enlightened' is meant 'spiritually enlightened'. It is one's own spiritual Nature in enlightenment that responds to the external world, comes in contact with objects, raises the eyebrows, winks the eyelids, and moves the hands and legs. This Nature is the Mind, and the Mind is the Buddha, and the Buddha is the Way, and the Way is Zen. This simple word, Zen, is beyond the comprehension both of the wise and the ignorant. To see directly into one's original Nature, this is Zen. Even if you are well learned in hundreds of the Sutras and Sastras, you still remain an ignoramus in Buddhism when you have not yet seen into your original Nature. Buddhism is not there [in mere learning]. The highest truth is unfathomably deep, is not an object of talk or discussion, and even the canonical texts have no way to bring it within our reach. Let us once see into our own original Nature and we have the truth, even when we are quite illiterate, not knowing a word. . . .

"Those who have not seen into their own Nature may read the Sutras, think of the Buddha, study long, work hard, practise religion throughout the six periods of the day, sit for a long time and never lie down for sleep, and may be wide in learning and well informed in all things; and they may believe that all this is Buddhism. All the Buddhas in successive ages only talk of seeing into one's Nature. All things are impermanent; until you get an insight into your Nature, do not say 'I have perfect knowledge'. Such is really committing a very grave crime. Ananda, one of the ten great disciples of the Buddha was known for his wide information, but did not have any insight into Buddhahood, because he was so bent on gaining information only. . . ."

The sixth patriarch, Hui-neng (Yeno), insists on this in a most unmistakable way when he answers the question: "As to your commission from the fifth patriarch of Huang-mei, how do you direct and instruct others in it?" The answer was, "No direction, no instruction there is; we speak only of seeing into one's Nature and not of practising dhyana and seeking deliverance thereby."

Elsewhere they are designated as the "confused" and "not worth consulting with"; they that are empty-minded and sit quietly, having no thoughts whatever; whereas "even ignorant ones, if they all of a sudden realize the truth and open their mental eyes, are, after all, wise men and may attain even to Buddhahood".

Again, when the patriarch was told of the method of instruction adopted by the masters of the Northern school of Zen, which consisted in stopping all mental activities, quietly absorbed in contemplation, and in sitting cross-legged for the longest while at a stretch, he declared such practices to be abnormal and not at all to the point, being far from the truth of Zen, and added this stanza which was quoted elsewhere:

> "While living one sits up and lies not,
> When dead, one lies and sits not;
> A set of ill-smelling skeleton!
> What is the use of toiling and moiling so?"

When at Demboin, Baso used to sit cross-legged all day and meditating. His master, Nangaku Yejo (Nan-yueh Huai-jang, 677–744), saw him and asked:

"What seekest thou here thus sitting cross-legged?"

"My desire is to become a Buddha."

Thereupon the master took up a piece of brick and began to polish it hard on the stone near by.

"What workest thou on so, my master?" asked Baso.

"I am trying to turn this into a mirror."

"No amount of polishing will make a mirror of the brick, sir."

"If so, no amount of sitting cross-legged as thou doest will make of thee a Buddha," said the master.

"What shall I have to do then?"

"It is like driving a cart; when it moveth not, wilt thou whip the cart or the ox?"

Baso made no answer.

The master continued: "Wilt thou practise this sitting cross-legged in order to attain dhyana or to attain Buddhahood? If it is dhyana, dhyana does not consist in sitting or lying; if it is Buddhahood, the Buddha has no fixed forms. As he has no abiding place anywhere, no one can take hold of him, nor can he be let go. If thou seekest Buddhahood by thus sitting cross-legged, thou murderest him. So long as thou freest thyself not from sitting so,[3] thou never comest to the truth."

These are all plain statements, and no doubts are left as to the ultimate end of Zen, which is not sinking oneself into a state of torpidity by sitting quietly after the fashion of a Hindu saint and trying to exclude all the mental ripplings that seem to come up from nowhere, and after a while pass away—where nobody knows. The Zen masters, as we see below, are always found trying to avail themselves of every apparently trivial incident of life in order to make the disciples' minds flow into a channel hitherto altogether unperceived. It is like picking a hidden lock, the flood of new experiences gushes forth from the opening. It is again like the clock's striking the hours; when the appointed time comes it clicks, and the whole percussion of sounds is released. The mind seems to have something of this mechanism; when a certain moment is reached, a hitherto

[3] That is, from the idea that this sitting cross-legged leads to Buddhahood. From the earliest periods of Zen in China, the quietest tendency has been running along the whole history with the intellectual tendency which emphasizes the satori element. Even today these currents are represented to a certain extent by the Soto on the one hand and the Rinzai on the other, while each has its characteristic features of excellence. My own standpoint is that of the intuitionalist and not that of the quietest; for the essence of Zen lies in the attainment of satori.

closed screen is lifted, an entirely new vista opens up, and the tone of one's whole life thereafter changes. This mental clicking or opening is called satori by the Zen masters and is insisted upon as the main object of their discipline.

In this connection the reader will find the following words of Meister Eckhart quite illuminative: "Upon this matter a heathen sage hath a fine saying in speech with another sage: 'I become aware of something in me which flashes upon my reason. I perceive of it that it is something, but what it is I cannot perceive. Only meseems that, could I conceive it, I should comprehend all truth.' "[4]

III

Here are some examples to show that the whole Zen discipline gains meaning when there takes place this turning of the mental hinge to a wider and deeper world. For when this wise and deeper world opens, everyday life, even the most trivial thing of it, grows loaded with the truths of Zen. On the one hand, therefore, satori is a most prosaic and matter-of-fact thing; on the other hand, a mystery. But after all, is not life itself filled with wonders, mysteries, and unfathomabilities, far beyond our discursive understanding?

A monk asked Joshu (Chao-chou Tsung-shen, 778–897) to be instructed in Zen. Said the master, "Have you had your breakfast or not?" "Yes, master, I have," answered the monk. "If so, have your dishes washed," was an immediate response, which, it is said, at once opened the monk's mind to the truth of Zen.

Tokusan (Teh-shan Hsuan-chien, 779–865) was a great scholar of the *Diamond Sutra* (*Vajracchedika*). Learning that there was such a thing as Zen ignoring all the written scriptures and directly laying hands on one's soul, he came to Ryutan (Lung-t'an) to be instructed in the doctrine. One day Tokusan was sitting outside trying to see into the mystery of

[4] W. Lehmann, *Meister Eckhart*. Gottingen, 1917, p. 243. Quoted by Professor Rudolf Otto in his *The Idea of the Holy*, p. 201.

Zen. Ryutan said, "Why don't you come in?" Replied Tokusan, "It is pitch dark." A candle was lighted and handed over to Tokusan. When the latter was at the point of taking it, Ryutan suddenly blew the light out, whereupon the mind of Tokusan was opened.[5]

Hyakujo (Pai-chang Huai-hai, 724–814) one day went out attending his master Baso (Ma-tsu). A flock of wild geese was seen flying and Baso asked:

"What are they?"

"They are wild geese, sir."

"Whither are they flying?"

"They have flown away, sir."

Baso abruptly taking hold of Hyakujo's nose gave it a twist. Overcome with pain, Hyakujo cried aloud: "Oh! Oh!"

"You say they have flown away," Baso said, "but all the same they have been here from the very beginning."

This made Hyakujo's back wet with cold perspiration. He had satori.

Is there any connection in any possible way between the washing of the dishes and the blowing out of a candle and the twisting of the nose? We must say with Ummon: If there is none, how could they all come to the realization of the truth of Zen? If there is, what inner relationship is there? What is this satori? What new point of viewing things is this? So long as our observation is limited to those conditions which preceded the opening of a disciple's eye we cannot perhaps fully comprehend where lies the ultimate issue. They are matters of everyday occurrence, and if Zen lies objectively among them, every one of us is a master before we are told of it. This is

[5] In Claud Field's *Mystics and Saints of Islam*, p. 25, we read under Hasan Basri: "Another time I saw a child coming toward me holding a lighted torch in his hand, 'Where have you brought the light from?' I asked him. He immediately blew it out, and said to me, 'O Hasan, tell me where it is gone, and I will tell you whence I fetched it.'" Of course the parallel is here only apparent, for Tokusan got his enlightenment from quite a different source than the mere blowing out of the candle. Still the parallel in itself is interesting enough to be quoted here.

partly true inasmuch as there is nothing artificially constructed in Zen, but if the nose is to be really twisted or the candle blown out in order to take the scale off the eye, our attention must be directed inwardly to the working of our minds, and it will be there where we are to take hold of the hidden relation existing between the flying geese and the washed dishes and the blown-out candle and any other happenings that weave our infinitely variegated patterns of human life.

Under Daiye (Tai-hui, 1089–1163), the great Zen teacher of the Sung dynasty, there was a monk named Doken (Tao-ch'ien) who had spent many years in the study of Zen, but who had not yet delved into its secrets, if there were any. He was discouraged when he was sent on an errand to a distant city. A trip requiring half a year to finish would surely be a hindrance rather than a help to his study. Sogen (Tsung-yuan), one of his fellow-monks, took pity on him and said: "I will accompany you on this trip and do all that I can for you. There is no reason why you cannot go on with your meditation even while travelling." They started together.

One evening Doken despairingly implored his friend to assist him in the solution of the mystery of life. The friend said: "I am willing to help you in every way, but there are five things in which I cannot be of any help to you. These you must look after yourself." Doken expressed the desire to know what they were. "For instance," said the friend, "when you are hungry or thirsty, my eating of food or drinking does not fill your stomach. You must drink and eat yourself. When you want to respond to the calls of nature, you must take care of them yourself, for I cannot be of any use to you. And then it will be nobody else but yourself that will carry this corpse of yours [i.e. the body] along this highway." This remark at once opened the mind of the truth-seeking monk, who, transported with his discovery, did not know how to express his joy.

Sogen now told him that his work was done and that his further companionship would have no meaning after this. So they parted company and Doken was left alone to continue the trip. After the half-year, Doken came back to his own monastery. Daiye, his teacher, happened to meet him on his way down the mountain, and made the following remark, "This time he knows it all." What was it, one may remark, that flashed through Doken's mind when his friend Sogen gave him such matter-of-fact advice?

Kyogen (Hsian-yen) was a disciple of Hyakujo. After the master's death he went to Yisan (Wei-shan, 771–853), who was a senior disciple of Hyakujo. Yisan asked him: "I am told that you have been under my late master Hyakujo, and also that you have remarkable intelligence; but the understanding of Zen through this medium necessarily ends in intellectual and analytical comprehension, which is not of much use. Yet you may have had an insight into the truth of Zen. Let me have your view as to the reason of birth-and-death; that is, as to your own being before your parents gave birth to you."

Thus asked, Kyogen did not know how to reply. He retired into his own room and assiduously made research among his notes which he had taken of the sermons given by his late master. He failed to come across a suitable passage he might present as his own view. He returned to Yisan and implored him to teach in the faith of Zen. But Yisan said: "I really have nothing to impart to you, and if I tried to do so you may have occasion to make me an object of ridicule later on. Besides, whatever I can instruct you is my own and will never be yours." Kyogen was disappointed and considered his senior disciple unkind. Finally he came to the decision to burn up all his notes and memorandums which were of no help to his spiritual welfare, and, retiring altogether from the world, to spend the rest of his life in solitude and simplicity in accordance with the Buddhist rules. He reasoned: "What is the use of studying Buddhism, so difficult to comprehend and too subtle to receive instructions from another? I shall be a plain homeless monk, troubled with no desire to master things too deep for thought." He left Yisan and built a hut near the tomb of Chu (Hui-chung), the National Master, at Nan-yang. One day he was weeding and sweeping the ground, and when a piece of rock brushed away struck a bamboo, the sound produced by the percussion unexpectedly elevated his mind to a state of satori. The question proposed by Yisan became transparent; his joy was boundless, he felt as if meeting again his lost parent. Besides, he came to realize the kindness of his abandoned senior brother monk who refused him instruction. For he now knew that this would not have happened to him if Yisan had been unkind enough to explain things for him.

Below is the verse he composed soon after his achievement, from which we may get an idea of his satori:

"One stroke has made me forget all my previous knowledge,
No artificial discipline is at all needed;
In every movement I uphold the ancient way,
And never fall into the rut of mere quietism;
Wherever I walk no traces are left,
And my senses are not fettered by rules of conduct;
Everywhere those who have attained to the truth,
All declare this to be of the highest order."

IV

There is something, we must admit, in Zen that defies explanation, and to which no master however ingenious can lead his disciples through intellectual analysis. Kyogen or Tokusan had enough knowledge of the canonical teachings or of the master's expository discourses; but when the real thing was demanded of them they significantly failed to produce it either to their inner satisfaction or for the master's approval. The satori, after all, is not a thing to be gained through the understanding. But once the key is within one's grasp, everything seems to be laid bare before him; the entire world assumes then a different aspect. By those who know, this inner change is recognized. The Doken before he started on his mission and the Doken after the realization were apparently the same person; but as soon as Daiye saw him he knew what had taken place in him, even when he uttered not a word.

Baso twisted Hyakujo's nose, and the latter turned into such a wild soul as to have the audacity to roll up the matting before his master's discourse had hardly begun (see below). The experience they have gone through within themselves is not a very elaborate, complicated, and intellectually demonstrable thing; for none of them ever try to expound it by a series of learned discourses; they do just this thing or that, or utter a single phrase unintelligible to outsiders, and the whole affair proves most satisfactory both to the master and to the disciple. The satori cannot be a phantasm, empty and contentless, and lacking in real value, but the simplest possible experience perhaps because it is the very foundation of all experiences.

As to the opening of satori, all that Zen can do is to indicate the way and leave the rest all to one's own experience; that is to say, following up the indication and arriving at the goal —this is to be done by oneself and without another's help. With all that the master can do, he is helpless to make the disciple take hold of the thing unless the latter is inwardly fully prepared for it. Just as we cannot make a horse drink against his will, the taking hold of the ultimate reality is to be done by oneself. Just as the flower blooms out of its inner necessity, the looking into one's own nature must be the outcome of one's own inner overflowing. This is where Zen is so personal and subjective, in the sense of being inner and creative.

Zen does not give us any intellectual assistance, nor does it waste time in arguing the point with us; but it merely suggests or indicates, not because it wants to be indefinite, but because that is really the only thing it can do for us. If it could, it would do anything to help us come to an understanding. In fact Zen is exhausting every possible means to do that, as we can see in all the great masters' attitudes towards their disciples.[6] When they are actually knocking them down, their kindheartedness is never to be doubted. They are just waiting for the time when their pupils' minds get all ripened for the final moment. When this is come, the opportunity of opening an eye to the truth of Zen lies everywhere. One can pick it up in the hearing of an inarticulate sound, or listening to an unintelligible remark, or in the observation of a flower blooming, or in the encountering of any trivial everyday incident

[6] See Chapter 5, "Practical Methods of Zen Instruction", pp. 111.

such as stumbling, rolling up a screen, using a fan, etc. These are all sufficient conditions that will awaken one's inner sense. Evidently a most insignificant happening, and yet its effect on the mind infinitely surpasses all that one could expect of it. A light touch of an ignited wire, and an explosion shaking the very foundations of the earth. In fact, all the causes of satori are in the mind. That is why when the clock clicks, all that has been lying there bursts up like a volcanic eruption or flashes out like a bolt of lightning.[7] Zen calls this "returning to one's own home"; for its followers will declare: "You have now found yourself; from the very beginning nothing has been kept away from you. It was yourself that closed the eye to the fact. In Zen there is nothing to explain, nothing to teach, that will add to your knowledge. Unless it grows out of yourself, no knowledge is really of value to you, a borrowed plumage never grows."

As Satori strikes at the primary fact of existence, its attainment marks a turning-point in one's life. The attainment, however, must be thorough-going and clear-cut in order to produce a satisfactory result. To deserve the name "satori" the mental revolution must be so complete as to make one really and sincerely feel that there took place a fiery baptism of the spirit. The intensity of this feeling is proportional to the amount of effort the opener of satori has put into the achievement. For there is a gradation in satori as to its intensity, as in all our mental activity. The possessor of a lukewarm satori may suffer no such spiritual revolution as Rinzai, or Bukko (Fo-kuang), whose case is quoted below. Zen is a matter of character and not of the intellect, which means that Zen grows out of the will as the first principle of life. A brilliant intellect may fail to unravel all the mysteries of Zen, but a strong soul will drink deep of the inexhaustible fountain. I do not know if the intellect is superficial and touches only the fringe of one's per-

---

[7] The lightning simile in the *Kena-Upanishad* (IV, 30), as is supposed by some scholars, is not to depict the feeling of inexpressive awe as regards the nature of Brahman, but it illustrates the bursting out of enlightenment upon consciousness. "A—a—ah" is most significant here.

sonality, but the fact is that the will is the man himself, and Zen appeals to it. When one becomes penetratingly conscious of the working of this agency, there is the opening of satori and the understanding of Zen. As they say, the snake has now grown into the dragon; or, more graphically, a common cur —a most miserable creature wagging its tail for food and sympathy, and kicked about by the street boys so mercilessly— has now turned into a golden-haired lion whose roar frightens to death all the feeble-minded.

Therefore, when Rinzai was meekly submitting to the "thirty blows" of Obaku, he was a pitiable sight; as soon as he attained satori he was quite a different personage, and his first exclamation was, "There is not much after all in the Buddhism of Obaku." And when he saw the reproachful Obaku again, he returned his favour by giving him a slap on the face. "What an arrogance, what an impudence!" Obaku exclaimed; but there was reason in Rinzai's rudeness, and the old master could not but be pleased with this treatment from his former tearful Rinzai.

When Tokusan gained an insight into the truth of Zen he immediately took up all his commentaries on the *Diamond Sutra*, once so valued and considered indispensable that he had to carry them wherever he went; he now set fire to them, reducing all the manuscripts to nothingness. He exclaimed, "However deep your knowledge of abstruse philosophy, it is like a piece of hair placed in the vastness of space; and however important your experience in things worldly, it is like a drop of water thrown into an unfathomable abyss."

On the day following the incident of the flying geese, to which reference is made elsewhere, Baso appeared in the preaching-hall, and was about to speak before a congregation, when Hyakujo came forward and began to roll up the matting.[8] Baso without protesting came down from his seat and returned to his own room. He then called Hyakujo and asked

---

[8] This is spread before the Buddha and on it the master performs his bowing ceremony, and its rolling up naturally means the end of a sermon.

him why he rolled up the matting before he had uttered a word.

"Yesterday you twisted my nose," replied Hyakujo, "and it was quite painful."

"Where," said Baso, "was your thought wandering then?"

"It is not painful any more today, master."

How differently he behaves now! When his nose was pinched, he was quite an ignoramus in the secrets of Zen. He is now a golden-haired lion, he is master of himself, and acts as freely as if he owned the world, pushing away even his own master far into the background.

There is no doubt that satori goes deep into the very root of individuality. The change achieved thereby is quite remarkable, as we see in the examples above cited.

When our consideration is limited to the objective side of satori as illustrated so far, it does not appear to be a very extraordinary thing—this opening an eye to the truth of Zen. The master makes some remarks, and if they happen to be opportune enough, the disciple will come at once to a realization and see into a mystery hitherto undreamed of. It seems all to depend upon what kind of mood or what state of mental preparedness one is in at the moment. Zen is after all a haphazard affair, one may be tempted to think; but when we know that it took Nangaku (Nanyueh) eight long years to answer the question "Who is he that thus cometh towards me?" we shall realize the fact that there was in him a great deal of mental anguish and tribulation which he had to go through before he could come to the final solution and declare, "Even when one asserts that it is a somewhat, one misses it altogether." We must try to look into the psychological aspect of satori, where is revealed the inner mechanism of opening the door to the eternal secrets of the human soul. This is done best by quoting some of the masters themselves whose introspective statements are on record.

Koho (Kao-feng, 1238–1285) was one of the great masters in the latter part of the Sung dynasty. When his master first let him attend to the "Joshu's Mu",[9] he exerted himself hard on the problem. One day his master, Setsugan (Hsueh-yen), suddenly asked him, "Who is it that carries for you this lifeless corpse of yours?" The poor fellow did not know what to make of the question, for the master was merciless and it was usually followed by a hard knocking down. Later, in the midst of his sleep one night, he recalled the fact that once when he was under another master he was told to find out the ultimate signification of the statement "All things return to one",[10] and this kept him up the rest of that night and through the several days and nights that succeeded. While in this state of an extreme mental tension he found himself one day looking at Goso Hoyen's verse on his own portrait, which partly read:

"One hundred years—thirty-six thousand morns,
This same old fellow moveth on for ever!"

This at once made him dissolve his eternal doubt as to "Who's carrying around this lifeless body of yours?" He was baptized and became an altogether new man.

He leaves us in his *Goroku* ("Sayings Recorded") an account of those days of the mental strain in the following narrative: "In olden days when I was at Sokei (Shuang-ching),

[9] This is one of the most noted ko-an and generally give to the uninitiated as an eye-opener. When Joshu was asked by a monk whether there was Buddha-Nature in the dog, the master answered "Mu!" (*wu* in Chinese), which literally means "no". But as it is nowadays understood by the followers of Rinzai, it does not mean anything negative as the term may suggest to us ordinarily, it refers to something most assuredly positive, and the novice is told to find it out by himself, not depending upon others (*aparapaccaya*), as no explanation will be given nor is any possible. This ko-an is popularly known as "Joshu's Mu or Muji". A ko-an is a theme or statement or question given to the Zen student for solution, which will lead him to a spiritual insight. The subject will be fully treated in the Second Series of the *Essays in Zen Buddhism*.

[10] Another ko-an for beginners. A monk once asked Joshu, "All things return to the One, but where does the One return?" To which the master answered, "When I was in the province of Seiju (Ts'ing-chou) I had a monkish garment made which weighed seven kin (*chin*).

and before one month was over after my return to the Meditation Hall there, one night while deep in sleep I suddenly found
myself fixing my attention on the question 'All things return
to the One, but where does this One return?' My attention was
so rigidly fixed on this that I neglected sleeping, forgot to eat,
and did not distinguish east from west, nor morning from
night. While spreading the napkin, producing the bowls, or
attending to my natural wants, whether I moved or rested,
whether I talked or kept silent, my whole existence was
wrapped up with the question 'Where does this one return?'
No other thoughts ever disturbed my consciousness; no, even
if I wanted to stir up the least bit of thought irrelevant to
the central one, I could not do so. It was like being screwed
up or glued; however much I tried to shake myself off, it refused to move. Though I was in the midst of a crowd or congregation, I felt as if I were all by myself. From morning till
evening, from evening till morning, so transparent, so tranquil,
so majestically above all things were my feelings! Absolutely
pure and not a particle of dust! My one thought covered
eternity; so calm was the outside world, so oblivious of the
existence of other people I was. Like an idiot, like an imbecile,
six days and nights thus elapsed when I entered the Shrine
with the rest, reciting the Sutras, and happened to raise my
head and looked at the verse by Goso. This made me all of a
sudden awake from the spell, and the meaning of 'Who carries
this lifeless corpse of yours?' burst upon me—the question once
given by my old master. I felt as if this boundless space itself
were broken up into pieces, and the great earth were altogether levelled away. I forgot myself, I forgot the world, it was
like one mirror reflecting another. I tried several ko-an in my
mind and found them so transparently clear! I was no more
deceived as to the wonderful working of Prajna (transcendental wisdom)." When Koho saw his old master later, the
latter lost no time in asking him, "Who is it that carries this
lifeless corpse of yours?" Koho burst out a "Kwats!" Thereupon
the master took up a stick ready to give him a blow, but
the disciple held it back, saying, "You cannot give me a blow
today." "Why can't I?" was the master's demand. Instead of

replying to him, however, Koho left the room briskly. The following day the master asked him, "All things return to the One, and where does the One return to?" "The dog is lapping the boiling water in the cauldron." "Where did you get this nonsense?" reprimanded the master. "You had better ask yourself," promptly came the response. The master rested well satisfied.

These cases show what mental process one has to go through before the opening of satori takes place. Of course these are prominent examples and highly accentuated, and every satori is not preceded by such an extraordinary degree of concentration. But an experience more or less like these must be the necessary antecedent to all satori, especially to that which is to be gone through at the outset of the study. The mirror of mind or the field of consciousness then seems to be so thoroughly swept clean as not to leave a particle of dust on it.

When thus all mentation is temporarily suspended, even the consciousness of an effort to keep an idea focused at the centre of attention is gone—that is, when, as the Zen followers say, the mind is so completely possessed or identified with its object of thought that even the consciousness of identity is lost as when one mirror reflects another, the subject feels as if living in a crystal palace, all transparent, refreshing, buoyant, and royal. But the end has not yet been reached, this being merely the preliminary condition leading to the consummation called satori. If the mind remains in this state of fixation, there will be no occasion for its being awakened to the truth of Zen. The state of "Great Doubt" (*tai-gi*), as it is technically known, is the antecedent. It must be broken up and exploded into the next stage, which is looking into one's nature or the opening of satori.

The explosion, as it is nothing else, generally takes place when this finely balanced equilibrium tilts for one reason or another. A stone is thrown into a sheet of water in perfect stillness, and the disturbance at once spreads all over the surface. It is somewhat like this. A sound knocks at the gate of consciousness so tightly closed, and it at once reverberates through the entire being of the individual. He is awakened in the most vivid sense of the word. He comes out baptized in the fire of creation. He has seen the work of God in his very workshop. The occasion may not necessarily be the hearing of a temple bell, it may be reading a stanza, or seeing something moving, or the sense of touch irritated, when a most highly accentuated state of concentration bursts out into a satori.

V. CHIEF CHARACTERISTICS OF SATORI

1. *Irrationality.* By this I mean that satori is not a conclusion to be reached by reasoning, and defies all intellectual determination. Those who have experienced it are always at a loss to explain it coherently or logically. When it is explained at all, either in words or gestures, its content more or less undergoes a mutilation. The uninitiated are thus unable to grasp it by what is outwardly visible, while those who have had the experience discern what is genuine from what is not. The satori experience is thus always characterized by irrationality, inexplicability, and incommunicability.

Listen to Tai-hui once more: "This matter [i.e. Zen] is like a great mass of fire; when you approach it your face is sure to be scorched. It is again like a sword about to be drawn; when it is once out of the scabbard, someone is sure to lose his life. But if you neither fling away the scabbard nor approach the fire, you are no better than a piece of rock or of wood. Coming to this pass, one has to be quite a resolute character full of spirit."[11] There is nothing here suggestive of cool reasoning and quiet metaphysical or epistemological analysis, but of a certain desperate will to break through an insurmountable barrier, of the will impelled by some irrational or unconscious power behind it. Therefore, the outcome also defies intellection or conceptualization.

2. *Intuitive insight.* That there is noetic quality in mystic experiences has been pointed out by James in his *Varieties of Religious Experience,* and this applies also to the Zen experi-

[11] Tai-hui's sermon at the request of Li Hsuan-chiao.

ence known as satori. Another name for satori is "ken-sho" (*chien-hsing* in Chinese) meaning "to see essence or nature", which apparently proves that there is "seeing" or "perceiving" in satori. That this seeing is of quite a different quality from what is ordinarily designated as knowledge need not be specifically noticed. Hui-k'e is reported to have made this statement concerning his satori which was confirmed by Bodhidharma himself: "[As to my satori], it is not a total annihilation; it is knowledge of the most adequate kind; only it cannot be expressed in words." In this respect Shen-hui was more explicit, for he says that "the one character *chih* (knowledge) is the source of all mysteries".[12]

Without this noetic quality satori will lose all its pungency, for it is really the reason of satori itself. It is noteworthy that the knowledge contained in satori is concerned with something universal and at the same time with the individual aspect of existence. When a finger is lifted, the lifting means, from the viewpoint of satori, far more than the act of lifting. Some may call it symbolic, but satori does not point to anything beyond itself, being final as it is. Satori is the knowledge of an individual object and also that of Reality which is, if I may say so, at the back of it.

3. *Authoritativeness*. By this I mean that the knowledge realized by satori is final, that no amount of logical argument can refute it. Being direct and personal it is sufficient unto itself. All that logic can do here is to explain it, to interpret it in connection with other kinds of knowledge with which our minds are filled. Satori is thus a form of perception, an inner perception, which takes place in the most interior part of consciousness. Hence the sense of authoritativeness, which means finality. So, it is generally said that Zen is like drinking water, for it is by one's self that one knows whether it is warm or cold. The Zen perception being the last term of experience, it cannot be denied by outsiders who have no such experience.

4. *Affirmation*. What is authoritative and final can never be

[12] *Miao* is a difficult term to translate; it often means "exquisiteness", "indefinable subtlety". In this case *miao* is the mysterious way in which things are presented to this ultimate knowledge. Tsung-mi on *Zen Masters and Disciples*.

negative. For negation has no value for our life, it leads us nowhere; it is not a power that urges, nor does it give one a place to rest. Though the satori experience is sometimes expressed in negative terms, it is essentially an affirmative attitude towards all things that exist; it accepts them as they come along regardless of their moral values. Buddhists call this *kshanti*, "patience", or more properly "acceptance", that is, acceptance of things in their suprarelative or transcendental aspect where no dualism of whatever sort avails.

Some may say that this is pantheistic. The term, however, has a definite philosophic meaning and I would not see it used in this connection. When so interpreted the Zen experience exposes itself to endless misunderstandings and "defilements". Tai-hui says in his letter to Miao-tsung: "An ancient sage says that the Tao itself does not require special disciplining, only let it not be defiled. I would say: To talk about mind or nature is defiling; to talk about the unfathomable or the mysterious is defiling; to practise meditation or tranquillization is defiling; to direct one's attention to it, to think about it is defiling; to be writing about it thus on paper with a brush is especially defiling. What then shall we have to do in order to get ourselves oriented, and properly apply ourselves to it? The precious vajra sword is right here and its purpose is to cut off the head. Do not be concerned with human questions of right and wrong. All is Zen just as it is, and right here you are to apply yourself." Zen is Suchness—a grand affirmation.

5. *Sense of the Beyond.* Terminology may differ in different religions, and in satori there is always what we may call a sense of the Beyond; the experience indeed is my own but I feel it to be rooted elsewhere. The individual shell in which my personality is so solidly encased explodes at the moment of satori. Not, necessarily, that I get unified with a being greater than myself or absorbed in it, but that my individuality, which I found rigidly held together and definitely kept separate from other individual existences, becomes loosened somehow from its tightening grip and melts away into something indescribable, something which is of quite a different order from what I am accustomed to. The feeling that follows is that of a complete release or a complete rest—the feeling that one has ar-

rived finally at the destination. "Coming home and quietly resting" is the expression generally used by Zen followers. The story of the prodigal son in the *Saddharmapundarika,* in the *Vajra-samadhi,* and also in the New Testament points to the same feeling one has at the moment of a satori experience.

As far as the psychology of satori is considered, a sense of the Beyond is all we can say about it; to call this the Beyond, the Absolute, or God, or a Person is to go further than the experience itself and to plunge into a theology or metaphysics. Even the "Beyond" is saying a little too much. When a Zen master says, "There is not a fragment of a tile above my head, there is not an inch of earth beneath my feet," the expression seems to be an appropriate one. I have called it elsewhere the Unconscious, though this has a psychological taint.

6. *Impersonal Tone.* Perhaps the most remarkable aspect of the Zen experience is that it has no personal note in it as is observable in Christian mystic experiences. There is no reference whatever in Buddhist satori to such personal and frequently sexual feelings and relationships as are to be gleaned from these terms: flame of love, a wonderful love shed in the heart, embrace, the beloved, bride, bridegroom, spiritual matrimony, Father, God, the Son of God, God's child, etc. We may say that all these terms are interpretations based on a definite system of thought and really have nothing to do with the experience itself. At any rate, alike in India, China, and Japan, satori has remained thoroughly impersonal, or rather highly intellectual.

Is this owing to the peculiar character of Buddhist philosophy? Does the experience itself take its colours from the philosophy or theology? Whatever this is, there is no doubt that in spite of its having some points of similitude to the Christian mystic experience, the Zen experience is singularly devoid of personal or human colourings. Chao-pien, a great government officer of the Sung dynasty, was a lay-disciple of Fach'uan of Chiang-shan. One day after his official duties were over, he found himself leisurely sitting in his office, when all of a sudden a clash of thunder burst on his ear, and he realized a state of satori. The poem he then composed depicts one aspect of the Zen experience:

"Devoid of thought, I sat quietly by the desk in my
official room,
With my fountain-mind undisturbed, as serene as
water;
A sudden clash of thunder, the mind-doors burst
open,
And lo, there sitteth the old man in all his homeliness."

This is perhaps all the personal tone one can find in the Zen
experience, and what a distance between "the old man in his
homeliness" and "God in all his glory", not to say anything
about such feelings as "the heavenly sweetness of Christ's excellent love", etc.! How barren, how unromantic satori is when
compared with the Christian mystic experiences!

Not only satori itself is such a prosaic and non-glorious event,
but the occasion that inspires it also seems to be unromantic
and altogether lacking in supersensuality. Satori is experienced
in connection with any ordinary occurrence in one's daily life.
It does not appear to be an extraordinary phenomenon as is
recorded in Christian books of mysticism. Someone takes hold
of you, or slaps you, or brings you a cup of tea, or makes some
most commonplace remark, or recites some passage from a
sutra or from a book of poetry, and when your mind is ripe
for its outburst, you come at once to satori. There is no ro-
mance of love-making, no voice of the Holy Ghost, no pleni-
tude of Divine Grace, no glorification of any sort. Here is
nothing painted in high colours, all is grey and extremely unob-
trusive and unattractive.

7. *Feeling of Exaltation.* That this feeling inevitably ac-
companies satori is due to the fact that it is the breaking-up of
the restriction imposed on one as an individual being, and this
breaking up is not a mere negative incident but quite a
positive one fraught with signification because it means an
infinite expansion of the individual. The general feeling,
though we are not always conscious of it, which characterizes
all our functions of consciousness, is that of restriction and
dependence, because consciousness itself is the outcome of two
forces conditioning or restricting each other. Satori, on the
contrary, essentially consists in doing away with the opposi-

tion of two terms in whatsoever sense—and this opposition is the principle of consciousness as before mentioned, while satori is to realize the Unconscious which goes beyond the opposition.

To be released of this, therefore, must make one feel above all things intensely exalted. A wandering outcast maltreated everywhere not only by others but by himself finds that he is the possessor of all the wealth and power that is ever attainable in this world by a mortal being—if this does not give him a high feeling of self-glorification, what could? Says a Zen master, "When you have satori you are able to reveal a palatial mansion made of precious stones on a single blade of grass; but when you have no satori, a palatial mansion itself is concealed behind a simple blade of grass."

Another Zen master, evidently alluding to the *Avatamsaka,* declares: "O monks, lo and behold! A most auspicious light is shining with the utmost brilliancy all over the great chiliocosm, simultaneously revealing all the countries, all the oceans, all the Sumerus, all the suns and moons, all the heavens, all the lands—each of which number as many as hundreds of thousands of kotis. O monks, do you not see the light?" But the Zen feeling of exaltation is rather a quiet feeling of self-contentment; it is not at all demonstrative, when the first glow of it passes away. The Unconscious does not proclaim itself so boisterously in the Zen consciousness.

8. *Momentariness.* Satori comes upon one abruptly and is a momentary experience. In fact, if it is not abrupt and momentary, it is not satori. This abruptness (*tun*) is what characterizes the Hui-neng school of Zen ever since its proclamation late in the seventh century. His opponent Shen-hsiu was insistent on a gradual unfoldment of Zen consciousness. Hui-neng's followers were thus distinguished as strong upholders of the doctrine of abruptness. This abrupt experience of satori, then, opens up in one moment (*ekamuhurtena*) an altogether new vista, and the whole existence is appraised from quite a new angle of observation.

IV. TECHNIQUES OF ZEN

CHAPTER 5

Practical Methods of
Zen Instruction

As I conceive it, Zen is the ultimate fact of all philosophy and religion. Every intellectual effort must culminate in it, or rather must start from it, if it is to bear any practical fruits. Every religious faith must spring from it if it has to prove at all efficiently and livingly workable in our active life. Therefore Zen is not necessarily the fountain of Buddhist thought and life alone; it is very much alive also in Christianity, Mohammedanism, in Taoism, and even in positivistic Confucianism. What makes all these religions and philosophies vital and inspiring, keeping up their usefulness and efficiency, is due to the presence in them of what I may designate as the Zen element. Mere scholasticism or mere sacerdotalism will never create a living faith. Religion requires something inwardly propelling, energizing, and capable of doing work. The intellect is useful in its place, but when it tries to cover the whole field of religion it dries up the source of life. Feeling or mere faith is so blind and will grasp anything that may come across and hold to it as the final reality. Fanaticism is vital enough as far as its explosiveness is concerned, but this is not a true religion, and its practical sequence is the destruction of the whole system, not to speak of the fate of its own being. Zen is what makes the religious feeling run through its legitimate channel and what gives life to the intellect.

Zen does this by giving one a new point of view on things, a new way of appreciating the truth and beauty of life and the world, by discovering a new source of energy in the inmost recesses of consciousness, and by bestowing on one a feeling of completeness and sufficiency. That is to say, Zen works miracles by overhauling the whole system of one's inner life and opening up a world hitherto entirely undreamt of. This may be called a resurrection. And Zen tends to emphasize the speculative element, though confessedly it opposes this more than anything else in the whole process of the spiritual revolution, and in this respect Zen is truly Buddhistic. Or it may be better to say that Zen makes use of the phraseology belonging to the sciences of speculative philosophy. Evidently, the feeling element is not so prominently visible in Zen as in the Pure Land sects where "bhakti" (faith) is all in all; Zen on the other hand emphasizes the faculty of seeing (*darsana*) or knowing (*vidya*) though not in the sense of reasoning out, but in that of intuitively grasping.

According to the philosophy of Zen, we are too much of a slave to the conventional way of thinking, which is dualistic through and through. No "interpenetration" is allowed, there takes place no fusing of opposites in our everyday logic. What belongs to God is not of this world, and what is of this world is incompatible with the divine. Black is not white, and white is not black. Tiger is tiger, and cat is cat, and they will never be one. Water flows, a mountain towers. This is the way things or ideas go in this universe of the senses and syllogisms. Zen, however, upsets this scheme of thought and substitutes a new one in which there exists no logic, no dualistic arrangement of ideas. We believe in dualism chiefly because of our traditional training. Whether ideas really correspond to facts is another matter requiring a special investigation. Ordinarily we do not inquire into the matter, we just accept what is instilled into our minds; for to accept is more convenient and practical, and life is to a certain extent, though not in reality, made thereby easier. We are in nature conservatives, not because we are lazy, but because we like repose and peace, even superficially. But the time comes when traditional logic holds true no more, for we begin to feel contradictions and splits and consequently spiritual anguish. We lose trustful repose which we experienced when we blindly followed the traditional ways of thinking. Eckhart says that we are all seeking repose whether consciously or not just as the stone cannot cease moving until it touches the earth. Evidently the repose we seemed to enjoy before we were awakened to the contradictions involved in our logic was not the real one, the stone has kept moving down towards the ground. Where then is the ground of non-dualism on which the soul can be really and truthfully tranquil and blessed? To quote Eckhart again, "Simple people conceive that we are to see God as if He stood on that side and we on this. It is not so; God and I are one in the act of my perceiving Him." In this absolute oneness of things Zen establishes the foundations of its philosophy.

The idea of absolute oneness is not the exclusive possession of Zen, there are other religions and philosophies that preach the same doctrine. If Zen, like other monisms or theisms, merely laid down this principle and did not have anything specifically to be known as Zen, it would have long ceased to exist as such. But there is in Zen something unique which makes up its life and justifies its claim to be the most precious heritage of Eastern culture. The following "mondo" or dialogue (literally questioning and answering) will give us a glimpse into the ways of Zen. A monk asked Joshu (Chaochou), one of the greatest masters in China, "What is the one ultimate word of truth?" Instead of giving him any specific answer he made a simple response saying, "Yes." The monk who naturally failed to see any sense in this kind of response asked for a second time, and to this the master roared back, "I am not deaf!"[1] See how irrelevantly (shall I say) the all-important

---

[1] Another time when Joshu was asked about the "first word", he coughed. The monk remarked, "Is this not it?" "Why, an old man is not even allowed to cough!"—this came quickly from the old master. Joshu had still another occasion to express his view on the one word. A monk asked, "What is the one word?" Demanded the master, "What do you say?" "What is the one word?"—the question was repeated when Joshu gave his verdict, "You make it two."

Shuzan (Shu-shan) was once asked, "An old master says, 'There is one word which when understood wipes out the sins of innumerable kalpas': what is this one word?" Shuzan answered, "Right under your nose!" "What is the ultimate meaning of it?" "This is all I can say":—this was the conclusion of the master.

problem of absolute oneness or of the ultimate reason is treated here! But this is characteristic of Zen, this is where Zen transcends logic and overrides the tyranny and misrepresentation of ideas. As I said before, Zen mistrusts the intellect, does not reply upon traditional and dualistic methods of reasoning, and handles problems after its own original manners.

To cite another instance before going further into the subject proper. The same old Joshu was asked another time, "One light divides itself into hundreds of thousands of lights; may I ask where this one light originates?"² This question like the last mentioned is one of the deepest and most baffling problems of philosophy. But the old master did not waste much time in answering the question, nor did he resort to any wordy discussion. He simply threw off one of his shoes without a remark. What did he mean by it? To understand all this, it is necessary that we should acquire a "third eye", as they say, and learn to look at things from a new point of view.

How is this new way of looking at things demonstrated by the Zen masters? Their methods are naturally very uncommon, unconventional, illogical, and consequently incomprehensible

² There are many mondoes on the same subject. The best known one by Joshu is quoted elsewhere; of others we mention the following. A monk asked Risan (Li-shan), "All things are reduced to emptiness, but where is emptiness reduced?" Risan answered, "The tongue is too short to explain it to you." "Why is it too short?" "Within and without, it is of one suchness," said the master.

A monk asked Keisan (Ch'i-shan), "When relations are dissolved, all is reduced to emptiness; but where is emptiness reduced?" The master called out to the monk, and the monk responded "Yes", whereupon the master called his attention, saying, "Where is emptiness?" Said the monk, "Pray, you tell me." Keisan replied, "It is like the Persian tasting pepper." While the one light is an etiological question as long as its origin is the point at issue, the questions here referred to are teleological because the ultimate reduction of emptiness is the subject for solution. But as Zen transcends time and history, it recognizes only one beginningless and endless course of becoming. When we know the origin of the one light, we also know where emptiness ends.

to the uninitiated. The object of the present chapter will be to describe those methods classified under the following general headings: I. Verbal Method, and II. Direct Method. The first method may be further divided into: 1. Paradox; 2. Going Beyond Opposites; 3. Contradiction; 4. Affirmation; 5. Repetition; and 6. Exclamation.

I. VERBAL METHOD

1. PARADOX

It is well known that all mystics are fond of paradoxes to expound their views. For instance, a Christian mystic may say: "God is real, yet he is nothing, infinite emptiness; he is at once all-being and no-being. The divine kingdom is real and objective; and at the same time it is within myself—I myself am heaven and hell." Eckhart's "divine darkness" or "immovable mover" is another example. I believe we can casually pick up any such statements in mystic literature and compile a book of mystic irrationalities.

Zen is no exception in this respect, but in its way of thus expressing the truth there is something we may designate characteristically Zen. It principally consists in the concreteness and vividness of expression. It generally refuses to lend an ear to abstractions. According to Fudaishi (Fu-ta-shih):

"Empty-handed I go and yet the spade is in my hands;
I walk on foot, and yet on the back of an ox I am riding:
When I pass over the bridge,
Lo, the water floweth not, but the bridge doth flow."

This sounds altogether out of reason, but in fact Zen abounds with such graphic irrationalities. "The flower is not red, nor is the willow green"—is one of the best known utterances of Zen, and is regarded as the same as its affirmative: "The flower is red and the willow is green." To put it in logical formula, it will run like this: "A is at once A and not-A." If so, I am I and yet you are I. An Indian philosopher asserts that *Tat twam asi*, Thou art it. If so, heaven is hell and God is Devil. To pious orthodox Christians, what a shocking doctrine this Zen is! When Mr. Chang drinks Mr. Li grows tipsy. The silent thundering Vimalakirti confessed that he was sick because all his fellow-beings were sick. All wise and loving souls must be said to be the embodiments of the Great Paradox of the universe.

But I am digressing. What I wanted to say was that Zen is more daringly concrete in its paradoxes than other mystical teachings. The latter are more or less confined to general statements concerning life or God or the world, but Zen carries its paradoxical assertions into every detail of our daily life. It has no hesitation in flatly denying all our most familiar facts of experience. "I am writing here and yet I have not written a word. You are perhaps reading this now and yet there is not a person in the world who reads. I am utterly blind and deaf, but every colour is recognized and every sound discerned." The Zen masters will go on like this indefinitely. Basho (Pa-chiao), a Korean monk of the ninth century, once delivered a famous sermon which ran thus: "If you have a staff (*shujo*, or *chu-chang* in Chinese), I will give you one; if you have not, I will take it away from you."

When Joshu, the great Zen master of whom mention was repeatedly made, was asked what he would give when a poverty-stricken fellow should come to him, he replied, "What is wanting in him?"[3] When he was asked on another occasion,

[3] Another time a monk was told, "Hold on to your poverty!" Nan-yin Yegu's (Nan-yuan Hui-yung's) answer to his poverty-stricken monk was more consoling: "You hold a handful of jewels yourself." The subject of poverty is the all-important one in our religious experience—poverty not only in the material but also in the spiritual sense. Asceticism must have as its ground-principle a far deeper sense than to be merely curbing human desires and passions; there must be in it something positive and highly religious. "To be poor in spirit", whatever meaning it may have in Christianity, is rich in signification for Buddhists, especially for Zen followers. A monk, Sei-jei (Ch'ing-shi), came to Sozan (Ts'ao-shan), a great master of the Soto school in China, and said, "I am a poor lonely monk: pray have pity on me." "O monk, come on forward!" Whereupon the monk approached the master, who then exclaimed,

"When a man comes to you with nothing, what would you say to him?" his immediate response was, "Cast it away!" We may ask him, When a man has nothing, what will he cast? When a man is poor, can he be said to be sufficient unto himself? Is he not in need of everything?

Whatever deep meaning there may be in these answers of Joshu, the paradoxes are quite puzzling and baffle our logically trained intellect. "Carry away the farmer's oxen, and make off with the hungry man's food" is a favourite phrase with the Zen masters, who think we can thus best cultivate our spiritual farm and fill up the soul hungry for the substance of things.

It is related that Okubo Shibun, famous for painting bamboo, was requested to execute a kakemono representing a bamboo forest. Consenting, he painted with all his known skill a picture in which the entire bamboo grove was in red. The patron upon its receipt marvelled at the extraordinary skill with which the painting had been executed, and, repairing to the artist's residence he said, "Master, I have come to thank you for the picture; but, excuse me, you have painted the bamboo red." "Well," cried the master, "in what colour would you desire it?" "In black, of course," replied the patron. "And who," answered the artist, "ever saw a black-leaved bamboo?" When one is so used to a certain way of looking at things, one finds it so full of difficulties to veer round and start on a new line of procedure. The true colour of the bamboo is perhaps neither red nor black nor green nor any other colour known to us. Perhaps it is red, perhaps it is black just as well. Who knows? The imagined paradoxes may be after all really not paradoxes.

2. GOING BEYOND THE OPPOSITES

The next form in which Zen expresses itself is the denial of opposites, somehow corresponding to the mystic "via negativa". The point is not to be "caught", as the masters would say, in any of the four propositions (*catushkotika*): 1. "It is

---

"After enjoying three cupfuls of fine *chiu* (liquor) brewed at Ch'ing-yuan, do you still protest that your lips are not at all wet?"

A"; 2. "It is not-A"; 3. "It is both A and not-A"; and 4. "It is neither A nor not-A." When we make a negation or an assertion, we are sure to get into one of these logical formulas according to the Indian method of reasoning. So long as the intellect is to move among the ordinary dualistic groove, this is unavoidable. It is in the nature of our logic that any statement we can make is to be so expressed. But Zen thinks that the truth can be reached when it is neither asserted nor negated. This is indeed the dilemma of life, but the Zen masters are ever insistent on escaping the dilemma. Let us see if they escape free.

According to Ummon, "In Zen there is absolute freedom; sometimes it negates and at other times it affirms; it does either way at pleasure." A monk asked, "How does it negate?" "With the passing of winter there cometh spring." "What happens when spring cometh?" "Carrying a staff across the shoulders, let one ramble about in the fields, East or West, North or South, and beat the old stumps to one's heart's content." This was one way to be free as shown by one of the greatest masters in China.

Kyogen (Hsiang-yen), a disciple of Isan (Wei-shan), with whom we got acquainted just now, said in one of his sermons: "It is like a man over a precipice one thousand feet high, he is hanging himself there with a branch of a tree between his teeth; the feet are far off the ground, and his hands are not taking hold of anything. Suppose another man coming to him to propose a question, 'What is the meaning of the first patriarch coming over here from the West?' If this man should open the mouth to answer, he is sure to fall and lose his life; but if he would make no answer, he must be said to ignore the inquirer. At this critical moment what should he do?" This is putting the negation of opposites in a most graphically illustrative manner. The man over the precipice is caught in a dilemma of life and death, and there can be no logical quibblings. The cat may be sacrificed at the altar of Zen, the mirror may be smashed on the ground, but how about one's own life? The Buddha in one of his former lives is said to have thrown himself down into the maw of a man-devouring monster, in order to get the whole stanza of the truth. Zen, being practical, wants us to make the same noble determination to give up our dualistic life for the sake of enlightenment and eternal peace. For it says that its gate will open when this determination is reached.

3. CONTRADICTION

We now come to the third class I have styled "Contradiction", by which I mean the Zen master's negation, implicitly or expressly, of what he himself has stated or what has been stated by another. To one and the same question his answer is sometimes "No", sometimes "Yes". Or to a well-known and fully established fact he gives an unqualified denial. From an ordinary point of view he is altogether unreliable, yet he seems to think that the truth of Zen requires such contradictions and denials; for Zen has a standard of its own, which, to our common-sense minds, consists just in negating everything we properly hold true and real. In spite of these apparent confusions, the philosophy of Zen is guided by a thorough-going principle whose topsy-turviness, when once grasped, becomes plainest truth.

A monk asked the sixth patriarch of the Zen sect in China, who flourished late in the seventh and early in the eighth centuries, "Who has attained to the secrets of Wobai (Huang-mei)?" Wobai is the name of the mountain where the fifth patriarch, Hung-jen, used to reside, and it was a well-known fact that Hui-neng, the sixth patriarch, studied Zen under him and succeeded in the orthodox line of transmission. The question was therefore really not a plain regular one, seeking an information about facts. It had quite an ulterior object. The reply of the sixth patriarch was, "One who understands Buddhism has attained to the secrets of Wobai."

"Have you then attained them?"

"No, I have not."

"How is it," asked the monk, "that you have not?"

The answer was, "I do not understand Buddhism."[4]

Did he not really understand Buddhism? Or is it that not to understand is to understand? This is also the philosophy of the *Kena-Upanishad*.

This contradiction, negation, or paradoxical statement is the inevitable result of the Zen way of looking at life. The whole emphasis of its discipline is placed on the intuitive grasping of the inner truth deeply hidden in our consciousness. And this truth thus revealed or awakened within oneself defies intellectual manipulation, or at least cannot be imparted to others through any of dialectical formulas. It must come out of oneself, grow within oneself, and become one with one's own being. What others—that is, ideas or images—can do is to indicate the way where lies the truth. This is what Zen masters do. And the indicators given by them are naturally unconventionally free and refreshingly original. As their eyes are always fixed on the ultimate truth itself, anything and everything they can command is utilized to accomplish the end, regardless of its logical conditions and consequences. This indifference to logic is sometimes asserted purposely, just to let us know that the truth of Zen is independent of the intellect. Hence the statement in the *Prajna-paramita-Sutra*, that "Not to have any Dharma to discourse about—this is discoursing about the Dharma."

Haikyu (P'ei Hsiu), a state minister of the T'ang dynasty, was a devoted follower of Zen under Obaku. One day he showed him a manuscript in which his understanding of Zen was stated. The master took it, and setting it down beside him, made no movement to read it, but remained silent for some little while. He then said, "Do you understand?" "Not quite," answered the minister. "If you have an understanding here," said the master, "there is something of Zen. But if it is committed to paper and ink, nowhere is our religion to be found."

Being a living fact, Zen is only where living facts are han-

---

[4] An analogous story is told of Sekito Kisen (Shih-t'ou Hsi-ch'ien), who is grandson in faith of the sixth patriarch. The story is quoted elsewhere.

dled. Appeal to the intellect is real and living as long as it issues directly from life. Otherwise, no amount of literary accomplishment or of intellectual analysis avails in the study of Zen.

4. AFFIRMATION

So far Zen appears to be nothing but a philosophy of negation and contradiction, whereas in fact it has its affirmative side, and in this consists the uniqueness of Zen. In most forms of mysticism, speculative or emotional, their assertions are general and abstract, and there is not much in them that will specifically distinguish them from some of the philosophical dictums. Sings Blake, for instance:

> "To see a world in a grain of sand,
>   And a heaven in a wild flower,
>   Hold infinity in the palm of your hand
>   And eternity in an hour."

Again, listen to the exquisite feelings expressed in the lines of Wither:

> "By the murmur of a spring,
>   Or the least bough's rustling;
>   By a daisy, whose leaves spread
>   Shut when Titan goes to bed;
>   Or a shady bush or tree—
>   She could more infuse in me
>   Than all nature's beauties can
>   In some other wiser men."

It is not very difficult to understand these poetic and mystical feelings as expressed by the highly sensitive souls, though we may not all realize exactly as they felt. Even when Eckhart declares that "the eye with which I see God is the same with which God sees me", or when Plotinus refers to "that which mind, when it turns back, thinks before it thinks itself", we do not find it altogether beyond our understanding to get at their meaning as far as the ideas are concerned which they try to convey in these mystical utterances. But when we come to statements by the Zen masters, we are entirely at sea how to take them. Their affirmations are so irrelevant, so inappropriate, so irrational, and so nonsensical—at least superficially—that those who have not gained the Zen way of looking at things can hardly make, as we say, head or tail of them.

The truth is that even with full-fledged mystics they are unable to be quite free from the taint of intellection, and leave, as a rule, "traces" by which their holy abode could be reached. Plotinus' "flight from alone to alone" is a great mystical utterance proving how deeply he delved into the inner sanctuary of our consciousness. But there is still something speculative or metaphysical about it, and when it is put side by side with the Zen utterances to be cited below, it has, as the masters would say, a mystic flavour on the surface. So long as the masters are indulging in negations, denials, contradictions, or paradoxes, the stain of speculation is not quite washed off them. Naturally, Zen is not opposed to speculation as it is also one of the functions of the mind. But Zen has travelled along a different path altogether unique, I think, in the history of mysticism, whether Eastern or Western, Christian or Buddhist. A few examples will suffice to illustrate my point.

A monk asked Joshu, "I read in the Sutra that all things return to the One, but where does this One return to?" Answered the master, "When I was in the province of Tsing I had a robe made which weighed seven *chin*." When Korin (Hsiang-lin Yuan) was asked what was the signification of Bodhi-Dharma's coming from the West, his reply was, "After a long sitting one feels fatigued." What is the logical relation between the question and the answer? Does it refer to Dharma's nine years' sitting against the wall, as the tradition has it? If so, was his propaganda much ado for nothing except his feeling fatigued? When Kwazan (He-shan) was asked what the Buddha was, he said, "I know how to play the drum, rub-a-dub, rub-a-dub!" (*chieh ta ku*). When Baso Doichi was sick, one of his disciples came and inquired about his condition, "How do you feel today?" "Nichimen-butsu, Gwachimen-butsu!" was the reply, which literally means "sun-faced Buddha, moon-faced Buddha!" A monk asked Joshu, "When the body crumbles all to pieces and returns to the dust, there eternally abides one thing. Of this I have been told, but where does this one thing abide?" The master replied, "It is windy again this morning." When Shuzan (Shou-shan) was asked what was the principal teaching of Buddhism, he quoted a verse:

> "By the castle of the king of Ch'u,
> Eastward flows the stream of Ju."

"Who is the teacher of all the Buddhas?" was the question put to Bokuju (Mu-chou), who in reply merely hummed a tune, "Ting-ting, tung-tung, ku-ti, ku-tung!" To the question what Zen was, the same master gave the following answer, "Namu-sambo!" The monk, however, confessed that he could not understand it, whereupon the master exclaimed, "O you miserable frog, whence is this evil karma of yours?" On another occasion the same question called forth a different answer, which was, "Makahannyaharamii!" When the monk failed to comprehend the ultimate meaning of the phrase, the master went on:

> "My robe is all worn out after so many years' usage,
> And parts of it in shreds loosely hanging, have been
> blown away to the clouds."

To quote another case from Bokuju, he was once asked by a monk, "What is the doctrine that goes beyond the Buddhas and Fathers?" The master, immediately holding up his staff, said to the congregation, "I call this a staff, and what would you call it?" No answer was forthcoming, whereupon the master, again holding forth the staff, asked the monk, "Did you not ask me about the doctrine that goes beyond the Buddhas and Fathers?"

When Nan-yin Ye-gu (Nan-yuan Hui-yung) was once asked what the Buddha was, he said, "What is not the Buddha?" Another time his answer was, "I never knew him." There was still another occasion when he said, "Wait until there is one, for then I will tell you." So far Nan-yin does not seem to be so very incomprehensible, but what follows will challenge our keenest intellectual analysis. When the inquiring monk replied to the master's third statement, saying, "If so, there is no Buddha in you," the master promptly asserted, "You are right there." This evoked a further question, "Where am I right, sir?" "This is the thirtieth day of the month," replied the master.

Perhaps this is sufficient to show how freely Zen deals with those abstruse philosophical problems which have been taxing all human ingenuity ever since the dawn of intelligence. Let me conclude this part with a sample sermon delivered by Goso Hoyen (Wu-tsu Fa-yen); for a Zen master occasionally—no, quite frequently—comes down to the dualistic level of understanding and tries to deliver a speech for the edification of his pupils. But being a Zen sermon we naturally expect something unusual in it. Goso was one of the ablest Zen masters of the twelfth century. He was the teacher of Yengo (Yuan-wu), famous as the author of the *Hekiganshu*. One of his sermons runs thus:

"Yesterday I came across one topic which I thought I might communicate to you, my pupils, today. But an old man such as I am is apt to forget, and the topic has gone off altogether from my mind. I cannot just recall it." So saying, Goso remained quiet for some little time, but at last he exclaimed, "I forget, I forget, I cannot remember!" He resumed, however: "I know there is a mantram in one of the Sutras known as *The King of Good Memory*. Those who are forgetful may recite it, and the thing forgotten will come again. Well, I must try." He then recited the mantram, "Om o-lo-lok-kei svaha!" Clapping his hands and laughing heartily, he said: "I remember, I remember; this it was: When you seek the Buddha, you cannot see him: when you look for the patriarch, you cannot see him. The muskmelon is sweet even to the stems, the bitter gourd is bitter even to the roots."

He then came down from the pulpit without further remark.

5. REPETITION

In one of his sermons Eckhart, referring to the mutual relationship between God and man, says: "It is as if one stood before a high mountain and cried, 'Art thou there?' The echo comes back, 'Art thou there?' If one cries, 'Come out!' the echo answers, 'Come out!' " Something like this is to be observed in the Zen masters' answers now classified under "Repetition". It may be found hard for the uninitiated to penetrate into the inner meaning of those parrot-like repetitions which sometimes sound like mimicry on the part of the master. In this case, indeed, the words themselves are mere sounds, and the inner sense is to be read in the echoing itself if anywhere. The understanding, however, must come out of one's own inner life, and what the echoing does is to give this chance of self-awakening to the earnest seekers of truth. When the mind is so tuned as to be all ready to break into a certain note, the master turns the key and it sings out its own melody, not learned from anybody else but discovered within itself.

Tosu Daido (T'ou-tzu Tai-t'ung), of the T'ang dynasty, who died in the year 914, answered "The Buddha" when he was questioned, "What is the Buddha?" He said "Tao" when the question was, "What is Tao?" He answered "The Dharma" to the question "What is the Dharma?"

Language is with the Zen masters a kind of exclamation or ejaculation as directly coming out of their inner spiritual experience. No meaning is to be sought in the expression itself, but within ourselves, in our own minds, which are awakened to the same experience. Therefore when we understand the language of the Zen masters, it is the understanding of ourselves and not the sense of the language which reflects ideas and not the experienced feelings themselves. Thus it is impossible to make those understand Zen who have not had any Zen experience yet, just as it is impossible for the people to realize the sweetness of honey who have never tasted it before. With such people, "sweet" honey will ever remain as an idea altogether devoid of sense; that is, the word has no life with them.

Hogen Mon-yeki (Fa-yen Wen-i), the founder of the Hogen branch of Zen Buddhism, flourished early in the tenth century. He asked one of his disciples, "What do you understand by this: 'Let the difference be even a tenth of an inch, and it will grow as wide as heaven and earth'?" The disciple said, "Let the difference be even a tenth of an inch, and it will grow as wide as heaven and earth." Hogen, however, told him that such an answer will never do. Said the disciple, "I cannot do otherwise; how do you understand?" The master at once replied, "Let the difference be even a tenth of an inch and it will grow as wide as heaven and earth."

Hogen was a great master of repetitions, and there is another interesting instance. After trying to understand the ultimate truth of Zen under fifty-four masters, Tokusho (Te-shao, 907–971) finally came to Hogen; but tired of making special efforts to master Zen, he simply fell in with the rest of the monks there. One day when the master ascended the platform, a monk asked, "What is one drop of water dripping from the source of So[5] (Ts'ao)?" Said the master, "That is one drop of water dripping from the source of So." The monk failed to make anything out of the repetition and stood as if lost; while Tokusho, who happened to be by him, had for the first time his spiritual eye opened to the inner meaning of Zen, and all the doubts he had been cherishing secretly down in his heart were thoroughly dissolved. He was altogether another man after that.

To conceive the truth as something external which is to be perceived by a perceiving subject is dualistic and appeals to the intellect for its understanding, but according to Zen we are living right in the truth, by the truth, from which we cannot be separated. Says Gensha (Hsuan-sha), "We are here as if immersed in water head and shoulders underneath the great ocean, and yet how piteously we are extending our hands for water!" Therefore, when he was asked by a monk, "What is my self?" he at once replied, "What would you do with a self?" When this is intellectually analysed, he means that when we begin to talk about self we immediately and inevitably establish the dualism of self and not-self, thus falling into the errors of intellectualism. We are in the water—this is the fact, and let

[5] That is, Ts'ao-ch'i, where the sixth patriarch of Zen used to reside. It is the birthplace of Chinese Zen Buddhism.

us remain so, Zen would say, for when we begin to beg for water we put ourselves in an external relation to it and what has hitherto been our own will be taken away from us.

While Gensha on a certain occasion was treating an army officer called Wei to tea, the latter asked, "What does it mean when they say that in spite of our having it every day we do not know it?" Gensha without answering the question took up a piece of cake and offered it to him. After eating the cake the officer asked the master again, who then remarked, "Only we do not know it even when we are using it every day." This is evidently an object lesson. Another time a monk came to him and wanted to know how to enter upon the path of truth. Gensha asked, "Do you hear the murmuring of the stream?" "Yes, I do," said the monk. "There is a way to enter."

6.   EXCLAMATION

The Zen masters frequently make an exclamatory utterance[6] in response to questions, instead of giving an intelligible answer. When words are used, if at all intelligible we may feel that we can somehow find a clue to get at the meaning, but when an inarticulate utterance is given we are quite at a loss how to deal with it, unless we are fortified with some previous knowledge such as I have at some length attempted to give to my readers.

Of all the Zen masters who used to give exclamatory utterance, the most noted ones are Ummon and Rinzai, the former for his "Kwan!" and the latter for his "Kwats!"

Rinzai distinguishes four kinds of "Kwats!" The first, according to him, is like the sacred sword of Vajraraja; the second is like the golden-haired lion squatting on the ground; the third is like the sounding rod or the grass used as a decoy; and the fourth is the one that does not at all function as a "Kwats!"

Rinzai once asked his disciple, Rakuho (Le-p'u), "One man has been using a stick and another resorting to the 'Kwats!' Which of them do you think is the more intimate to the truth?"

[6] Does this not remind us of an old mystic who defined God as an unutterable sign?

Answered the disciple, "Neither of them!" "What is the most intimate then?" Rakuho cried out, "Kwats!" Whereupon Rinzai struck him. This swinging of a stick was the most favourite method of Tokusan and stands generally contrasted to the crying utterance of Rinzai; but here the stick is used by Rinzai and the latter's speciality is taken up in a most telling manner by his disciple Rakuho.

Besides these "skilful contrivances" (*upaya-kausalya*) so far enumerated under seven headings, there are a few more "contrivances", though I am not going to be very exhaustive here on the subject.

One of them is "silence". Vimalakirti was silent when Manjusri asked him as to the doctrine of non-duality, and his silence was later commented upon by a master as "deafening like thunder". A monk asked Basho Yesei (Pa-chiao Hui-ch'ing) to show him the "original face" without the aid of any intermediary conception, and the master, keeping his seat, remained silent. When Shifuku (Tzu-fu) was asked as to a word befitting the understanding of the inquirer, he did not utter a word, he simply kept silent. Bunki (Wen-hsi) of Koshu (Hang-chou) was a disciple of Kyozan (Yang-shan); he was asked by a monk, "What is the self?" but he remained silent. As the monk did not know what to make of it, he asked again, to which the master replied, "When the sky is clouded, the moon cannot shine out." A monk asked Sozan (Ts'ao-shan), "How is the silence inexpressible to be revealed?" "I do not reveal it here." "Where would you reveal it?" "At midnight last night," said the master, "I lost three pennies by my bed."

Sometimes the masters sit quiet "for some little while" (*liang-chiu*), either in response to a question or when in the pulpit. This *liang-chiu* does not always merely indicate the passage of time, as we can see in the following cases: A monk came to Shuzan (Shou-shan) and asked, "Please play me a tune on a stringless harp." The master was quiet for some little while, and said, "Do you hear it?" "No, I do not hear it." "Why," said the master, "did you not ask louder?"

A monk asked Hofuku (Pao-fu), "I am told that when one

wants to know the path of the uncreate, one should know the source of it. What is the source, sir?" Hofuku was silent for a while, and then asked his attendant, "What did the monk ask me now?" When that monk repeated the question, the master ejected him, exclaiming, "I am not deaf!"

II. THE DIRECT METHOD

We now come to the most characteristic feature of Zen Buddhism, by which it is distinguished not only from all the other Buddhist schools, but from all forms of mysticism that are ever known to us. So far the truth of Zen has been expressed through words, articulate or otherwise, however enigmatic they may superficially appear; but now the masters appeal to a more direct method instead of verbal medium. In fact, the truth of Zen is the truth of life, and life means to live, to move, to act, not merely to reflect. Is it not the most natural thing for Zen, therefore, that its development should be towards acting or rather living its truth instead of demonstrating or illustrating it in words; that is to say, with ideas? In the actual living of life there is no logic, for life is superior to logic. We imagine logic influences life, but in reality man is not a rational creature so much as we make him out; of course he reasons, but he does not act according to the result of his reasoning pure and simple. There is something stronger than ratiocination. We may call it impulse, or instinct, or, more comprehensively, will. Where this will acts there is Zen, but if I am asked whether Zen is a philosophy of will I rather hesitate to give an affirmative answer. Zen is to be explained, if at all explained it should be, rather dynamically than statically. When I raise the hand thus, there is Zen. But when I assert that I have raised the hand, Zen is no more there. Nor is there any Zen when I assume the existence of somewhat that may be named will or anything else. Not that the assertion or assumption is wrong, but that the thing known as Zen is three thousand miles away, as they say. An assertion is Zen only when it is in itself an act and does not refer to anything that is asserted in it. In the finger pointed at the moon there is no Zen, but when the pointing finger itself is considered, altogether independent of any external references, there is Zen.

Life delineates itself on the canvas called time; and time never repeats: once gone, forever gone; and so is an act: once done, it is never undone. Life is a *sumiye*-painting, which must be executed once and for all time and without hesitation, without intellection, and no corrections are permissible or possible. Life is not like an oil-painting, which can be rubbed out and done over time and again until the artist is satisfied. With a *sumiye*-painting, any brush stroke painted over a second time results in a smudge; the life has left it. All corrections show when the ink dries. So is life. We can never retract what we have once committed to deeds; nay, what has once passed through consciousness can never be rubbed out. Zen therefore ought to be caught while the thing is going on, neither before nor after. It is an act of one instant. When Dharma was leaving China, as the legend has it, he asked his disciples what was their understanding of Zen, and one of them who happened to be a nun, replied, "It is like Ananda's looking into the kingdom of Akshobhya Buddha, it is seen once and has never been repeated." This fleeting, unrepeatable, and ungraspable character of life is delineated graphically by Zen masters who have compared it to lightning or a spark produced by the percussion of stones: *shan tien kuang, chi shih huo.*

The idea of direct method appealed to by the masters is to get hold of this fleeting life as it flees and not after it has flown. While it is fleeing, there is no time to recall memory or to build ideas. No reasoning avails here. Language may be used, but this has been associated too long with ideation, and has lost directness or being by itself. As soon as words are used, they express meaning, reasoning; they represent something not belonging to themselves; they have no direct connection with life, except being a faint echo or image of something that is no longer here. This is the reason why the masters often avoid such expressions or statements as are intelligible in any logical way. Their aim is to have the pupil's attention concentrated in the thing itself which he wishes to grasp and not in anything that is in the remotest possible connection liable to disturb him.

Therefore when we attempt to find meaning in dharanis or ex-clamations or a nonsensical string of sounds taken as such, we are far away from the truth of Zen. We must penetrate into the mind itself as the spring of life, from which all these words are produced. The swinging of a stick, the crying of a "Kwats!", or the kicking of a ball must be understood in this sense; that is, as the directest demonstration of life—no, even as life itself. The direct method is thus not always the violent assertion of life-force, but a gentle movement of the body, the responding to a call, the listening to a murmuring stream, or to a singing bird, or any of our most ordinary everyday assertions of life.

Reiun (Ling-yun) was asked, "How were things *before* the appearance of the Buddha in the world?" He raised his hossu. "How were things *after* the appearance of the Buddha?" He again raised the hossu. This raising of the hossu was quite a favourite method with many masters to demonstrate the truth of Zen. As I stated elsewhere, the hossu and the staff were the religious insignias of the master, and it was natural that they would be in much display when the monks approached with questions. One day Obaku Kiun (Huang-po Hsi-yun) as-cended the pulpit, and as soon as monks were gathered, the master took up his staff and drove them all out. When they were about all out, he called them, and they turned their heads back. The master said, "The moon looks like a bow, less rain and more wind." The staff was thus wielded effectively by the masters, but who would ever have thought of a cane being made an instrument of illustrating the most profound truth of religion?

As some Zen masters remarked, Zen is our "ordinary mind-edness"; that is to say, there is in Zen nothing supernatural or unusual or highly speculative that transcends our everyday life. When you feel sleepy, you retire; when you are hungry, you eat, just as much as the fowls of the air and the lilies of the field, taking "no thought for your life, what ye shall eat, or what ye shall drink; nor yet for your body, what ye shall put on". This is the spirit of Zen.

Ryutan Soshin (Lung-t'an Sui-hsin) was a disciple of Tenno Dogo (Tao-wu). He served the master as one of his personal attendants. He was with him for some time, when one day he said to the master, "Since I came to you, I have not at all been instructed in the study of mind." Replied the master, "Ever since you came to me, I have always been pointing to you how to study mind." "In what way, sir?" "When you brought me a cup of tea, did I not accept it? When you served me with food, did I not partake of it? When you made bows to me, did I not return them? When did I ever neglect in giving you instructions?" Ryutan kept his head hanging for some time, when the master told him, "If you want to see, see directly into it; but when you try to think about it, it is altogether missed."

So far the direct method has not been of any violent character as to involve a bodily injury or nervous shock, but the masters had no qualms if they thought necessary to shake the pupils roughly. Rinzai for one was noted for the directness and incisiveness of his dealings; the point of his sword cut through the heart of the opponent. The monk Jo (Ting) was one of his disciples, and when he asked the master what the fundamental principle of Buddhism was, Rinzai came down from his straw chair, and taking hold of the monk slapped him with the palm of his hand, and let him go. Jo stood still without knowing what to make of the whole procedure, when a bystanding monk blamed him for not bowing to the master. While doing so, Jo all of a sudden awoke to the truth of Zen. Later, when he was passing over a bridge, he happened to meet a party of three Buddhist scholars, one of whom asked Jo: "The river of Zen is deep, and its bottom must be sounded. What does this mean?" Jo, disciple of Rinzai, at once seized the questioner and was at the point of throwing him over the bridge, when his two friends interceded and asked Jo's merciful treatment of the offender. Jo released the scholar, saying, "If not for the intercession of his friends I would at once let him sound the bottom of the river himself." With these people Zen was no joke, no mere play of ideas; it was, on the contrary, a most serious thing on which they would stake their lives, a way of action.

Let me conclude these remarks on the Direct Method with

a sermon from Goso (Wu-tsu), of whom mention has already been made:

If people ask me what Zen is like I will say that it is like learning the art of burglary. The son of a burglar saw his father growing older and thought: "If he is unable to carry out his profession, who will be the bread-winner of this family, except myself? I must learn the trade." He intimated the idea to his father, who approved of it. One night the father took the son to a big house, broke through the fence, entered the house, and opening one of the large chests, told the son to go in and pick out the clothings. As soon as he got into it the lid was dropped and the lock securely applied. The father now came out to the courtyard, and loudly knocking at the door woke up the whole family, whereas he himself quietly slipped away by the former hole in the fence. The residents got excited and lighted candles, but found that the burglars had already gone. The son, who remained all the time in the chest securely confined, thought of his cruel father. He was greatly mortified, when a fine idea flashed upon him. He made a noise which sounded like the gnawing of a rat. The family told the maid to take a candle and examine the chest. When the lid was unlocked, out came the prisoner, who blew out the light, pushed away the maid, and fled. The people ran after him. Noticing a well by the road, he picked up a large stone and threw it into the water. The pursuers all gathered around the well trying to find the burglar drowning himself in the dark hole. In the meantime he was safely back in his father's house. He blamed the latter very much for his narrow escape. Said the father: "Be not offended, my son. Just tell me how you got off." When the son told him all about his adventures the father remarked, "There you are, you have learned the art!"

CHAPTER 6

The Reason of Unreason: the Koan Exercise

I

What is a koan?

A koan, according to one authority, means "a public document setting up a standard of judgment", whereby one's Zen understanding is tested as to its correctness. A koan is generally some statement made by an old Zen master, or some answer of his given to a questioner. The following are some that are commonly given to the uninitiated:

1. A monk asked Tung-shan, "Who is the Buddha?" "Three *chin* of flax."

2. Yun-men was once asked, "When not a thought is stirring in one's mind, is there any error here?" "As much as Mount Sumeru."

3. Chao-chou answered, "*Wu!*" (*mu* in Japanese) to a monk's question, "Is there Buddha-nature in a dog?" *Wu* literally means "not" or "none", but when this is ordinarily given as a koan, it has no reference to its literal signification; it is "*Wu*" pure and simple.

4. When Ming the monk overtook the fugitive Hui-neng, he wanted Hui-neng to give up the secret of Zen. Hui-neng replied, "What are your original features which you have even prior to your birth?"

5. A monk asked Chao-chou, "What is the meaning of the First Patriarch's visit to China?" "The cypress tree in the front courtyard."

6. When Chao-chou came to study Zen under Nan-ch'uan, he asked, "What is the Tao (or the Way)?" Nan-ch'uan replied, "Your everyday mind, that is the Tao."

7. A monk asked, "All things are said to be reducible to the

One, but where is the One to be reduced?" Chao-chou answered, "When I was in the district of Ch'ing I had a robe made that weighed seven *chin.*"

8. When P'ang the old Zen adept first came to Ma-tsu in order to master Zen, he asked, "Who is he who has no companion among the ten thousand things of the world?" Matsu replied, "When you swallow up in one draught all the water in the Hsi Ch'iang, I will tell you."

When such problems are given to the uninitiated for solution, what is the object of the master? The idea is to unfold the Zen psychology in the mind of the uninitiated, and to reproduce the state of consciousness, of which these statements are the expression. That is to say, when the koans are understood the master's state of mind is understood, which is satori and without which Zen is a sealed book.

In the beginning of Zen history a question was brought up by the pupil to the notice of the master, who thereby gauged the mental state of the questioner and knew what necessary help to give him. The help thus given was sometimes enough to awaken him to realization, but more frequently than not puzzled and perplexed him beyond description, and the result was an ever-increasing mental strain or "searching and contriving" on the part of the pupil, of which we have already spoken in the foregoing pages. In actual cases, however, the master would have to wait for a long while for the pupil's first question, if it were coming at all. To ask the first question means more than half the way to its own solution, for it is the outcome of a most intense mental effort for the questioner to bring his mind to a crisis. The question indicates that the crisis is reached and the mind is ready to leave it behind. An experienced master often knows how to lead the pupil to a crisis and to make him successfully pass it. This was really the case before the koan exercise came in vogue, as was already illustrated by the examples of Lin-chi, Nan-yueh, and others.

As time went on there grew up many "questions and answers" (*mondo* in Japanese) which were exchanged between masters and pupils. And with the growth of Zen literature it was perfectly natural now for Zen followers to begin to attempt an intellectual solution or interpretation of it. The "questions and answers" ceased to be experiences and intuitions of Zen consciousness, and became subjects of logical inquiry. This was disastrous, yet inevitable. Therefore the Zen master who wished for the normal development of Zen consciousness and the vigorous growth of Zen tradition would not fail to recognize rightly the actual state of things, and to devise such a method as to achieve finally the attainment of the Zen truth.

The method that would suggest itself in the circumstances was to select some of the statements made by the old masters and to use them as pointers. A pointer would then function in two directions: (1) To check the working of the intellect, or rather to let the intellect see by itself how far it can go, and also that there is a realm into which it as such can never enter; (2) To effect the maturity of Zen consciousness which eventually breaks out into a state of satori.

When the koan works in the first direction there takes place what has been called "searching and contriving". Instead of the intellect, which taken by itself forms only a part of our being, the entire personality, mind and body, is thrown out into the solution of the koan. When this extraordinary state of spiritual tension, guided by an experienced master, is made to mature, the koan works itself out into what has been designated as the Zen experience. An intuition of the truth of Zen is now attained, for the wall against which the Yogin has been beating hitherto to no purpose breaks down, and an entirely new vista opens before him. Without the koan the Zen consciousness loses its pointer, and there will never be a state of satori. A psychological *impasse* is the necessary antecedent of satori. Formerly, that is, before the days of the koan exercise, the antecedent pointer was created in the consciousness of the Yogin by his own intense spirituality. But when Zen became systematized owing to the accumulation of Zen literature in the shape of "questions and answers" the indispensability of the koan had come to be universally recognized by the masters.

The worst enemy of Zen experience, at least in the beginning, is the intellect, which consists and insists in discriminating subject from object. The discriminating intellect, therefore, must be cut short if Zen consciousness is to unfold itself, and the koan is constructed eminently to serve this end.

On examination we at once notice that there is no room in the koan to insert an intellectual interpretation. The knife is not sharp enough to cut the koan open and see what are its contents. For a koan is not a logical proposition but the expression of a certain mental state resulting from the Zen discipline. For instance, what logical connection can there be between the Buddha and "three *chin* of flax"? or between the Buddha-nature and *"Wu"*? or between the secret message of Bodhidharma and "a cypress tree"? In a noted Zen textbook known as *Hekiganshu* (*Pi-yen-chi* in Chinese)[1] Yuan-wu gives the following notes concerning the "three *chin* of flax", showing how the koan was interpreted by those pseudo-Zen followers who failed to grasp Zen:

"There are some people these days who do not truly understand this koan; this is because there is no crack in it to insert their intellectual teeth. By this I mean that it is altogether too plain and tasteless. Various answers have been given by different masters to the question, 'What is the Buddha?' One said, 'He sits in the Buddha Hall.' Another said, 'The one endowed with the thirty-two marks of excellence.' Still another, 'A bamboo-root whip.' None, however, can excell T'ung-shan's 'three *chin* of flax' as regards its irrationality, which cuts off all passage of speculation. Some comment that T'ung-shan was weighing flax at the moment, hence the answer. Others say that it was a trick of equivocation on the part of T'ung-shan; and still others think that as the questioner was not conscious of the fact that he was himself the Buddha, T'ung-shan answered him in this indirect way.

"Such [commentators] are all like corpses, for they are utterly unable to comprehend the living truth. There are still others, however, who take the 'three *chin* of flax' as the Bud-

---

[1] This is one of the most favourite vademecums of Zen Buddhists. For further explanation see below.

dha [thus giving it a pantheistic interpretation]. What wild and fantastic remarks they make! As long as they are beguiled by words, they can never expect to penetrate into the heart of T'ung-shan, even if they live to the time of Maitreya Buddha. Why? Because words are merely a vehicle on which the truth is carried. Not comprehending the meaning of the old master, they endeavour to find it in his words only, but they will find therein nothing to lay their hands on. The truth itself is beyond all description, as is affirmed by an ancient sage, but it is by words that the truth is manifested.

"Let us, then, forget the words when we gain the truth itself. This is done only when we have an insight through experience into that which is indicated by words. The 'three *chin* of flax' is like the royal thoroughfare to the capital; when you are once on it every step you take is in the right direction. When Yun-men was once asked what was the teaching that went beyond the Buddhas and the patriarchs, he said 'Dumpling'. Yun-men and T'ung-shan are walking the same road hand in hand. When you are thoroughly cleansed of all the impurities of discrimination, without further ado the truth will be understood. Later the monk who wanted to know what the Buddha was went to Chih-men and asked him what T'ung-shan meant by 'three *chin* of flax'. Said Chih-men, 'A mass of flowers, a mass of brocade'. He added, 'Do you understand?' The monk replied, 'No.' 'Bamboos in the South, trees in the North,' was the conclusion of Men."

Technically speaking, the koan given to the uninitiated is intended "to destroy the root of life", "to make the calculating mind die", "to root out the entire mind that has been at work since eternity", etc. This may sound murderous, but the ultimate intent is to go beyond the limits of intellection, and these limits can be crossed over only by exhausting oneself once for all, by using up all the psychic powers at one's command. Logic then turns into psychology, intellection into conation and intuition. What could not be solved on the plane of empirical consciousness is now transferred to the deeper recesses of the mind. So, says a Zen master, "Unless at one time perspiration has streamed down your back, you cannot see the boat sailing before the wind." "Unless once you have been thoroughly drenched in a perspiration you cannot expect to see the revelation of a palace of pearls on a blade of grass."

The koan refuses to be solved under any easier conditions. But once solved the koan is compared to a piece of brick used to knock at a gate; when the gate is opened the brick is thrown away. The koan is useful as long as the mental doors are closed, but when they are opened it may be forgotten. What one sees after the opening will be something quite unexpected, something that has never before entered even into one's imagination. But when the koan is re-examined from this newly acquired point of view, how marvellously suggestive, how fittingly constructed, although there is nothing artificial here!

II. PRACTICAL INSTRUCTIONS REGARDING THE KOAN EXERCISE

The following are some of the practical suggestions that have been given by Zen masters of various ages, regarding the koan exercise; and from them we can gather what a koan is expected to do towards the development of Zen consciousness, and also what tendency the koan exercise has come to manifest as time goes on. As we will see later on, the growth of the koan exercise caused a new movement among the Zen masters of the Ming dynasty to connect it with the Nembutsu, that is, the recitation of the Buddha-name. This was owing to the presence of a common denominator between the psychological mechanism of the koan exercise and the recitation of the Buddha-name. (The subject will be given special treatment later on.)

A Zen master of Huang-po Shan, probably of early Sun, gives the following instruction in the study of Zen:

"O you brother-monks! You may talk glibly and perhaps intelligently about Zen, about Tao, and scoff at the Buddhas and patriarchs; but when the day comes to reckon up all your accounts, your lip-Zen will be of no avail. Thus far you have been beguiling others, but today you will find that you have been beguiling yourselves. O you brother-monks! While still strong and healthy in body try to have a real understanding as to what Zen is. After all it is not such a difficult thing to take hold of the lock; but simply because you have not made up your minds to die in the last ditch, if you do not find a way to realization, you say, 'It is too difficult; it is beyond my power.' It is absurd! If you are really men of will, you will find out what your koan means. A monk once asked Chao-chou, 'Has a dog the Buddha-nature?' to which the master answered, '*Wu!*' Now devote yourselves to this koan and try to find its meaning. Devote yourselves to it day and night, whether sitting or lying, whether walking or standing; devote yourselves to its solution during the entire course of the twelve periods. Even when dressing or taking meals, or attending to your natural wants, have your every thought fixed on the koan. Make resolute efforts to keep it always before your mind. Days pass, years roll on, but in the fullness of time when your mind is so attuned and recollected there will be a sudden awakening within yourselves—an awakening into the mentality of the Buddhas and the patriarchs. You will then, for the first time, and wherever you may go, never again be beguiled by a Zen master."[2]

I-an Chen of Fo-chi monastery gives this advice:

"The old saying runs, 'When there is enough faith, there is enough doubt which is a great spirit of inquiry, and when there is a great spirit of inquiry there is an illumination.' Have everything thoroughly poured out that has accumulated in your mind—learning, hearing, false understanding, clever or witty sayings, the so-called truth of Zen, Buddha's teachings, self-conceit, arrogance, etc. Concentrate yourself on the koan, of which you have not yet had a penetrating comprehension. That is to say, cross your legs firmly, erect your spinal column straight, and paying no attention to the periods of the day, keep up your concentration until you grow unaware of your whereabouts, east, west, south, north, as if you were a living corpse.

[2] From the *Zenkwan Sakushin* ("Breaking Through the Zen Frontier Gate").

"The mind moves in reponse to the outside world and when it is touched it knows. The time will come when all thoughts cease to stir and there will be no working of consciousness. It is then that all of a sudden you smash your brain to pieces and for the first time realize that the truth is in your own possession from the very beginning. Would not this be great satisfaction to you in your daily life?"

Tai-hui was a great koan advocate of the twelfth century. One of his favourite koans was Chao-chou's "*Wu*", but he had also one of his own. He used to carry a short bamboo stick which he held forth before an assembly of monks, and said: "If you call this a stick, you affirm; if you call it not a stick, you negate. Beyond affirmation and negation what would you call it?" In the following extract from his sermons titled *Tai-hui Pu-shuo,* compiled by T'su-ching, 1190, he gives still another koan to his gardener-monk, Ching-kuang.

"The truth (*dharma*) is not to be mastered by mere seeing, hearing, and thinking. If it is, it is no more than the seeing, hearing, and thinking; it is not at all seeking after the truth itself. For the truth is not in what you hear from others or learn through the understanding. Now keep yourself away from what you have seen, heard, and thought, and see what you have within yourself. Emptiness only, nothingness, which eludes your grasp and to which you cannot fix your thought. Why? Because this is the abode where the senses can never reach. If this abode were within the reach of your sense it would be something you could think of, something you could have a glimpse of; it would then be something subject to the law of birth and death.

"The main thing is to shut off all your sense-organs and make your consciousness like a block of wood. When this block of wood suddenly starts up and makes a noise, that is the moment you feel like a lion roaming about freely with no-body disturbing him, or like an elephant that crosses a stream not minding its swift current. At that moment there is no fidgeting, nothing doing, just this and no more. Says P'ing-t'ien the Elder:

" 'The celestial radiance undimmed,
The norm lasting for ever more;
For him who entereth this gate,
No reasoning, no learning.'

"You should know that it is through your seeing, hearing, and thinking that you enter upon the path, and it is also through the seeing, hearing, and thinking that you are prevented from entering. Why? Let you be furnished with the double-bladed sword that destroys and resuscitates life where you have your seeing, hearing, and thinking, and you will be able to make good use of the seeing, hearing, and thinking. But if the sword that cuts both ways, that destroys as well as resuscitates, is missing, your seeing, hearing, and thinking will be a great stumbling-block, which will cause you to prostrate again and again on the ground. Your truth-eye will be completely blinded; you will be walking in complete darkness, not knowing how to be free and independent. If you want, however, to be the free master of yourself by doing away with your seeing, hearing, and thinking, stop your hankering monkey-like mind from doing mischief; keep it quietly under control; keep your mind firmly collected regardless of what you are doing—sitting or lying, standing or walking, remaining silent or talking; keep your mind like a line stretched taut; do not let it slip out of your hand. Just as soon as it slips out of your control you will find it in the service of the seeing, hearing, and thinking. In such a case is there any remedy? What remedy is applicable here?

"A monk asked Yun-men, 'Who is the Buddha?' 'The dried-up dirt-cleaner.' This is the remedy; whether you are walking or sitting or lying, let your mind be perpetually fixed on this 'dirt-cleaner'. The time will come when your mind will suddenly come to a stop like an old rat who finds himself in a *cul-de-sac*. Then there will be a plunging into the unknown with the cry, 'Ah, this!' When this cry is uttered you have discovered yourself. You find at the same time that all the teachings of the ancient worthies expounded in the Buddhist Tripitaka, the Taoist Scriptures, and the Confucian Classics,

are no more than commentaries upon your own sudden cry,
'Ah, this!' "

Tai-hui was never tired of impressing upon his disciples the
importance of having satori which goes beyond language and
reasoning and which bursts out in one's consciousness by over-
stepping the limits of consciousness. His letters and sermons
are filled with advice and instructions directed towards this
end. I quote one or two of them. That he was so insistent on
this point proves that Zen in his day was degenerating to a
form of mere quietism on the one hand and on the other to
the intellectual analysis of the koans left by the old masters.

"The study of Zen must end in satori. It is like a holiday
race-boat which is ordinarily put away in some quiet corner,
but which is designed for winning a regatta. This has been
the case with all the ancient masters of Zen, for we know that
Zen is really won only when we have satori. You have to have
satori somehow, but you will never get what you want by trying to be quiet with yourself, by sitting like a dead man. Why?
Does not one of the patriarchs say that when you attempt to
gain quietness by suppressing activity your quietness will all
the more be susceptible to disturbance? However earnestly you
may try to quiet your confused mind, the result will be altogether contrary to what you expect to realize so long as your
reasoning habit continues.

"Abandon, therefore, this reasoning habit; have the two
characters, 'birth' and 'death', pasted on your forehead, and
fix your attention exclusively on the following koan, as if you
were oppressed under the obligation of a very heavy debt.
Think of the koan regardless of what you are doing, regardless of what time of the day it is, day or night. A monk asked
Chao-chou, 'Has a dog the Buddha-nature, or not?' Said
Chou, 'Wu!' Collect your thoughts upon this 'Wu!' and see
what is contained in it. As your concentration goes on you will
find the koan altogether devoid of taste, that is, without any
intellectual clue whereby to fathom its content. Yet in the
meantime you may have a feeling of joy stealing into your
heart, which, however, is soon followed by another feeling,
this time a feeling of disquietude. Paying no attention to this

interweaving of emotions, exert yourself to go ahead with the koan, when you will become aware that you have pushed yourself like the old rat into a blind alley. A turning back will then be necessary, but this can never be accomplished by the weak-minded, who are ever faltering and hesitating."

In another place Tai-hui says: "Just steadily go on with your koan every moment of your life. If a thought rises, do not attempt to suppress it by conscious effort; only renew the attempt to keep the koan before the mind. Whether walking or sitting, let your attention be fixed upon it without interruption. When you begin to find it entirely devoid of flavour, the final moment is approaching; do not let it slip out of your grasp. When all of a sudden something flashes out in your mind, its light will illumine the entire universe, and you will see the spiritual land of the Enlightened Ones fully revealed at the point of a single hair, and the great wheel of the Dharma revolving in a single grain of dust."[3]

K'ung-ku Ching-hung[4] has a similar advice for monks. He says:

"Chao-chou's 'Wu!', before you have penetrated into its meaning, is like a silver mountain or an iron wall [against which you stand nonplussed]. But as you go on with 'Wu!' day after day trying to get into its content, and do not give even a moment's rest to yourself, the supreme moment will inevitably come upon you, just as a flood makes its own channel; and then you will see that the iron wall and the silver mountain were not, after all, very formidable. The main point is not to put any reliance on learning, but to put a stop to all hankering, and to exert yourself to the utmost to solve the great problem of birth and death. Do not waste your time by merely thinking of 'Wu!' as if you were no more than a simpleton, make no attempt to give a false solution to it by

---

[3] Tai-hui's passages are taken from a collection of his letters, sermons, discourses, and sayings known as his *Pu-shao, Yu-lu,* and *Shu.* He was very well acquainted with the *Avatamsaka* (or *Gandavyuha*), and there are many allusions by him to its teachings, as we find in this last sentence here.
[4] Still living in 1466.

means of speculation and imagination. Resolutely put yourself, heart and soul, into the unravelling of the problem of 'Wu!' When suddenly, as you let go of your hold, there comes a grand over-turning of the whole system of consciousness, and for the first time you realize in a most luminous manner what all this finally comes to."

The author of *The Mirror for Zen Students*[5] confirms all that has already been quoted, and describes fully the psychology of the koan exercise.

"What is required of Zen devotees is to see into the phrase[6] that liveth and not into the one which is dead. Try to search for the sense of the koan you have, putting your whole mental strength into the task like the mother-hen sitting on her eggs, like a cat trying to catch a rat, like a hungry one eagerly looking everywhere for food, like a thirsty one seeking for water, like a child thinking of its mother. If you exert yourself as seriously and as desperately as that, the time will surely come when the sense of the koan will dawn upon you.

"There are three factors making for success in the study of Zen: (1) great faith, (2) great resolution, and (3) great spirit of inquiry. When any one of these is lacking it is like a cauldron with a broken leg, it limps. At all moments of your life, regardless of what you are doing, exert yourself to see into the meaning of Chao-chou's 'Wu'. Keep the koan always before your mind and never release the spirit of inquiry. As the inquiry goes on steadily and uninterruptedly you will come to see that there is no intellectual clue in the koan, that it is altogether devoid of sense as you ordinarily understand that word, that it is entirely flat, devoid of taste, has nothing appetizing about

[5] Compiled by T'ui-yin, a Korean Zen master of the Ming era (A.D. 1368–1650). The book appeared in 1579.

[6] That is, *chu.* The Zen masters generally distinguish two kinds of *chu;* the live one and the dead one. By the "live *chu*" are meant such statements as give no clues whatever to their rational interpretations but put an end to the functioning of the empirical consciousness; whereas the "dead *chu*" are those that lend themselves to logical or philosophical treatment and therefore that can be learned from others and committed to memory. This according to T'ui-yin.

it, and that you are beginning to have a certain feeling of uneasiness and impatience. When you come to this state it is the
moment for you to cast aside the scabbard, throw yourself
down into the abyss, and by so doing lay a foundation for
Buddhahood.

"Do not think that the meaning of the koan is at the moment
of your holding it up for solution; do not reason about it or
exercise your imagination over it; do not wait for satori to
come over you by clearing your mind of its confused ideas;
only collect yourself on the unintelligibility of the koan over
which the mind evidently has no control.[7] You will finally find
yourself like an old rat getting into the furthest corner of the
barn where it suddenly perceives by veering clear round the

[7] In *Essays in Zen Buddhism* I have given more advice regarding the Zen Yogin's attitude towards the koan, which afford interesting and illuminating materials for the psychological
student of Zen consciousness. T'ui-yin cautions his koan students on the following ten points: (1) Do not calculate according to your imagination; (2) Let not your attention be
drawn where the master raises his eyebrows or twinkles his
eyes; (3) Do not try to extract meaning from the way the koan
is worded; (4) Do not try to demonstrate on the words; (5)
Do not think that the sense of the koan is to be grasped where
it is held out as an object of thought; (6) Do not take Zen for
a state of mere passivity; (7) Do not judge the koan with the
dualistic standard of *yu* (*asti*) and *wu* (*nasti*); (8) Do not
take the koan as pointing to absolute emptiness; (9) Do not
ratiocinate on the koan; and (10) Do not keep your mind in
the attitude of waiting for satori to turn up. The koan exercise
is confused with so-called meditation, but from all these warnings given by an old master regarding the exercise it is evident
that Zen is not an exercise in meditation or in passivity. If Zen
is to be properly understood by its students, Eastern and Western, this characteristic aspect of it must be fully comprehended.
Zen has its definite object, which is "to open our minds to
satori" as we say, and in order to bring about this state of
consciousness a koan is held out before the mental eye, not to
meditate on, nor to keep the mind in a state of receptivity, but
to use the koan as a kind of pole with which to leap over the
stream of relativity to the other side of the Absolute. And the
unique feature of Zen Buddhism is that all this is accomplished
without resorting to such religious conceptions as sin, faith,
God, grace, salvation, a future life, etc.

way of escape. To measure the koan by an intellectual standard, as you ordinarily do with other things, to live your life up
and down in the stream of birth and death, to be always assailed by feelings of fear, worry, and uncertainty, all this is
owing to your imagination and calculating mind. You ought to
know how to rise above the trivialities of life, in which most
people are found drowning themselves. Do not waste time asking how to do it, just put your whole soul into the business. It
is like a mosquito biting at an iron bull; at the very moment
the iron absolutely rejects your frail proboscis, you for once
forget yourself, you penetrate, and the work is done."

Sufficient authorities have now been quoted to show where
lies the function of the koan in bringing about what is known
as satori, and also to show what the Zen master had in mind
when he first began to exercise the minds of his disciples towards the maturing of their Zen consciousness. In the way of
summary I conclude this part of the present chapter with a
passage from the writings of Hakuin, who is father of the
modern Japanese Rinzai school of Zen. In this we will see
how the psychology of Zen has been going on without much
change for more than a thousand years, since the days of
Hui-neng and his Chinese followers.

"If you want to get at the unadulterated truth of egolessness,
you must once for all let go your hold and fall over the
precipice, when you will rise again newly awakened and in
full possession of the four virtues of eternity, bliss, freedom,
and purity, which belong to the real ego. What does it mean
to let go of your hold on the precipice? Suppose a man has
wandered out among the remote mountains, where no one
else has ever ventured. He comes to the edge of a precipice
unfathomably deep, the rugged rock covered with moss is
extremely slippery, giving him no sure foothold; he can neither
advance nor retreat, death is looking at him in the face. His
only hope lies in holding on to the vine which his hands have
grasped; his very life depends on his holding on to it. If he
should by carelessness let go his hold, his body would be
thrown down to the abyss and crushed to pieces, bones and
all.

"It is the same with the student of Zen. When he grapples with a koan single-handedly he will come to see that he has reached the limit of his mental tension, and he is brought to a standstill. Like the man hanging over the precipice he is completely at a loss what to do next. Except for occasional feelings of uneasiness and despair, it is like death itself. All of a sudden he finds his mind and body wiped out of existence, together with the koan. This is what is known as 'letting go your hold'. As you become awakened from the stupor and regain your breath it is like drinking water and knowing for yourself that it is cold. It will be a joy inexpressible."

III. HISTORICAL GENERALIZATIONS ON THE KOAN EXERCISE

The innovation of the koan exercise was inevitable owing to the following circumstances:

1. If the study of Zen had run its natural course it would soon have come to its own extinction owing to the aristocratic nature of its discipline and experience.

2. As Zen gradually exhausted its creative originality in two or three hundred years of development after the time of Hui-neng, the sixth patriarch, it found that a new life must be awakened in it, if it were to survive, by using some radical method which would vigorously stir up the Zen consciousness.

3. With the passing of the age of creative activity there was an accumulation of materials known as "stories" (*hua-t'ou*), or "conditions" (*chi-yuan*), or "questions and answers" (*men-ta*), which made up the bulk of Zen history; and this tended to invite intellectual interpretation, ruinous to the maturing of the Zen experience.

4. The rampant growth of Zen quietism since the beginning of Zen history most dangerously threatened the living experience of Zen. The two tendencies, quietism or the school of "silent illumination", and intuitionalism or the school of noetic experience, had been from the beginning, covertly if not openly, at war with each other.

Because of these conditions, the koan exercise adopted by

the Zen masters of the tenth and the eleventh century was designed to perform the following functions:

1. To popularize Zen in order to counteract native aristocracy which tended to its own extinction;

2. To give a new stimulus to the development of Zen consciousness, and thus to accelerate the maturing of the Zen experience;

3. To check the growth of intellectualism in Zen;

4. To save Zen from being buried alive in the darkness of quietism.

From the various quotations which have been given concerning the koan exercise, the following psychic facts may be gathered:

1. The koan is given to the student first of all to bring about a highly wrought-up state of consciousness.

2. The reasoning faculty is kept in abeyance, that is, the more superficial activity of the mind is set at rest so that its more central and profounder parts which are found generally deeply buried can be brought out and exercised to perform their native functions.

3. The affective and conative centres which are really the foundations of one's personal character are charged to do their utmost in the solution of the koan. This is what the Zen master means when he refers to "great faith" and "great spirit of inquiry" as the two most essential powers needed in the qualification of a successful Zen devotee. The fact that all great masters have been willing to give themselves up, body and soul, to the mastery of Zen, proves the greatness of their faith in ultimate reality, and also the strength of their spirit of inquiry known as "seeking and contriving", which never suspends its activity until it attains its end, that is, until it has come into the very presence of Buddhata itself.

4. When the mental integration thus reaches its highest mark there obtains a neutral state of consciousness which is erroneously designated as "ecstasy" by the psychological student of the religious consciousness. This Zen state of consciousness essentially differs from ecstasy in this: Ecstasy is the suspension of the mental powers while the mind is passively

engaged in contemplation; the Zen state of consciousness, on the other hand, is the one that has been brought about by the most intensely active exercise of all the fundamental faculties constituting one's personality. They are here positively concentrated on a single object of thought, which is called a state of oneness (*ekagra*). It is also known as a state of *daigi* or "fixation".

This is the point where the empirical consciousness with all its contents both conscious and unconscious is about to tip over its border-line, and get noetically related to the Unknown, the Beyond, the Unconscious. In ecstasy there is no such tipping or transition, for it is a static finality not permitting further unfoldment. There is nothing in ecstasy that corresponds to "throwing oneself down the precipice", or "letting go the hold".

5. Finally, what at first appears to be a temporary suspense of all psychic faculties suddenly becomes charged with new energies hitherto undreamed of. This abrupt transformation has taken place quite frequently by the intrusion of a sound, or a vision, or a form of motor activity. A penetrating insight is born of the inner depths of consciousness, as the source of a new life has been tapped, and with it the koan yields up its secrets.

A philosophical explanation of these psychic facts is offered by Zen Buddhists in the following manner. It goes without saying that Zen is neither psychology nor philosophy, but that it is an experience charged with deep meaning and laden with living, exalting contents. The experience is final and its own authority. It is the ultimate truth, not born of relative knowledge, that gives full satisfaction to all human wants. It must be realized directly within oneself: no outside authorities are to be relied upon. Even the Buddha's teachings and the master's discourses, however deep and true they are, do not belong to one so long as they have not been assimilated into his being, which means that they are to be made to grow directly out of one's own living experiences. This realization is called satori. All koans are the utterances of satori with no intellectual mediations; hence their uncouthness and incomprehensibility.

The Zen master has no deliberate scheme on his part to

make his statements of satori uncouth or logically unpalatable; the statements come forth from his inner being, as flowers burst out in spring-time, or as the sun sheds its rays. Therefore to understand them we have to be like flowers or like the sun; we must enter into their inner being. When we reproduce the same psychic conditions out of which the Zen masters have uttered these koans, we shall know them. The masters thus avoid all verbal explanations, which only serve to create in the minds of his disciples an intellectual curiosity to probe into the mystery. The intellect being a most obtrusive hindrance, or rather a deadly enemy, at least in the beginning of Zen study, it must be banished for a while from the mind. The koan is, indeed, a great baffler to reasoning. For this reason, Zen is ever prone to give more value to the psychic facts than to conceptualism. As the facts are directly experienced and prove quite satisfactory, they appeal irresistibly to the "seeking and contriving" mind of the Zen follower.

As facts of personal experience are valued in Zen, we have such koans as Yun-men's "dried-up dirt-cleaner", or Chao-chou's "cypress-tree", T'ung-shan's "three *chin* of flax", etc., which are all familiar incidents in everyone's life. Compared with the Indian expressions such as "All is empty, unborn, and beyond causation" or "The whole universe is contained in one particle of dust", how homely the Chinese are!

Owing to this fact, Zen is better designed to exclude the intellect and to lead our empirical consciousness to its deeper sources. If a noetic experience of a radically different order is to be attained, which sets all our strivings and searchings at rest, something that does not at all belong to the intellectual categories is to be devised. More precisely speaking, something illogical, something irrational, something that does not yield itself to an intellectual treatment is to be the special feature of Zen. The koan exercise was thus the natural development of Zen consciousness in the history of human strivings to reach the ultimate. By means of the koan the entire system of our psychic apparatus is made to bear upon the maturing of the satori state of consciousness.

IV. AN UNSYSTEMATIC CLASSIFICATION OF
ZEN QUESTIONS

1. The question asking for instruction. This is what is generally asked by a novice of the master, wishing to be enlightened on such subjects as Buddha, the signification of Bodhi-Dharma's visit to China, the essence of the Buddhist teaching, the Dharmakaya, etc.

2. The question in which the questioner asks for the master's judgment by describing his own mental condition. When a monk said to Chao-chou, "What do you say to one who has nothing to carry about?" he was analysing his own state of mind. To this Chao-chou replied, "Carry it along."

3. The question whereby the questioner attempts to see where the master stands. A monk came to Tung-feng who lived in a mountain hut and asked him, "If a tiger should suddenly appear here, what would you do?" The hut-keeper roared like a tiger; the monk behaved as if terrified; whereupon the keeper laughed heartily.

4. The question in which the questioner shows that he still has a doubt as to his attainment and expresses his desire for confirmation. A monk asked Tao-wu of T'ien-huang, "What shall I do when there is still a shadow of doubt?" Wu replied, "Even oneness when held on to is wide of the mark."

5. The question whereby the questioner is anxious to find out the master's attitude. A monk asked Chao-chou, "All things are reducible to the One; but where is the One reducible?" Chou said, "When I was in the district of Ch'ing I had a robe made that weighed seven *chin*."

6. The question asked by one who is at a loss as to how to go on with his study of Zen. A monk asked Hsing-hua: "I am unable to distinguish black from white. Pray enlighten me somehow." The question was hardly out when the master gave him a good slashing.

7. The question asked with the intention to probe into the attainment of the master. This kind of question must have been in vogue when the Zen monasteries were everywhere estab-

lished and the monks travelled from one master to another. A monk asked Feng-hsueh, "How is it that one who understands not, never cherishes a doubt?" Replied the master, "When a tortoise walks on the ground, he cannot help leaving traces in the mud."

8. The question of ignorance. This does not seem to differ from the sixth. A monk asked Hsuan-sha, "I am a newcomer in the monastery; please tell me how to go on with my study." "Do you hear the murmuring stream?" "Yes, master." "If so, here is the entrance."

9. The question proposed by one who has his own view of Zen and wishes to see how the master takes it. "As to worldly knowledge and logical cleverness, I have nothing to do with them; pray let me have a Zen theme." When this was asked by a monk, the master gave him a hearty blow.

10. The question in which an ancient master's saying is referred to. A monk said to Yun-men, "What would one do when no boundaries are seen, however wide the eyes are open?" Said Men, "Look!"

11. The question containing words from the sutras. "According to the sutra, all beings are endowed with the Buddha-nature; how is it then that they know it not?" "They know," replied Shou-shan.

12. The question containing references to a known fact. "The ocean is said to contain the precious gem; how can a man lay hands on it?" Replied Feng-hsueh: "When Wang-hsiang comes, its brightness is dazzling; when Li-lou goes, the waves roll as high as the sky. The more one tries to take hold of it, the farther it vanishes; the more one attempts to see it, the darker it grows."

13. The question that starts from an immediate fact of observation. "I see that you belong to the Brotherhood, what is the Buddha? What is the Dharma?" San-sheng replied, "This is the Buddha, this is the Dharma, knowest thou?"

14. The question containing a hypothetical case. "This Buddha sits in the Hall; what is the other Buddha?" Ching-shan's answer was, "This Buddha sits in the Hall."

15. The question embodying a real doubt. "All things are

such as they are from the beginning; what is that which is beyond existence?" "Your statement is quite plain; what is the use of asking me?" was a master's solution.

16. The question with an aggressive intent. "The Patriarch came from India and what did he design to do here?" Mu-chou retorted, "You tell; what did he design?" The monk gave no reply, so Mu-chou struck him.

17. The question plainly and straightforwardly stated. A non-Buddhist philosopher asked the Buddha, "Words or no-words, I ask neither." The Buddha remained silent. The philosopher said: "The Blessed One is indeed full of mercy and compassion. He has cleared off clouds of confusion for my sake, showing me how to enter upon the path."

18. The question not expressed in words. A non-Buddhist philosopher came to the Buddha and stood before him without uttering a word. The Buddha then said, "Abundantly indeed, O philosopher!" The philosopher praised him, saying, "It is all owing to the Blessed One's mercy that I now enter upon the path."

V. ZEN AND THE UNCONSCIOUS

CHAPTER 7

The Zen Doctrine of No-Mind

I. HUI-NENG'S ATTACK UPON QUIETISM

What distinguishes Hui-neng most conspicuously and characteristically from his predecessors as well as from his contemporaries is his doctrine of "hon-rai mu-ichi-motsu" (*pen-lai wu-i-wu*). This is one of the lines declared against Shen-hsiu's *gatha* to which reference has already been made. The whole *gatha* by Hui-neng runs thus:

> There is no Bodhi-tree,
> Nor stand of mirror bright.
> Since all is void,
> Where can the dust alight?

"From the first not a thing is"—this was the first proclamation made by Hui-neng. It is a bomb thrown into the camp of Shen-hsiu and his predecessors. By it Hui-neng's Zen came to be sharply outlined against the background of the dust-brushing type of Zen meditation. Shen-hsiu was not exactly wrong in his view, for there is reason to suppose that Shen-hsiu's own teacher, Hung-jen, the Fifth Patriarch, who was also Hui-neng's teacher, had a similar view, though this was not so explicitly stated as Shen-hsiu's. In fact, Hung-jen's teaching could be construed in either way, in that of Shen-hsiu or in that of Hui-neng. Hung-jen was a great master of Zen and from him grew up many strong personalities who became great spiritual leaders of the time. Of them Shen-hsiu and Hui-neng were the most distinguished in many ways, and the camp came to be divided between them. Shen-hsiu interpreted Hung-jen in his own light, and Hui-neng in his, and, as already explained, the latter as time went on proved to be the winner as being in better accord with the thought and psychology of the Chinese people.

In all likelihood there was in Hung-jen's teaching itself something which tended to that of Shen-hsiu, for Hung-jen seems to have instructed his pupils to "keep their guard on the Mind" all the time. He, of course, being a follower of Bodhi-Dharma, believed in the Mind from which this universe with all its multiplicities issues, but which in itself is simple, undefiled, and illuminating as the sun behind the clouds. "To keep one's guard on this original Mind" means to keep it clear from the beclouding mists of individualization, so that its pure light may be retained intact and ever illuminating. But in this view the conception of the Mind and of its relation to the world of multiplicities is not clearly defined, and there is every probability of getting these concepts confused.

If the Mind is originally pure and undefiled, why is it necessary to brush off its dust, which comes from nowhere? Is not this dust-wiping, which is the same thing as "keeping one's guard", an unwarranted process on the part of the Zen Yogin? The wiping is indeed an altogether unnecessary contrivance. If from the Mind arises this world, why not let the latter rise as it pleases? To try to stop its rising by keeping one's guard on the Mind—is not this interfering with the mind? The most logical and most natural thing to do in relation to the Mind would be to let it go on with its creating and illuminating.

Hung-jen's teaching of guarding the Mind may mean to guard on the part of the Yogin his own individual mind from getting in the way of the original Mind. But at the same time there is the danger of the Yogin's acting exactly contrary to the doctrine of non-interference. This is a delicate point, and the masters have to be quite definite about it—not only in concepts but in the practical methods of training. The master himself may have a well-defined idea of what he desires to accomplish in the pupil's mind, but the latter too frequently fails to move in unison with the master. For this reason, methods must vary not only with persons but with ages. And again, for this reason differences are more vehemently asserted among the disciples than between two masters advocating different methods.

Shen-hsiu was perhaps more inclined to teach the self-guarding or dust-wiping process than the letting-alone process. This latter, however, has in its turn deep pitfalls into which its devotees may fall. For it is fundamentally the outcome of the doctrine of emptiness or nothingness; that is, the idea that "from the first not a thing is".

When Hui-neng declared, "From the first not a thing is," the keynote of his Zen thought was struck, and from it we recognize the extent of difference there is between him and his predecessors and contemporaries. This keynote was never so clearly struck before. When the Masters who followed him pointed to the presence of the Mind in each individual mind and also to its absolute purity, this idea of presence and purity was understood somehow to suggest the existence of an individual body, however ethereal and transparent it may be conceived. And the result was to dig out this body from the heap of obscuring materials. On the other hand, Hui-neng's concept of nothingness (*wu-i-wu*) may push one down into a bottomless abyss, which will no doubt create a feeling of utter forlornness. The philosophy of Prajnaparamita, which is also that of Hui-neng, generally has this effect. To understand it a man requires a deep religious intellectual insight into the truth of Sunyata. When Hui-neng is said to have had an awakening by listening to the *Vajracchedika Sutra* (*Diamond Sutra*) which belongs to the Prajnaparamita group of the Mahayana texts, we know at once where he has his foothold.

The dominant idea prevailing up to the time of Hui-neng was that the Buddha-nature with which all beings are endowed is thoroughly pure and undefiled as to its self-being. The business of the Yogin is therefore to bring out his self-nature, which is the Buddha-nature, in its original purity. But, as I said before, in practice this is apt to lead the Yogin to the conception of something separate which retains its purity behind all the confusing darkness enveloping his individual mind. His meditation may end in clearing up the mirror of consciousness in which he expects to see the image of his original pure self-being reflected. This may be called static meditation. But serenely reflecting or contemplating on the purity of the Mind has a suicidal effect on life, and Hui-neng vehemently protested against this type of meditation.

In the *T'an-ching*, and other Zen works after it, we often come across the term *"K'an-ching"*, meaning "to keep an eye on Purity", and this practice is condemned. "To keep an eye on purity" is no other than a quietistic contemplation of one's self-nature or self-being. When the concept of "original purity" issues in this kind of meditation, it goes against the true understanding of Zen. Shen-hsiu's teaching was evidently strongly coloured with quietism or the reflection type. So, when Hui-neng proclaimed, "From the first not a thing is," the statement was quite original with him, though ultimately it goes back to the *Prajnaparamita*. It really revolutionized the Zen practice of meditation, establishing what is really Buddhist and at the same time preserving the genuine spirit of Bodhi-Dharma.

Hui-neng and his followers now came to use the new term *chien-hsing* instead of the old *k'an-ching*. *Chien-hsing* means "to look into the nature [of the Mind]". *K'an* and *chien* both relate to the sense of sight, but the character *k'an*, which consists of a hand and an eye, is to watch an object as independent of the spectator; the seen and the seeing are two separate entities. *Chien*, composed of an eye alone on two outstretched legs, signifies the pure act of seeing. When it is coupled with *hsing*, Nature, or Essence, or Mind, it is seeing into the ultimate nature of things, and not watching, as the Samkhya's Purusha watches the dancing of Prakrit. The seeing is not reflecting on an object as if the seer had nothing to do with it. The seeing, on the contrary, brings the seer and the object seen together, not in mere identification but the becoming conscious of itself, or rather of its working. The seeing is an active deed, involving the dynamic conception of self-being; that is, of the Mind. The distinction made by Hui-neng between *k'an* and *chien* may thus be considered revolutionary in the history of Zen thought.

The utterance, "From the first not a thing is," thus effectively destroys the error which attaches itself too frequently to the idea of purity. Purity really means nothingness (*sunyata*); it is the negation of all qualities, a state of absolute no-ness, but it somehow tends to create a separate entity outside the "one who sees". The fact that *k'an* has been used with it proves that the error has actually been committed. When the idea "from the first not a thing is" is substituted for "the self-nature of the Mind is pure and undefiled", all the logical and psychological pedestals which have been given to one are now swept from underneath one's feet and one has nowhere to stand. And this is exactly what is needed for every sincere Buddhist to experience before he can come to the realization of the Mind. The seeing is the result of his having nothing to stand upon. Hui-neng is thus in one way the father of Chinese Zen.

It is true that he sometimes uses terms as suggesting the older type of meditation when he speaks about "cleansing the mind" (*ching-hsin*), "self-being's originally being pure and undefiled", "the sun being covered with clouds", etc. Yet his unmistakable condemnation of quietistic meditation rings clearly through his works: "When you sit quietly with an emptied mind, this is falling into a blank emptiness"; and again, "There are some people with the confused notion that the greatest achievement is to sit quietly with an emptied mind, where not a thought is allowed to be conceived." Hui-neng thus advises "neither to cling to the notion of a mind, nor to cling to the notion of purity, nor to cherish the thought of immovability; for these are not our meditation". "When you cherish the notion of purity and cling to it, you turn purity into falsehood. . . . Purity has neither form nor shape, and when you claim an achievement by establishing a form to be known as purity, you obstruct your own self-nature, you are purity-bound." From these passages we can see where Hui-neng wants us to look for final emancipation.

There are as many kinds of binding as there are kinds of clinging. When we cling to purity we thereby make a form of it, and we are purity-bound. For the same reason, when we cling to or abide with emptiness, we are emptiness-bound; when we abide with Dhyana or tranquillization, we are

Dhyana-bound. However excellent are the merits of these spiritual exercises, they inevitably lead us to a state of bondage in one way or another. In this there is no emancipation. The whole system of Zen discipline may thus be said to be nothing but a series of attempts to set us absolutely free from all forms of bondage. Even when we talk of "seeing into one's self-nature", this seeing has also a binding effect on us if it is construed as having something in it specifically set up; that is, if the seeing is a specific state of consciousness. For this is the "binding".[1]

The Master (Shen-hui) asked Teng, "What exercise do you recommend in order to see into one's self-nature?"

Teng answered: "First of all it is necessary to practise meditation by quietly sitting cross-legged. When this exercise is fully mastered, Prajna (intuitive knowledge) grows out of it, and by virtue of this Prajna the seeing into one's self-nature is attained."

Shen-hui inquired: "When one is engaged in meditation, is this not a specifically contrived exercise?"

"Yes, it is."

"If so, this specific contrivance is an act of limited consciousness, and how could it lead to the seeing of one's self-nature?"

"For this seeing we must exercise ourselves in meditation (*dhyana*): if not for this exercise, how can one ever see into one's self-nature?"

Shen-hui commented: "This exercising in meditation owes its function ultimately to an erroneous way of viewing the truth; and as long as this is the case, exercises of such nature would never issue in [true] meditation (*dhyana*)."

Teng explained: "What I mean by attaining meditation by exercising oneself in meditation is this. When meditation is attained, an illumination inside and outside comes by itself upon one; and because of this illumination inside and outside, one sees purity; and because of one's mind being pure it is known as seeing into one's nature."

Shen-hui, however, argued further: "When the seeing into

[1] See the *Sayings of Shen-hui,* § 11.

one's nature is spoken of, we make no reference to this nature as having inside and outside. If you speak of an illumination taking place inside and outside, this is seeing into a mind of error, and how can it be real seeing into one's self-nature? We read in a Sutra: If you are engaged in the mastery of all kinds of Samadhi, that is moving and not sitting in meditation. The mind flows out as it comes in contact with the environment. How can it be called meditation (*dhyana*)? If this kind of meditation is to be held as genuine, Vimalakirti would not take Sariputra to task when the latter claimed to be exercising himself in meditation."

In these critical questionings Shen-hui exposes the position of Teng and his followers, the advocates of purity; for in them there are still traces of clinging, i.e. setting up a certain state of mind and taking it for ultimate emancipation. So long as the seeing is something to see, it is not the real one; only when the seeing is no-seeing—that is, when the seeing is not a specific act of seeing into a definitely circumscribed state of consciousness—is it the "seeing into one's self-nature". Paradoxically stated, when seeing is no-seeing there is real seeing; when hearing is no-hearing there is real hearing. This is the intuition of the Prajnaparamita.

When thus the seeing of self-nature has no reference to a specific state of consciousness, which can be logically or relatively defined as a something, the Zen Masters designate it in negative terms and call it "no-thought" or "no-mind", *wu-nien* or *wu-hsin*. As it is "no-thought" or "no-mind", the seeing is really the seeing. Elsewhere I intend to analyse this concept of "no-mind" (*wu-hsin*), which is the same thing as "no-thought" (*wu-nien*), but here let me deal in further detail with the ideas of purity, illumination, and self-nature in order to shed more light on the thought of Hui-neng as one of the greatest Zen Masters in the early history of Chinese Zen. To do this, I will take another quotation from *Shen-hui's Sayings*, in which we have these points well illustrated by the most eloquent disciple of Hui-neng.

Chang-yen King asked [Shen-hui]: "You discourse ordinarily on the subject of Wu-nien ('no-thought' or 'no-consciousness'), and make people discipline themselves in it. I wonder if there is a reality corresponding to the notion of Wu-nien, or not?"

Shen-hui answered: "I would not say that Wu-nien is a reality, nor that it is not."

"Why?"

"Because if I say it is a reality, it is not in the sense in which people generally speak of reality; if I say it is a non-reality, it is not in the sense in which people generally speak of non-reality. Hence Wu-nien is neither real nor unreal."

"What would you call it then?"

"I would not call it anything."

"If so, what could it be?"

"No designation whatever is possible. Therefore I say that Wu-nien is beyond the range of wordy discourse. The reason we talk about it at all is because questions are raised concerning it. If no questions are raised about it, there would be no discourse. It is like a bright mirror. If no objects appear before it, nothing is to be seen in it. When you say that you see something in it, it is because something stands against it."

"When the mirror has nothing to illuminate, the illumination itself loses its meaning, does it not?"

"When I talk about objects presented and their illumination, the fact is that this illumination is something eternal belonging to the nature of the mirror, and has no reference to the presence or absence of objects before it."

"You say that it has no form, it is beyond the range of wordy discourse, the notion of reality or non-reality is not applicable to it; why then do you talk of illumination? What illumination is it?"

"We talk of illumination because the mirror is bright and its self-nature is illumination. The mind which is present in all things being pure, there is in it the light of Prajna, which illuminates the entire world-system to its furthest end."

"This being so, when is it attained?"

"Just see into nothingness (*tan chien wu*)."

"Even if it is nothingness, it is seeing something."

"Though it is seeing, it is not to be called something."

"If it is not to be called something, how can there be the seeing?"

"Seeing into nothingness—this is true seeing and eternal seeing."

II. HUI-NENG'S DOCTRINE OF MINDLESSNESS

The first declaration made by Hui-neng regarding his Zen experience was that "From the first not a thing is", and then he went on to the "Seeing into one's self-nature", which self-nature, being "not a thing", is nothingness. Therefore, "seeing into one's self-nature" is "seeing into nothingness", which is the proclamation of Shen-hui. And this seeing is the illuminating of this world of multiplicity by the light of Prajna. Prajna thus becomes one of the chief issues discussed in the *T'an-ching*, and this is where the current of Zen thought deviates from the course it had taken from the time of Bodhi-Dharma.

In the beginning of Zen history the centre of interest was in the Buddha-nature or Self-nature, which was inherent in all beings and absolutely pure. This is the teaching of the *Nirvana Sutra,* and all Zen followers since Bodhi-Dharma are firm believers in it. Hui-neng was, of course, one of them. He was evidently acquainted with this doctrine even before he came to the Fifth Patriarch, Hung-jen, because he insisted on the identity of the Buddha-nature in all beings regardless of the racial or national differences which might be found between himself and his Master. The biography of Hui-neng known as the *Tsao-chi Tai-chi Pieh Tien,* perhaps the earliest literary composition recording his life, has him as listening to the *Nirvana Sutra* recited by a nun, who was sister to his friend Lin. If Hui-neng were just a student of the *Vajracchedika,* which we gather from the *T'an-ching,* he could never have talked with Hung-jen as described in the *T'an-ching.* His allusion to the Buddha-nature must no doubt have come from the *Nirvana Sutra.* With this knowledge, and what he had gained at Hung-jen's, he was able to discourse on the original purity of self-nature and our seeing into this truth as fundamental in the understanding of Zen thought. In Hung-jen, the teacher of Hui-neng, the idea of Prajna was not so emphatically brought out as in the disciple. With the latter, the problem of Prajna, especially in the relation to Dhyana, is all-absorbing.

Prajna is primarily one of the three subjects of the Buddhist Triple Discipline, which is Morality (*sila*), Meditation (*dhyana*), and Wisdom (*prajna*). Morality consists in observing all the precepts laid down by the Buddha for the spiritual welfare of his disciples. Meditation is the exercise to train oneself in tranquillization, for as long as the mind is not kept under control by means of meditation it was of no use just to observe mechanically the rules of conduct; in fact, the latter were really meant for spiritual tranquillization. Wisdom or Prajna is the power to penetrate into the nature of one's being, as well as the truth itself thus intuited. That all these three are needed for a devoted Buddhist goes without saying. But after the Buddha, as time went on, the Triple Discipline was split into three individual items of study. The observers of the rules of morality set down by the Buddha became teachers of the Vinaya; the Yogins of meditation were absorbed in various Samadhis, and even acquired something of supernatural faculties, such as clairvoyance, mind-reading, telepathy, knowledge of one's past lives, etc.; and lastly, those who pursued Prajna became philosophers, dialecticians, or intellectual leaders. This one-sided study of the Triple Discipline made the Buddhists deviate from the proper path of the Buddhist life, especially in Dhyana (meditation) and Prajna (wisdom or intuitive knowledge).

This separation of Dhyana and Prajna became particularly tragic as time went on, and Prajna came to be conceived as dynamically seeing into the truth. The separation at its inception had no thought of evil. Yet Dhyana became the exercise of killing life, of keeping the mind in a state of torpor and making the Yogins socially useless; while Prajna, left to itself, lost its profundity, for it was identified with intellectual subtleties which dealt in concepts and their analysis. Then the question arose as to whether or not Dhyana and Prajna were two distinct notions, each of which was to be pursued independently of the other. At the time of Hui-neng, the idea of separation was emphasized by Shen-hsiu and his followers, and the result was exercises in purification; that is, in dust-wiping meditation. We can say that Shen-hsiu was the advocate of Dhyana first and Prajna second, while Hui-neng almost reversed this, saying that Dhyana without Prajna leads to a grave error, but when Prajna is genuine, Dhyana comes along with it. According to Hui-neng, Dhyana is Prajna and Prajna is Dhyana, and when this relation of identity between the two is not grasped there will be no emancipation.

To begin with Dhyana, Hui-neng's definition is: "Dhyana (*tso-ch'an*) is not to get attached to the mind, is not to get attached to purity, nor is it to concern itself with immovability. . . . What is Dhyana, then? It is not to be obstructed in all things. Not to have any thought stirred up by the outside conditions of life, good and bad—this is *tso* (*dhyana*). To see inwardly the immovability of one's self-nature—this is *ch'an* (*dhyana*). . . . Outwardly, to be free from the notion of form —this is *ch'an*. Inwardly, not to be disturbed—this is *ting* (*dhyana*).

"When, outwardly, a man is attached to form, his inner mind is disturbed. But when outwardly he is not attached to form, his mind is not disturbed. His original nature is pure and quiet as it is in itself; only when it recognizes an objective world, and thinks of it as something, is it disturbed. Those who recognize an objective world, and yet find their mind undisturbed, are in true *Dhyana*. . . . In the *Vimalakirti* it is said that 'when a man is instantly awakened, he comes back to his original mind', and in the *Bodhisattva-sila,* that 'My own original self-nature is pure and non-defiled.' Thus, O friends, we recognize in each one of the thoughts [we may conceive] the pureness of our original self-nature; to discipline ourselves in this and to practise by ourselves [all its implications]—this is by ourselves to attain Buddha's truth."

In this we see that Hui-neng's idea of Dhyana is not at all the traditional one as has been followed and practised by most of his predecessors, especially by those of the Hinayana inclination. His idea is that advocated in the Mahayana, notably by

Vimalakirti, Subhuti, Manjusri and other great Mahayana figures.

Hui-neng's attitude towards Dhyana, meditation, will be more fully illustrated by the following story told of one of his disciples[2]:

"In the eleventh year of Kai-yuan (723 C.E.) there was a Zen master in T'an-chou known as Chih-huang, who once studied under Jen, the great master. Later, he returned to Lu-shan monastery at Chang-sha, where he was devoted to the practice of meditation (*tso-chan=dhyana*), and frequently entered into a Samadhi (*ting*). His reputation reached far and wide.

"At the time there was another Zen master whose name was Tai-yung. He went to Ts'ao-ch'i and studied under the great master for thirty years. The master used to tell him: 'You are equipped for missionary work.' Yung at last bade farewell to his master and returned north. On the way, passing by Huang's retreat, Yung paid a visit to him and respectfully inquired: 'I am told that your reverence frequently enters into a Samadhi. At the time of such entrances, is it supposed that your consciousness still continues, or that you are in a state of unconsciousness? If your consciousness still continues, all sentient beings are endowed with consciousness and can enter into a Samadhi like yourself. If, on the other hand, you are in a state of unconsciousness, plants and rocks can enter into a Samadhi.'

"Huang replied: 'When I enter into a Samadhi, I am not conscious of either condition.'

"Yung said: 'If you are not conscious of either condition, this is abiding in eternal Samadhi, and there can be neither entering into a Samadhi nor rising out of it.'

"Huang made no reply. He asked: 'You say you come from Neng, the great master. What instruction did you have under him?'

"Yung answered: 'According to his instruction, no-tranquil-lization (*ting-Samadhi*), no-disturbance, no-sitting (*tso*), no-

[2] In the *Pieh-chuan* (another "biography" of the Great Master of Ts'ao-ch'i—that is, of Hui-neng), and also in the current edition of the *T'an-ching*.

meditation (*ch'an*)—this is the Tathagata's Dhyana. The five Skandhas are not realities; the six objects of sense are by nature empty. It is neither quiet nor illuminating; it is neither real nor empty; it does not abide in the middle way; it is not-doing, it is no-effect-producing, and yet it functions with the utmost freedom: the Buddha-nature is all-inclusive.'

"This said, Huang at once realized the meaning of it and sighed: 'These thirty years I have sat[3] to no purpose!'"

Another quotation from the *Life of Ts'ao-ch'i, the Great Master* will make the import of the above passages much clearer. The emperor Chung-tsung of the T'ang dynasty, learning of the spiritual attainment of Hui-neng, despatched a messenger to him, but he refused to come up to the capital. Whereupon the messenger, Hsieh-chien, asked to be instructed in the doctrine he espoused, saying: "The great masters of Zen in the capital invariably teach their followers to practise meditation (*ts'o-ch'an, dhyana*), for according to them no emancipation, no spiritual attainment is possible without it."

To this Hui-neng replied: "The Truth is understood by the mind (*hsin*), and not by sitting (*ts'o*) in meditation. According to the *Vajracchedika:* 'If people say that the Tathagata sits or lies, they fail to understand my teaching. For the Tathagata comes from nowhere and departs nowhither; and therefore he is called the Tathagata ("Thus come").' Not coming from anywhere is birth, and not departing anywhither is death. Where there is neither birth nor death, there we have the purity-dhyana of the Tathagata. To see that all things are empty is to practise sitting (in meditation). . . . Ultimately, there is neither attainment nor realization; how much less sitting in meditation!"

Hui-neng further argued: "As long as there is a dualistic way of looking at things there is no emancipation. Light stands against darkness; the passions stand against enlightenment. Unless these opposites are illuminated by Prajna, so that the gap between the two is bridged, there is no understanding of the

---

[3] "To sit" technically means "to sit cross-legged in meditation", "to practise Dhyana", and it is generally used coupled with *ch'an* (*Zen=dhyana*).

Mahayana. When you stay at one end of the bridge and are
not able to grasp the oneness of the Buddha-nature, you are
not one of us. The Buddha-nature knows neither decrease nor
increase, whether it is in the Buddha or in common mortals.
When it is within the passions, it is not defiled; when it is
meditated upon, it does not thereby become purer. It is neither
annihilated nor abiding; it neither comes nor departs; it is
neither in the middle nor at either end; it neither dies nor is
born. It remains the same all the time, unchanged in all
changes. As it is never born, it never dies. It is not that we
replace death with life but that the Buddha-nature is above
birth and death. The main point is not to think of things good
and bad and thereby to be restricted, but to let the mind move
on as it is in itself and perform its inexhaustible functions. This
is the way to be in accord with the Mind-essence."

Hui-neng's conception of Dhyana, we can now see, was not
that traditionally held by followers of the two vehicles. His
Dhyana was not the art of tranquillizing the mind so that its
inner essence, pure and undefiled, may come out of its casings.
His Dhyana was not the outcome of dualistically conceiving
the Mind. The attempt to reach light by dispelling darkness is
dualistic, and this will never lead the Yogin to the proper understanding of the mind. Nor is the attempt to annihilate the
distinction the right one. Hui-neng therefore insisted on the
identity of Dhyana and Prajna, for so long as Prajna is kept
apart from Dhyana and Dhyana from Prajna, neither of the
two is legitimately valued. One-sided Dhyana is sure to tend
towards quietism and death, as has abundantly been exempli-
fied in the history of Zen and of Buddhism. For this reason
we cannot treat Hui-neng's Dhyana apart from his Prajna.

The motive of the compiler of the *T'an-ching* was evidently
to expound as the chief object of his work Hui-neng's idea of
Prajna, and to distinguish it from its traditional understanding.
The title of the Tun-huang MS. unmistakably indicates this
motive. It reads: "The Sutra of Mahaprajnaparamita, of the
Very Highest Mahayana, (belonging to) the Southern School,
and (Expounding its) Doctrine of Abrupt Awakening", while

what follows reads something like a sub-title, "The Platform Sermons (*sutra=ching*) (containing) the Doctrine Given out by Hui-neng the Great Teacher, the Sixth Patriarch, at Tai-fan Ssu, of Shao-chou". As these titles stand, it is difficult to tell which is the principal one. We know, however, that the Sutra contains the sermons on Prajna or Prajnaparamita as given out by Hui-neng, and that this doctrine belongs to the highest order of the Mahayana and of the Southern school, and is concerned with the Abrupt Doctrine which has come to characterize since the time of Hui-neng the teaching of all Zen schools.

After these titles, the opening passage acquaints us at once with the subject of the Sermon, perhaps the first ever given by Hui-neng, which deals with the doctrine of Prajnaparamita. Indeed, Hui-neng himself begins his sermon with the exhortation: "O my good friends, if you wish to see your minds purified, think of Mahaprajnaparamita." And according to the text, Hui-neng remains silent for a while, cleansing his own heart. While I suspect his previous knowledge of the *Nirvana Sutra,* he at once, in the beginning of this Sermon, refers to the fact that he listened to the *Vajracchedika Sutra* before he came to Hung-jen. And, as we know, this is the Sutra which became the principal authority for the teaching of Zen, and the one of all the sutras belonging to Prajnaparamita literature in which the doctrine of Prajna is most concisely expounded. There is no doubt that Hui-neng was deeply connected with the Prajnaparamita from the outset of his career.

Even the teaching of Hung-jen, under whom Hui-neng studied Buddhism, is stated to have made specific reference to Prajna. While it is doubtful whether Hung-jen was such an enthusiastic advocate of the doctrine of Prajna as Hui-neng, at least the *T'an-ching* compiler took him as one. For Hung-jen's proclamation runs: ". . . Retire to your quarters, all of you, and by yourselves meditate on *Chih-hui* (the Chinese equivalent for Prajna), and each compose a *gatha* which treats of the nature of Prajna in your original mind, and let me see it." Does this not already anticipate Hui-neng? Hung-jen might have said something more, but this was at least what most impressed Hui-neng, and through him his compiler. It is also significant that Hung-jen refers to the *Vajracchedika* when he expresses his intention to retain Shen-hsiu's poem on the wall where he first planned to have Lo-kung-feng's pictures of Zen history.

In fact, the doctrine of Prajna is closely connected with that of Sunyata (emptiness), which is one of the most fundamental ideas of the Mahayana—so much so, indeed, that the latter altogether loses its significance when the Sunyata idea is dropped from its philosophy. The Hinayana also teaches the emptiness of all things, but its emptiness does not penetrate so deeply as the Mahayana's into the constitution of our knowledge. The two notions of the Hinayana and of the Mahayana regarding emptiness, we can say, are of different orders. When emptiness was raised to a higher order than formerly, the Mahayana began its history. To grasp this, Prajna was needed, and naturally in the Mahayana Prajna and Sunyata go hand in hand. Prajna is no more mere knowledge dealing with relative objects; it is knowledge of the highest order permitted to the human mind, for it is the spark of the ultimate constituent of all things.

In the terminology of Chinese philosophy, *hsing* stands in most cases for the ultimate constituent, or that which is left after all that accidentally belongs to a thing is taken away from it. It may be questioned what is accidental and what is essential in the constitution of an individual object, but I will not stop to discuss the point, for I am more concerned with the exposition of the *T'an-ching* than with Chinese philosophy. Let us take it for granted that there is such a thing as *hsing*, which is something ultimate in the being of a thing or a person, though it must not be conceived as an individual entity, like a kernel or nucleus which is left when all the outer casings are removed, or like a soul which escapes from the body after death. *Hsing* means something without which no existence is possible, or thinkable as such. As its morphological construction suggests, it is "a heart or mind which lives" within an individual. Figuratively, it may be called vital force.

And this *hsing* is defined by Hui-neng in the following manner: "The *hsin* (mind or heart) is the dominion, *hsing* is the lord: the lord rules over his dominion, there is *hsing,* and there is the lord; *hsing* departs, and the lord is no more; *hsing* is and the body and mind (*hsin*) subsists, *hsing* is not and the body and mind is destroyed. The Buddha is to be made within *hsing* and not to be sought outside the body. . . ."[4]

In this, Hui-neng attempts to give us a clearer understanding of what he means by *hsing.* *Hsing* is the dominating force over our entire being; it is the principle of vitality, physical and spiritual. Not only the body but also the mind in its highest sense is active because of *hsing* being present in them. When *hsing* is no more, all is dead, though this does not mean that *hsing* is something apart from the body and mind, which enters into it to actuate it, and departs at the time of death. This mysterious *hsing,* however, is not a logical *a priori* but an actuality which can be experienced, and it is designated by Hui-neng as *tzu-hsing,* self-nature or self-being, throughout his *T̔an-ching.*

Self-nature, otherwise expressed, is self-knowledge; it is not mere being but knowing. We can say that because of knowing itself, it is; knowing is being, and being is knowing. This is the meaning of the statement made by Hui-neng that: "In original Nature itself there is Prajna-knowledge, and because of this self-knowledge. Nature reflects itself in itself, which is self-illumination not to be expressed in words" (par. 30). When Hui-neng speaks of Prajna-knowledge as if it is born of self-nature (par. 27), this is due to the way of thinking which then prevailed, and often involves us in a complicated situation, resulting in the dualism of self-nature and Prajna, which is altogether against the spirit of Hui-neng's Zen thought. We must, therefore, be on the watch when interpreting the *T̔an-ching* in regard to the relation of Prajna to self-nature.

However this may be, we have now come to Prajna, which must be explained in the light of Dhyana, whose Mahayanist signification we have just examined. But before doing this I wish to say a few more words about self-nature and Prajna. In Mahayana philosophy there are three concepts which have

[4] Par. 37.

been resorted to by scholars to explain the relation between substance and its function. They are *tai* (body), *hsiang* (form), and *yung* (use), which first appeared in *The Awakening of Faith in the Mahayana,* usually ascribed to Asvaghosha. Body corresponds to substance, Form to appearance, and Use to function. The apple is a reddish, round-shaped object: this is its Form, in which it appeals to our senses. Form belongs to the world of senses, i.e. appearance. Its Use includes all that it does and stands for, its value, its utility, its function, and so on. Lastly, the Body of the apple is what constitutes its apple-ship, without which it loses its being, and no apple, even with all the appearances and functions ascribed to it, is an apple without it. To be a real object these three concepts, Body, Form, and Use, must be accounted for.

To apply these concepts to our object of discourse here, self-nature is the Body and Prajna its Use, whereas there is nothing here corresponding to Form, because the subject does not belong to the world of form. There is the Buddha-nature, Hui-neng would argue, which makes up the reason of Buddha-hood; and this is present in all beings, constituting their self-nature. The object of Zen discipline is to recognize it, and to be released from error, which are the passions. How is the recognition possible, one may inquire? It is possible because self-nature is self-knowledge. The Body is no-body without its Use, and the Body is the Use. To be itself is to know itself. By using itself, its being is demonstrated, and this using is, in Hui-neng's terminology, "seeing into one's own Nature". Hands are no hands, have no existence, until they pick up flowers and offer them to the Buddha; so with legs, they are no legs, non-entities, unless their Use is set to work, and they walk over the bridge, ford the stream, and climb the mountain. Hence the history of Zen after Hui-neng developed this philosophy of Use to its fullest extent: the poor questioner was slapped, kicked, beaten, or called names to his utter bewilderment, and also to that of the innocent spectators. The initiative to this "rough" treatment of the Zen students was given by Hui-neng, though he seems to have refrained from making any practical application of his philosophy of Use.

When we say, "See into thy self-nature," the seeing is apt to be regarded as mere perceiving, mere knowing, mere statically reflecting on self-nature, which is pure and undefiled, and which retains this quality in all beings as well as in all the Buddhas. Shen-hsiu and his followers undoubtedly took this view of the "seeing". But as a matter of fact, the seeing is an act, a revolutionary deed on the part of the human understanding whose functions have been supposed all the time to be logically analysing ideas, ideas sensed from their dynamic signification. The "seeing", especially in Hui-neng's sense, was far more than a passive deed of looking at, a mere knowledge obtained from contemplating the purity of self-nature; the seeing with him was self-nature itself, which exposes itself before him in all nakedness, and functions without any reservation. Herein we observe the great gap between the Northern school of Dhyana and the Southern school of Prajna.

Shen-hsiu's school pays more attention to the Body aspect of self-nature, and tells its followers to concentrate their effects on the clearing up of consciousness, so as to see in it the reflection of self-nature, pure and undefiled. They have evidently forgotten that self-nature is not a somewhat whose Body can be reflected on our consciousness in the way that a mountain can be seen reflected on the smooth surface of a lake. There is no such Body in self-nature, for the Body itself is the Use; besides the Use there is no Body. And by this Use is meant the Body's seeing itself in itself. With Shen-hsiu this self-seeing or Prajna aspect of self-nature is altogether ignored. Hui-neng's position, on the contrary, emphasizes the Prajna aspect we can know of self-nature.

This fundamental discrepancy between Hui-neng and Shen-hsiu in the conception of self-nature, which is the same thing as the Buddha-nature, has caused them to run in opposite directions as regards the practice of Dhyana; that is, in the method of *tso-ch'an* (*zazen* in Japanese). Read the following *gatha*[5] by Shen-hsiu:

[5] The *T'an-ching* (Koshoji edition), par. 6.

Our body is the Bodhi-tree,
And our mind a mirror bright;
Carefully we wipe them hour by hour
And let no dust alight.

In the dust-wiping type of meditation (*tso-ch'an, zazen*) it
is not easy to go further than the tranquillization of the mind;
it is so apt to stop short at the stage of quiet contemplation,
which is designated by Hui-neng "the practice of keeping
watch over purity". At best it ends in ecstasy, self-absorption,
a temporary suspension of consciousness. There is no "seeing"
in it, no knowing of itself, no active grasping of self-nature, no
spontaneous functioning of it, no *chen-hsing* ("Seeing into Nature") whatever. The dust-wiping type is therefore the art of
binding oneself with a self-created rope, an artificial construction which obstructs the way to emancipation. No wonder that
Hui-neng and his followers attacked the Purity school.

The quietistic, dust-wiping, and purity-gazing type of meditation was probably one aspect of Zen taught by Hung-jen,
who was the master of Hui-neng, Shen-hsiu, and many other.
Hui-neng, who understood the real spirit of Zen most likely
because he was not hampered by learning, and consequently
by the conceptual attitude towards life, rightly perceived the
danger of quietism, and cautioned his followers to avoid it by
all means. But most other disciples of Hung-jen were more or
less inclined to adopt quietism as the orthodox method of
Dhyana practice. Before Tao-i, popularly known as Ma-tsu,
saw Huai-jang, of Nan-yueh, he was also a quiet-sitter who
wanted to gaze at the pure nothingness of self-nature. He had
been studying Zen under one of Hung-jen's disciples when he
was still young. Even when he came up to Nan-yueh, he continued his old practice, keeping up his *tso-ch'an* ("sitting in
meditation"). Hence the following discourse between himself
and Huai-jang, who was one of the greatest disciples of Hui-
neng.

Observing how assiduously Ma-tsu was engaged in practising *tso-ch'an* every day, Yuan Huai-jang said: "Friend, what
is your intention in practising *tso-ch'an*?" Ma-tsu said: "I wish
to attain Buddhahood." Thereupon Huai-jang took up a brick

and began to polish it. Ma-tsu asked: "What are you engaged in?" "I want to make a mirror of it." "No amount of polishing makes a mirror out of a brick." Huai-jang at once retorted: "No amount of practising *tso-ch'an* will make you attain Buddahood." "What do I have to do then?" asked Ma-tsu. "It is like driving a cart," said Huai-jang. "When it stops, what is the driver to do? To whip the cart, or to whip the ox?" Matsu remained silent.

Another time Huai-jang said: "Do you intend to be master of *tso-ch'an*, or do you intend to attain Buddhahood? If you wish to study Zen, Zen is neither in sitting cross-legged nor in lying down. If you wish to attain Buddahood by sitting cross-legged in meditation, the Buddha has no specified form. When the Dharma has no fixed abode, you cannot make any choice in it. If you attempt to attain Buddhahood by sitting cross-legged in meditation, this is murdering the Buddha. As long as you cling to this sitting posture you can never reach the Mind."

Thus instructed, Ma-tsu felt as if he were taking a most delicious drink. Making bows, he asked: "How should I prepare myself in order to be in accord with the Samadhi of formlessness?" The master said: "Disciplining yourself in the study of Mind is like sowing seeds in the ground; my teaching in the Dharma is like pouring rain from above. When conditions are matured, you will see the Tao.[6]

Asked Ma-tsu again: "The Tao has no form, and how can it be seen?"

The master replied: "The Dharma-eye belonging to the Mind is able to see into the Tao. So it is with the Samadhi of formlessness."

MA-TSU: "Is it subject to completion and destruction?"

MASTER: "If one applies to it such notions as completion and destruction, collection and dissipation, we can never have insight into it."

In one sense Chinese Zen can be said to have really started with Ma-tsu and his contemporary Shih-tou, both of whom

[6] Literally, "Way", meaning truth, the Dharma, ultimate Reality.

were the lineal descendants of Hui-neng. But before Ma-tsu
was firmly established in Zen he was still under the influence
of the dust-wiping and purity-gazing type of Dhyana, applying himself most industriously to the practice of *tso-ch'an*, sitting cross-legged in meditation. He had no idea of the self-
seeing type, no conception that self-nature which is self-being
was self-seeing, that there was no Being besides Seeing which
is Acting, that these three terms Being, Seeing, and Acting
were synonymous and interchangeable. The practice of
Dhyana was therefore to be furnished with an eye of Prajna,
and the two were to be considered one and not two separate
concepts.

To go back to Hui-neng. We now understand why he had
to insist on the importance of Prajna, and theorize on the oneness of Dhyana and Prajna. In the *T'an-ching* he opens his
Sermon with the seeing into one's self-nature by means of
Prajna, with which every one of us, whether wise or ignorant,
is endowed. Here he adopts the conventional way of expressing
himself, as he is no original philosopher. In our own reasoning
which we followed above, self-nature finds its own being when
it sees itself, and this seeing takes place by Prajna. But as
Prajna is another name given to self-nature when the latter
sees itself, there is no Prajna outside self-nature. The seeing
(*chien*) is also called recognizing or understanding, or, better, experiencing (*wu* in Chinese and *satori* in Japanese). The
character *Wu* is composed of "heart" (or "mind"), and "mine";
that is, "mine own heart", meaning "to feel in my own heart",
or "to experience in my own mind".

Self-nature is Prajna, and also Dhyana when it is viewed,
as it were, statically or ontologically. Prajna is more of epistemological significance. Now Hui-neng declares the oneness
of Prajna and Dhyana. "O good friends, in my teaching what
is most fundamental is Dhyana (*ting*) and Prajna (*chin*). And,
friends, do not be deceived and led to thinking that Dhyana
and Prajna are separable. They are one, and not two. Dhyana
is the Body of Prajna, and Prajna is the Use of Dhyana. When
Prajna is taken up, Dhyana is in Prajna; when Dhyana is taken
up, Prajna is in it. When this is understood, Dhyana and Prajna

go hand in hand in the practice (of meditation). O followers of the truth (*tao*), do not say that Dhyana is first attained and then Prajna awakened, or that Prajna is first attained and then Dhyana awakened; for they are separate. Those who advocate this view make a duality of the Dharma; they are those who affirm with the mouth and negate in the heart. They regard Dhyana as distinct from Prajna. But with those whose mouth and heart are in agreement, the inner and the outer are one, and Dhyana and Prajna are regarded as equal (i.e. as one).[7]

Hui-neng further illustrates the idea of this oneness by the relation between the lamp and its light. He says: "It is like the lamp and its light. As there is a lamp, there is light; if no lamp, no light. The lamp is the Body of the light, and the light is the Use of the lamp. They are differently designated, but in substance they are one. The relation between Dhyana and Prajna is to be understood in like manner."

This analogy of the lamp and its light is quite a favourite one with Zen philosophers. Shen-hui also makes use of it in his Sermon discovered by the author at the National Library of Peiping. In his *Sayings* (par. 19) we have Shen-hui's view on the oneness of Dhyana and Prajna, which was given as an answer to one of his questioners. "Where no thoughts are awakened, and emptiness and nowhereness prevails, this is right Dhyana. When this non-awakening of thought, emptiness, and nowhereness suffer themselves to be the object of perception, there is right Prajna. Where this (mystery) takes place, we say that Dhyana, taken up by itself, is the Body of Prajna, and is not distinct from Prajna, and is Prajna itself; and further, that Prajna, taken up by itself, is the Use of Dhyana, and is not distinct from Dhyana, and is Dhyana itself. (Indeed) when Dhyana is to be taken up by itself, there is no Dhyana; when Prajna is to be taken up by itself, there is no Prajna. Why? Because (Self-) nature is suchness, and this is what is meant by the oneness of Dhyana and Prajna."

In this, Hui-neng and Shen-hui are of the same view. But being still too abstract for the ordinary understanding, it may

---

[7] The *T῾an-ching*, (Koshoji edition), par. 14.

be found difficult to grasp what is really meant by it. In the following, Shen-hui is more concrete or more accessible in his statement.

Wang-wei was a high government officer greatly interested in Buddhism, and when he learned of the disagreement between Shen-hui and Hui-ch'eng, who was evidently a follower of Shen-hsiu, regarding Dhyana and Prajna, he asked Shen-hui: "Why this disagreement?"

Shen-hui answered: "The disagreement is due to Ch'eng's holding the view that Dhyana is to be practised first and that it is only after its attainment that Prajna is awakened. But according to my view, the very moment I am conversing with you, there is Dhyana, there is Prajna, and they are the same. According to the *Nirvana Sutra,* when there is more of Dhyana and less of Prajna, this helps the growth of ignorance; when there is more of Prajna and less of Dhyana, this helps the growth of false views; but when Dhyana and Prajna are the same, this is called seeing into the Buddha-nature. For this reason, I say we cannot come to an agreement."

WANG: "When are Dhyana and Prajna said to be the same?"

SHEN-HUI: "We speak of Dhyana, but as to its Body there is nothing attainable in it. Prajna is spoken of when it is seen that this Body is unattainable, remaining perfectly quiescent and serene all the time, and yet functioning mysteriously in ways beyond calculation. Herein we observe Dhyana and Prajna to be identical."

Both Hui-neng and Shen-hsiu lay stress on the significance of the Prajna-eye, which, being turned on itself, sees into the mysteries of Self-nature. The unattainable is attained, the eternally serene is perceived, and Prajna identifies itself with Dhyana in its varied functionings. Therefore, while Shen-hui is talking with Wang-wei, Shen-hui declares that in this talking Dhyana as well as Prajna is present, that this talking itself is Prajna and Dhyana. By this he means that Prajna is Dhyana and Dhyana is Prajna. If we say that only while sitting cross-legged in meditation there is Dhyana, and that when this type of sitting is completely mastered, there for the first time Prajna is awakened, we effect a complete severance of Prajna and

Dhyana, which is a dualism always abhorred by Zen followers. Whether moving or not-moving, whether talking or not-talking, there must be Dhyana in it, which is ever-abiding Dhyana. Again, we must say that being is seeing and seeing is acting, that there is no being, i.e. Self-nature, without seeing and acting, and that Dhyana is Dhyana only when it is at the same time Prajna. The following is a quotation from Ta-chu Hui-hai, who was a disciple of Ma-tsu:

Q.: "When there is no word, no discourse, this is Dhyana; but when there are words and discourses, can this be called Dhyana?"

A.: "When I speak of Dhyana, it has no relationship to discoursing or not discoursing; my Dhyana is ever-abiding Dhyana. Why? Because Dhyana is all the while in Use. Even when words are uttered, discoursing goes on, or when discriminative reasoning prevails, there is Dhyana in it, for all is Dhyana.

"When a mind, thoroughly understanding the emptiness of all things, faces forms, it at once realizes their emptiness. With it emptiness is there all the time, whether it faces forms or not, whether it discourses or not, whether it discriminates or not. This applies to everything which belongs to our sight, hearing, memory, and consciousness generally. Why is it so? Because all things in their self-nature are empty; and wherever we go we find this emptiness. As all is empty, no attachment takes place; and on account of this non-attachment there is a simultaneous Use (of Dhyana and Prajna). The Bodhisattva always knows how to make Use of emptiness, and thereby he attains the Ultimate. Therefore it is said that by the oneness of Dhyana and Prajna is meant Emancipation."

That Dhyana has nothing to do with mere sitting cross-legged in meditation, as is generally supposed by outsiders, or as has been maintained by Shen-hsiu and his school ever since the days of Hui-neng, is here asserted in a most unmistakable manner. Dhyana is not quietism, nor is it tranquillization; it is rather acting, moving, performing deeds, seeing, hearing, thinking, remembering; Dhyana is attained where there is, so to speak, no Dhyana practised; Dhyana is Prajna, and Prajna is Dhyana, for they are one. This is one of the themes constantly stressed by all the Zen masters following Hui-neng.

Ta-chu Hui-hai continues: "Let me give you an illustration, that your doubt may be cleared up and you may feel refreshed. It is like a brightly-shining mirror reflecting images on it. When the mirror does this, does the brightness suffer in any way? No, it does not. Does it then suffer when there are no images reflected? No, it does not. Why? Because the Use of the bright mirror is free from affections, and therefore its reflection is never obscured. Whether images are reflected or not, there are no changes in its brightness. Why? Because that which is free from affections knows no change in all conditions.

"Again, it is like the sun illumining the world. Does the light suffer any change? No, it does not. How, when it does not illumine the world? There are no changes in it, either. Why? Because the light is free from affections, and therefore whether it illumines objects or not, the unaffected sunlight is ever above change.

"Now the illumining light is Prajna, and unchangeability is Dhyana. The Bodhisattva uses Dhyana and Prajna in their oneness, and thereby attains enlightenment. Therefore it is said that by using Dhyana and Prajna in their oneness emancipation is meant. Let me add that to be free from affections means the absence of the passions and not that of the noble aspirations (which are free from the dualistic conception of existence)."

In Zen philosophy, in fact in all Buddhist philosophy, no distinctions are made between logical and psychological terms, and the one turns into the other quite readily. From the viewpoint of life no such distinctions can exist, for here logic is psychology and psychology is logic. For this reason Ta-chu Hui-hai's psychology becomes logic with Shen-hui, and they both refer to the same experience. We read in Shen-hui's *Sayings* (par. 32): "A bright mirror is set up on a high stand; its illumination reaches the ten-thousand things, and they are all reflected in it. The masters are wont to consider this phenomenon most wonderful. But as far as my school is concerned it is not to be considered wonderful. Why? As to this bright mirror, its illumination reaches the ten-thousand things, and these ten-thousand things are not reflected in it. This is what I would declare to be most wonderful. Why? The Tathagata discriminates all things with non-discriminating Prajna (*chih*). If he has any discriminating mind, do you think he could discriminate all things?"

The Chinese term for "discrimination" is *fen-pieh*, which is a translation of the Sanskrit *vikalpa*, one of the important Buddhist terms used in various Sutras and Sastras. The original meaning of the Chinese characters is "to cut and divide with a knife", which exactly corresponds to the etymology of the Sanskrit *viklp*. By "discrimination", therefore, is meant analytical knowledge, the relative and discursive understanding which we use in our everyday worldly intercourse and also in our highly speculative thinking. For the essence of thinking is to analyse—that is, to discriminate; the sharper the knife of dissection, the more subtle the resulting speculation. But according to the Buddhist way of thinking, or rather according to the Buddhist experience, this power of discrimination is based on non-discriminating Prajna (*chih* or *chih-hui*). This is what is most fundamental in the human understanding, and it is with this that we are able to have an insight into the Self-nature possessed by us all, which is also known as Buddha-nature. Indeed, Self-nature is Prajna itself, as has been repeatedly stated above. And this non-discriminating Prajna is what is "free from affections", which is the term Ta-chu Hui-hai uses in characterizing the mind-mirror.

Thus, "non-discriminating Prajna", "to be free from affections", "from the first not a thing is"—all these expressions point to the same source, which is the fountainhead of Zen experience.

Now the question is: How is it possible for the human mind to move from discrimination to non-discrimination, from affections to affectionlessness, from being to non-being, from relativity to emptiness, from the ten-thousand things to the contentless mirror-nature or Self-nature, or, Buddhistically expressed, from *mayoi* (*mi* in Chinese) to *satori* (*wu*)?[8] How this movement is possible is the greatest mystery not only in Buddhism but in all religion and philosophy. So long as this world, as conceived by the human mind, is a realm of opposites, there is no way to escape from it and to enter into a world of emptiness where all opposites are supposed to merge. The wiping-off of the multitudes known as the ten-thousand things in order to see into the mirror-nature itself is an absolute impossibility. Yet Buddhists all attempt to achieve it.

Philosophically stated, the question is not properly put. It is not the wiping-off of the multitudes, it is not moving from discrimination to non-discrimination, from relativity to emptiness, etc. Where the wiping-off process is accepted, the idea is that when the wiping-off is completed, the mirror shows its original brightness, and therefore the process is continuous on one line of movement. But the fact is that the wiping itself is the work of the original brightness. The "original" has no reference to time, in the sense that the mirror was once, in its remote past, pure and undefiled, and that as it is no more so, it must be polished up and its original brightness be restored. The brightness is there all the time, even when it is thought to be covered with dust and not reflecting objects as it should. The brightness is not something to be restored; it is not something appearing at the completion of the procedure; it has never departed from the mirror. This is what is meant when the *T'an-ching* and other Buddhist writings declare the Buddha-nature to be the same in all beings, including the ignorant as well as the wise.

As the attainment of the Tao does not involve a continuous movement from error to truth, from ignorance to enlightenment, from *mayoi* to *satori*, the Zen masters all proclaim that there is no enlightenment whatever which you can claim to have attained. If you say you have attained something, this is the surest proof that you have gone astray. Therefore, not to

[8] *Mayoi* means "standing on a cross-road", and not knowing which way to go; that is, "going astray", "not being in the way of truth". It stands contrasted with *satori* (*wu*), which is the right understanding, realization of truth.

have is to have; silence is thunder; ignorance is enlightenment; the holy disciples of the Purity-path go to hell while the precept-violating Bhikshus attain Nirvana; the wiping-off means dirt-accumulating; all these paradoxical sayings—and Zen literature is filled with them—are no more than so many negations of the continuous movement from discrimination to non-discrimination, from affectibility to non-affectibility, etc., etc.

The idea of a continuous movement fails to account for the facts, first, that the moving process stops at the originally bright mirror, and makes no further attempt to go on indefinitely, and secondly, that the pure nature of the mirror suffers itself to be defiled, i.e. that from one object comes another object absolutely contradicting it. To put this another way: absolute negation is needed, but can it be possible when the process is continuous? Here is the reason why Hui-neng persistently opposes the view cherished by his opponents. He does not espouse the doctrine of continuity which is the Gradual School of Shen-hsiu. All those who hold the view of a continuous movement belong to the latter. Hui-neng, on the other hand, is the champion of the Abrupt school. According to this school the movement from *mayoi* to *satori* is abrupt and not gradual, discrete and not continuous.

That the process of enlightenment is abrupt means that there is a leap, logical and psychological, in the Buddhist experience. The logical leap is that the ordinary process of reasoning stops short, and what has been considered irrational is perceived to be perfectly natural, while the psychological leap is that the borders of consciousness are overstepped and one is plunged into the Unconscious which is not, after all, unconscious. This process is discrete, abrupt, and altogether beyond calculation; this is "Seeing into one's Self-nature". Hence the following statement by Hui-neng:

"O friends, while under Jen the Master I had a *satori* (*wu*) by just once listening to his words, and abruptly saw into the original nature of Suchness. This is the reason why I wish to see this teaching propagated, so that seekers of the truth may also abruptly have an insight into Bodhi, see each by himself

what his mind (*hsin*) is, what his original nature is. . . . All
the Buddhas of the past, present, and future, and all the Sutras
belonging to the twelve divisions are in the self-nature of each
individual, where they were from the first. . . . There is
within oneself that which knows, and thereby one has a *satori*.
If there rises an erroneous thought, falsehoods and perversions
obtain; and no outsiders, however wise, are able to instruct
such people, who are, indeed, beyond help. But if there takes
place an illumination by means of genuine Prajna, all falsehoods vanish in an instant. If one's self-nature is understood,
one's *satori* is enough to make one rise to a state of Buddhahood. O friends, when there is a Prajna illumination, the inside as well as the outside becomes thoroughly translucent,
and a man knows by himself what his original mind is, which
is no more than emancipation. When emancipation is obtained, it is the Prajna-samadhi, and when this Prajna-samadhi
is understood, there is realized a state of *mu-nen* (*wu-nien*),
'thought-less-ness'."

The teaching of abrupt *satori* is then fundamental in the
Southern school of Hui-neng. And we must remember that this
abruptness or leaping is not only psychological, but dialectical.

Prajna is really a dialectical term denoting that this special
process of knowing, known as "abruptly seeing", or "seeing at
once", does not follow general laws of logic; for when Prajna
functions one finds oneself all of a sudden, as if by a miracle,
facing Sunyata, the emptiness of all things. This does not take
place as the result of reasoning, but when reasoning has been
abandoned as futile, and psychologically when the will-power
is brought to a finish.

The Use of Prajna contradicts everything that we may conceive of things worldly; it is altogether of another order than
our usual life. But this does not mean that Prajna is something
altogether disconnected with our life and thought, something
that is to be given to us by a miracle from some unknown and
unknowable source. If this were the case, Prajna would be of
no possible use to us, and there would be no emancipation for
us. It is true that the functioning of Prajna is discrete, and

interrupting to the progress of logical reasoning, but all the time it underlies it, and without Prajna we cannot have any reasoning whatever. Prajna is at once above and in the process of reasoning. This is a contradiction, formally considered, but in truth this contradiction itself is made possible because of Prajna.

That almost all religious literature is filled with contradictions, absurdities, paradoxes, and impossibilities, and demands to believe them, to accept them, as revealed truths, is due to the fact that religious knowledge is based on the working of Prajna. Once this viewpoint of Prajna is gained, all the essential irrationalities found in religion become intelligible. It is like appreciating a fine piece of brocade. On the surface there is an almost bewildering confusion of beauty, and the connoisseur fails to trace the intricacies of the threads. But as soon as it is turned over all the intricate beauty and skill is revealed. Prajna consists in this turning-over. The eye has hitherto followed the surface of the cloth, which is indeed the only side ordinarily allowed us to survey. Now, the cloth is abruptly turned over; the course of the eyesight is suddenly interrupted; no continuous gazing is possible. Yet by this interruption, or rather disruption, the whole scheme of life is suddenly grasped; there is the "seeing into one's self-nature".

The point I wish to make here is that the reason side has been there all the time, and that it is because of this unseen side that the visible side has been able to display its multiple beauty. This is the meaning of discriminative reasoning being always based on non-discriminating Prajna; this is the meaning of the statement that the mirror-nature of emptiness (*sunyata*) retains all the time its original brightness, and is never once beclouded by anything outside which is reflected on it; this is again the meaning of all things being such as they are in spite of their being arranged in time and space and subject to the so-called laws of nature.

This something conditioning all things and itself not being conditioned by anything assumes various names as it is viewed from different angles. Spatially, it is called "formless", against all that can be subsumed under form; temporarily, it is "non-abiding", as it moves on for ever, not being cut up into pieces called thoughts and as such detained and retained as something abiding; psychologically it is "the unconscious" (*wu-nien* =*mu-nen*) in the sense that all our conscious thoughts and feelings grow out of the Unconscious, which is Mind (*hsin*), or Self-nature (*tzu-hsing*).

As Zen is more concerned with experience and hence with psychology, let us go further into the idea of the Unconscious. The original Chinese is *Wu-nien* (*mu-nen*) or *Wu-hsin* (*mu-shin*), and literally means "no-thought", or "no-mind". But *nien* or *hsin* means more than thought or mind. This I have elsewhere explained in detail. It is rather difficult to give here an exact English equivalent for *nien* or *hsin*. Hui-neng and Shen-hui use principally *nien* instead of *hsin,* but there are other Zen masters who prefer *hsin* to *nien*. In point of fact, the two designate the same experience: *wu-nien* and *wu-hsin* point to the same state of consciousness.

The character *hsin* originally symbolizes the heart as the organ of affection, but has later come to indicate also the seat of thinking and willing. *Hsin* has thus a broad connotation, and may be taken largely to correspond to consciousness. *Wu-nien* is "no-consciousness", thus the unconscious. The character *nien* has *chien* "now", over the heart, and might originally have meant anything present at the moment in consciousness. In Buddhist literature, it frequently stands for the Sanskrit *Kshana,* meaning "a thought", "a moment regarded as a unit of time", "an instant"; but as a psychological term it is generally used to denote "memory", "intense thinking", and "consciousness". *Wu-nien* thus also means "the unconscious".

What, then, do the Zen masters mean by "the unconscious"?

It is evident that in Zen Buddhism the unconscious is not a psychological term either in a narrower or in a broader sense. In modern psychology the scientists refer to the unconscious as underlying consciousness, where a large mass of psychological factors are kept buried under one name or another. They appear in the field of consciousness sometimes in response to a call, and therefore by a conscious effort, but quite frequently unexpectedly and in a disguised form. To define this unconsciousness baffles the psychologists just because it is the unconscious. The fact is, however, that it is a reservoir of mysteries and a source of superstitions. And for this reason the concept of the unconscious has been abused by unscrupulous religionists, and some people hold that Zen is also guilty of this crime. The accusation is justifiable if Zen philosophy is no more than a psychology of the unconscious in its ordinary definition.

According to Hui-neng, the concept of the unconscious is the foundation of Zen Buddhism. In fact he proposes three concepts as constituting Zen, and the unconscious is one of them; the other two are "formlessness" (*wu-hsing*) and "non-abiding" (*wu-chu*). Hui-neng continues: "By formlessness is meant to be in form and yet to be detached from it; by the unconscious is meant to have thoughts and yet not to have them; as to non-abiding it is the primary nature of man."

His further definition of the unconscious is: "O good friends, not to have the Mind tainted while in contact with all conditions of life,[9]—this is to be Unconscious. It is to be always detached from objective conditions in one's own consciousness, not to let one's mind be roused by coming in contact with objective conditions. . . . O good friends, why is the Unconscious established as fundamental? There are some people with confused ideas who talk about seeing into their own nature, but whose consciousness is not liberated from objective conditions, and (my teaching) is only for the sake of such people. Not only are they conscious of objective conditions, but they contrive to cherish false views, from which all worldly worries and vagaries rise. But in self-nature there is from the first not a thing which is attainable. If anything attainable is here conceived, fortune and misfortune will be talked about; and this is no more than worrying and giving oneself up to vagaries. Therefore in my teaching, unconsciousness is established as fundamental.

"O good friends, what is there for *wu* (of *wu-nien*, uncon-

[9] *Ching* in Chinese. It means "boundaries", "an area enclosed by them", "environment", "objective world". In its technical sense it stands contrasted with *hsin*, mind.

sciousness) to negate? And what is there for *nien* to be conscious of? *Wu* is to negate the notion of two forms (dualism), and to get rid of a mind which worries over things, while *Nien* means to become conscious of the primary nature of Suchness (*tathata*); for Suchness is the Body of Consciousness, and Consciousness is the Use of Suchness. It is the self-nature of Suchness to become conscious of itself; it is not the eye, ear, nose, and tongue that is conscious; as Suchness has (self-) nature, consciousness rises in it; if there were no Suchness, then eye and ear, together with forms and sounds, would be destroyed. In the self-nature of Suchness there rises consciousness; while in the six senses there is seeing, hearing, remembering, and recognizing; the self-nature is not tainted by objective conditions of all kinds; the true nature moves with perfect freedom, discriminating all forms in the objective world and inwardly unmoved in the first principle."

While it is difficult and often misleading to apply the modern way of thinking to those ancient masters, especially masters of Zen, we must to a certain extent hazard this application, for otherwise there will be no chance of even a glimpse into the secrets of Zen experience. For one thing, we have what Hui-neng calls self-nature, which is the Buddha-nature of the *Nirvana Sutra* and other Mahayana writings. This self-nature in terms of the *Prajnaparamita* is Suchness (*tathata*), and Emptiness (*sunyata*). Suchness means the Absolute, something which is not subject to laws of relativity, and therefore which cannot be grasped by means of form. Suchness is thus formlessness. In Buddhism, form (*rupa*) stands against noform (*arupa*), which is the unconditioned. This unconditioned, formless, and consequently unattainable is Emptiness (*sunyata*). Emptiness is not a negative idea, nor does it mean mere privation, but as it is not in the realm of names and forms it is called emptiness, or nothingness, or the Void.

Emptiness is thus unattainable. "Unattainable" means to be beyond perception, beyond grasping, for emptiness is on the other side of being and non-being. All our relative knowledge is concerned with dualities. But if emptiness is absolutely beyond all human attempts to take hold of in any sense whatever it has no value for us; it does not come into the sphere of human interest; it is really non-existent, and we have nothing to do with it. But the truth is otherwise. Emptiness constantly falls within our reach; it is always with us and in us, and conditions all our knowledge, all our deeds, and is our life itself. It is only when we attempt to pick it up and hold it forth as something before our eyes that it eludes us, frustrates all our efforts, and vanishes like vapour. We are ever lured towards it, but it proves a will-o'-the-wisp.

It is Prajna which lays its hands on Emptiness, or Suchness, or Self-nature. And this laying-hands-on is not what it seems. This is self-evident from what has already been said concerning things relative. Inasmuch as self-nature is beyond the realm of relativity, its being grasped by Prajna cannot mean a grasping in its ordinary sense. The grasping must be no-grasping, a paradoxical statement which is inevitable. To use Buddhist terminology, this grasping is accomplished by non-discrimination; that is, by non-discriminating discrimination. The process is abrupt, discrete, an act of the conscious; not an unconscious act but an act rising from self-nature itself, which is the Unconscious.

Hui-neng's Unconscious is thus fundamentally different from the psychologists' Unconscious. It has a metaphysical connotation. When Hui-neng speaks of the Unconscious in Consciousness, he steps beyond psychology; he is not referring even to the Unconscious forming the basis of consciousness, which goes to the remotest part when the mind has not yet evolved, the mind being still in a state of mere sustenance. Nor is Hui-neng's Unconscious a kind of world-spirit which is found floating on the surface of chaos. It is timeless, and yet contains all time with its minutest periods as well as all its aeons.

Shen-hui's definition of the Unconscious which we have in his *Sayings* (par. 14) will shed further light on the subject. When preaching to others on the *Prajnaparamita* he says: "be not attached to form. Not to be attached to form means Suchness. What is meant by Suchness? It means the Unconscious. What is the Unconscious? It is not to think of being and non-being; it is not to think of good and bad; it is not to think

of having limits or not having limits; it is not to think of measurements (or of non-measurements); it is not to think of enlightenment, nor is it to think of being enlightened; it is not
to think of Nirvana, nor is it to think of attaining Nirvana: this
is the Unconscious. The Unconscious is no other than Prajnaparamita itself. Prajnaparamita is no other than the Samadhi
of Oneness.

"O friends, if there are among you some who are still in
the stage of learners, let them turn their illumination (upon
the source of consciousness) whenever thoughts are awakened
in their minds. When the awakened mind is dead, the conscious illumination vanishes by itself—this is the Unconscious.
This Unconscious is absolutely free from all conditions, for if
there are any conditions it cannot be known as the Unconscious.

"O friends, that which sees truly sounds the depths of the
Dharmadhatu, and this is known as the Samadhi of Oneness.
Therefore, it is said in the *Smaller Prajnaparamita*: 'O good
men, this is Prajnaparamita, that is to say, not to have any
(conscious) thoughts in regard to things. As we live in that
which is unconscious, this golden-coloured body, with the
thirty-two marks of supreme manhood, emits rays of great ef-
fulgence, contains Prajna altogether beyond thinking, is endowed with all the highest Samadhis attained by the Buddhas,
and with incomparable knowledge. All the merits (accruing
from the Unconscious) cannot be recounted by the Buddhas,
much less by the Sravakas and the Pratyeka-Buddhas.' He who
sees the Unconscious is not tainted by the six senses; he who
sees the Unconscious is enabled to turn towards the Buddha-
knowledge; he who sees the Unconscious is called Reality; he
who sees the Unconscious is the Middle Way and the first
truth; he who sees the Unconscious is furnished at once with
merits of the Ganga; he who sees the Unconscious is able
to produce all things; he who sees the Unconscious is able to
take in all things."

This view of the Unconscious is thoroughly confirmed by
Tachu Hui-hai, a chief disciple of Ma-tsu, in his *Essential
Teaching of the Abrupt Awakening*: "The Unconscious means

to have no-mind in all circumstances, that is to say, not to be determined by any conditions, not to have any affections or hankerings. To face all objective conditions, and yet to be eternally free from any form of stirring, this is the Unconscious. The Unconscious is thus known as to be truly conscious of itself. But to be conscious of consciousness is a false form of the Unconscious. Why? The Sutra states that to make people become conscious of the six vijnanas is to have the wrong consciousness; to cherish the six vijnanas is false; where a man is free from the six vijnanas, he has the right consciousness."

"To see the Unconscious" does not mean any form of self-consciousness, nor is to sink into a state of ecstasy or indifference or apathy, where all traces of ordinary consciousness are wiped out. "To see the Unconscious" is to be conscious and yet to be unconscious of self-nature. Because self-nature is not to be determined by the logical category of being and non-being, to be so determined means to bring self-nature into the realm of empirical psychology, in which it ceases to be what it is in itself. If the Unconscious, on the other hand, means the loss of consciousness, it then spells death, or at best a temporary suspension of life itself. But this is impossible inasmuch as self-nature is the Mind itself. This is the sense of the following passage which we come across everywhere in the *Prajnaparamita* and other Mahayana sutras: "To be unconscious in all circumstances is possible because the ultimate nature of all things is emptiness, and because there is after all not a form which one can say one has laid hands on. This unattainability of all things is Reality itself, which is the most exquisite form of the Tathagata." The Unconscious is thus the ultimate reality, the true form, the most exquisite body of Tathagatahood. It is certainly not a hazy abstraction, not a mere conceptual postulate, but a living experience in its deepest sense.

Further descriptions of the Unconscious from Shen-hui are as follows:

"To see into the Unconscious is to understand self-nature; to understand self-nature is not to take hold of anything; not to take hold of anything is the Tathagata's Dhyana. . . . Self-nature is from the first thoroughly pure, because its Body is not to be taken hold of. To see it thus is to be on the same standing with the Tathagata, to be detached from all forms, to have all the vagaries of falsehood at once quieted, to equip oneself with merits of absolute stainlessness, to attain true emancipation, etc."

"The nature of Suchness is our original Mind, of which we are conscious; and yet there is neither the one who is conscious nor that of which there is a consciousness."

"To those who see the Unconscious, karma ceases to function, and what is the use for them to cherish an erroneous thought and to try to destroy karma by means of confusion?"

"To go beyond the dualism of being and non-being, and again to love the track of the Middle Way—this is the Unconscious. The Unconscious means to be conscious of the absolutely one; to be conscious of the absolutely one means to have all-knowledge, which is Prajna. Prajna is the Tathagata-Dhyana."

We are back again here at the relationship of Prajna and Dhyana. This is in fact one of the recurring subjects in the philosophy of Buddhism, and we cannot get away from it, especially in the study of Zen. The difference between Shen-hsiu's and Hui-neng's school is no more than the difference which exists between them in regard to this relationship. Shen-hsiu approaches the problem from the point of view of Dhyana, while Hui-neng upholds Prajna as the most important thing in the grasping of Zen. The latter tells us first of all "to see" self-nature, which means to wake up in the Unconscious; Shen-hsiu, on the other hand, advises us "to sit in meditation", so that all our passions and disturbing thoughts may be quieted, and the inherent purity of self-nature shine out by itself. These two tendencies have been going on side by side in the history of Zen thought, probably due to the two psychological types to be found in us, intuitive and moral, intellectual and practical.

Those who emphasize Prajna, like Hui-neng and his school, tend to identify Dhyana with Prajna, and insist on an abrupt, instantaneous awakening in the Unconscious. This awakening in the Unconscious may be, logically speaking, a contradiction, but as Zen has another world in which to live its own life, it does not mind contradictory expressions and continues to use its peculiar phraseology.

Hui-neng's school thus objects to Shen-hsiu's on the grounds that those who spend their time in sitting cross-legged in meditation, trying to realize the state of tranquillity, are seekers after some tangible attainment; they are upholders of the doctrine of original purity, which they consider to be something intellectually demonstrable; they are gazers at a special object which can be picked up among other relative objects and shown to others as one points at the moon; they cling to this specific object as something most precious, forgetting that this clinging degrades the value of their cherished object because it is thereby brought down to the same order of being as themselves; because of this clinging to it and abiding in it, they cherish a certain definite state of consciousness as the ultimate point they should attain; therefore they are never truly emancipated, they have not cut the last string which keeps them still on this side of existence.

According to Hui-neng's Prajna school, Prajna and Dhyana become identical in the Unconscious, for when there is an awakening in the Unconscious, this is no awakening, and the Unconscious remains all the time in Dhyana, serene and undisturbed.

The awakening is never to be taken for an attainment or for an accomplishment as the result of such strivings. As there is no attainment in the awakening of Prajna in the Unconscious, there is no abiding in it either. This is the point most emphatically asserted in all the Prajnaparamita Sutras. No attainment, and therefore no clinging, no abiding, which means abiding in the Unconscious or abiding in non-abiding.

In Ta-chu Hui-hai we have this dialogue:

Q. "What is meant by the simultaneous functioning of the Triple Discipline?"

A. "To be pure and undefiled is Sila (precept). The mind

unmoved remaining ever serene in all conditions is Dhyana (meditation). To perceive the mind unmoved, and yet to raise no thoughts as to its immovability; to perceive the mind pure and undefiled, and yet to raise no thoughts as to its purity; to discriminate what is bad from what is good, and yet to feel no defilement by them, and to be absolute master of oneself: this is known as Prajna. When one perceives thus that Sila, Dhyana, and Prajna are all beyond attainability, one at once realizes that there is no discrimination to be made between them, and that they are of one and the same Body. This is the simultaneous functioning of the Triple Discipline."

Q. "When the mind abides in purity, is this not clinging to it?"

A. "When abiding in purity, one may have no thoughts of abiding in it, and then one is said not to be clinging to it."

Q. "When the mind abides in emptiness, is this not clinging to it?"

A. "When one has thoughts as to thus abiding, there is a clinging in one."

Q. "When the mind abides in the non-abiding, is this not clinging to the non-abiding?"

A. "When one cherishes no thoughts as to emptiness, there is no clinging. If you wish to understand when the mind comes to realize the moment of non-abiding, sit in the right meditation posture, and purge your mind thoroughly of thoughts—thoughts about all things, thoughts about goodness and badness of things. Events past are already past; therefore have no thoughts of them, and your mind is disconnected from the past. Thus past events are done away with. Present events are already here before you; then have no attachment to them. Not to have attachment means not to rouse any feeling of hate or love. Your mind is then disconnected from the present, and the events before your eyes are done away with. When the past, present, and future are thus in no way taken in, they are completely done away with. When thoughts come and go, do not follow them, and your pursuing mind is cut off. When abiding (with thoughts) do not tarry in them, and your abiding mind is cut off. When thus freed from abiding (with thoughts), you are said to be abiding with the non-abiding. If you have a thoroughly clear perception of yourself, you may remain abiding with thoughts, and yet what remains abiding is thoughts (and as to your Unconscious), it has neither an abiding place nor a non-abiding place. If you have a thoroughly clear perception as to the mind having no abiding place anywhere, this is known as having a thoroughly clear perception of one's own being. This very Mind which has no abiding place anywhere is the Buddha-Mind itself; it is called Emancipation-Mind, Enlightenment-Mind, the Unborn Mind, and Emptiness of Materiality and Ideality. It is what is designated in the sutras as Recognition of the Unborn. . . . All this is understood when one has the Unconscious in evidence anywhere."

The doctrine of the Unconscious as expounded here is, psychologically translated, that of absolute passivity or absolute obedience. It may also be represented as the teaching of humility. Our individual consciousness merged into the Unconscious must become like the body of a dead man, as used by St. Francis of Assisi to illustrate his idea of the perfect and highest obedience.

To make oneself like a corpse or a piece of wood or rock, though from a very different standpoint, seems to have been a favourite simile with Zen Buddhists too.

In Huang-po Hsi-yun we have this:

Q. "What is meant by worldly knowledge?"

A. "What is the use of involving yourself in such complexities? (The Mind) is thoroughly pure from the first, and no wordy discussions are needed about it. Only have no mind of any kind, and this is known as undefiled knowledge. In your daily life, whether walking or standing, sitting or lying, let not your speech of any nature be attached to things of the world; then whatever words you utter and in whichever way your eyes blink, they are all of undefiled knowledge. The world is at present on the way to general decline, and most Zen students are attached to things material and worldly. What concern have they after all with Mind? Let your mind be like vacuity of space, like a chip of dead wood and a piece of stone, like cold ashes and burnt-out coal. When this is done, you may feel some correspondence (to the true Mind). If otherwise, some day you will surely be taken to task by the old man of the other world. . . ."

Ignatius Loyola's recommendation of obedience as the foundation of his Order differs naturally in spirit from the idea of the Zen masters' recommendation of what may be called absolute indifference. They are indifferent to things happening to them, because they consider them as not touching the Unconscious which lies at the back of their surface consciousness. As they hold themselves intimately to the Unconscious, all the outer happenings, including what is popularly known as belonging to one's consciousness, are like shadows. Being so, they are suffered to assail the Zen master, while his Unconscious remains undisturbed. This suffering is, to use Christian terminology, a sacrifice, a holocaust consumed for the honour of God.

William James quotes Lejeune's *Introduction à la Vie Mystique* in his *Varieties of Religious Experience* (p. 312): "By poverty he immolates his exterior possessions; by chastity he immolates his body; by obedience he completes the sacrifice, and gives to God all that he yet holds as his own, his two most precious goods, his intellect and his will." By this sacrifice of the intellect and the will Catholic discipline is completed; that is to say, the devotee turns into a block of wood, a mere mass of burnt coal and cold ashes, and is identified with the Unconscious. And this experience is told by Catholic writers in terms of God, as a sacrifice to him; whereas Zen masters resort to more intellectual or psychological phraseology.

To quote further from Ignatius's *Sayings:* "I must consider myself as a corpse which has neither intelligence nor will: be like a mass of matter which without resistance lets itself be placed wherever it may please anyone; like a stick in the hand of an old man, who uses it according to his needs and places it where it suits him." This is the attitude he advises his followers to take towards the Order. The intent of the Catholic discipline is altogether different from that of Zen, and therefore Ignatius's admonition takes on quite a different colouring on the surface. But so far as its psychological experience is concerned, both the Zen masters and the Catholic leaders aim at bringing about the same state of mind, which is no other than realizing the Unconscious in our individual consciousnesses.

The Jesuit Rodriguez gives a very concrete illustration[10] in regard to the virtue of obedience: "A religious person ought in respect to all the things that he uses to be like a statue which one may drape with clothing, but which feels no grief and makes no resistance when one strips it again. It is in this way that you should feel towards your clothes, your books, your cell and everything else that you make use of. . . ." For your clothes, your books, etc., substitute your griefs, worries, joys, aspirations, etc., which are your psychological possessions just as much as are your physical goods. Avoid using these psychological possessions as if they were your private property, and you are Buddhists living in the Unconscious or with the Unconscious.

Some may say that physical goods are not the same as psychological functions, that without the latter there is no mind and without a mind no sentient being. But I say, without these physical possessions which you are supposed to be in need of, where is your body? Without the body, where is the mind? After all, these psychological functions do not belong to you to the same extent as your clothes, your table, your family, your body, etc., belong to you. You are always controlled by them, instead of your controlling them. You are not master even of your own body which seems to be most intimate to you. You are subject to birth and death. With the body your mind is most closely connected, and this seems to be still more out of your control. Are you not throughout your life a mere plaything of all your sensations, emotions, imaginations, ambitions, passions, etc.?

When Hui-neng and other Zen masters speak of the Unconscious, they may appear to be advising us to turn into cold dead

[10] James, pp. 315–16.

ashes with no mentality, with no feelings, with no inner mechanism commonly associated with humanity, to turn into mere nothingness, absolute emptiness; but in truth this is the advice given by all religionists, this is the final goal all religious discipline aspires to reach. Apart from their theological or philosophical interpretations, to my mind Christians and Buddhists refer to the same fact of experience when they talk about sacrifice and obedience. A state of absolute passivity dynamically interpreted, if such is possible, is the basis of the Zen experience.

The Unconscious is to let "thy will be done", and not to assert my own. All the doings and happenings, including thoughts and feelings, which I have or which come to me are of the divine will as long as there are on my part no clingings, no hankerings, and "my mind is wholly disconnected with things of the past, present, and future" in the way described above. This is again the spirit of Christ when he utters: "Take therefore no thought for the morrow: for the morrow shall take thought for the things of itself. Sufficient unto the day is the evil thereof." Replace "the morrow" with "the future" and "the day" with "the present", and what Christ says is exactly what the Zen master would say, though in a more philosophical manner. "The day" would not mean for the Zen master a period of twenty-four hours as popularly reckoned, but an instant or a thought which passes even before one utters the word. The Unconscious reflects on its surface all such thought-instants, which pass with the utmost rapidity while it itself remains serene and undisturbed. These passing thoughts constitute my consciousness, and in so far as the latter is regarded as belonging to me it has no connection with the Unconscious, and there are attachments, hankerings, worries, disappointments, and all kinds of "evil thereof". When they are, however, connected with the Unconscious, they fall away from my consciousness; they cease to be evils, and I share the serenity of the Unconscious. This is, I may say, a phase of absolute passivity.

The conception of the Unconscious leads to many wrong interpretations when it is taken as pointing to the existence of an entity to be designated "the Unconscious". Zen masters do not assume such an entity behind our empirical consciousness. Indeed, they are always against assumptions of this nature; they aim at destroying them by all possible means. The Chinese *wu-hsin,* "without mind", and *wu-nien,* "without thought" or "no-thought", mean both the Unconscious and being unconscious. This being so, I sometimes find myself at a loss to present the exact meaning of the Chinese writers whose translations are given in this Essay. The Chinese sentences are very loosely strung together, and each component character is not at all flexible. While read in the original, the sense seems to be clear enough, but when it is to be presented in translation more precision is required to comply with the construction of the language used, in our case English. To do this, much violence is to be practised on the genius of the original Chinese, and instead of a translation it is necessary to have an exposition, or an interpretation, or a paraphrasing; and, as a consequence, the continuous thread of thought woven around the original Chinese characters, with all their grammatical and structural peculiarities, is broken. What we may call the artistic effect of the original is inevitably lost.

In the following dialogue quoted from Hui-chung's sermons[11], arguments are developed around the ideas *wu-hsin* ("no-mind"=unconscious), *yung-hsin* ("using the mind"=conscious striving), *yu-hsin* ("to have a mind"=being conscious), *wu* (as an independent privative particle, "not", as a prefix, "dis-", "un-", etc., as a noun, "nothingness" or "no-ness", or "non-entity"), and *ch'eng-fo* ("attaining Buddhahood", "becoming a Buddha"). Hui-chung was one of the disciples of Hui-neng, and naturally was anxious to develop the doctrine of *wu-hsin* which means *wu-nien,* the term principally used by Hui-neng, his master. The dialogue opens with the question by Ling-chiao, one of his new followers:

Q. "I have left my home to become a monk, and my aspiration is to attain Buddhahood. How should I use my mind?"

[11] *Transmission of the Lamp* (Kokyoshoin edition), fas. 28, fol. 103–4.

A. "Buddhahood is attained when there is no mind which is to be used for the task."[12]

Q. "When there is no mind to be used for the task, who can ever attain Buddhahood?"

A. "By no-mind the task is accomplished by itself. Buddha, too, has no mind."[13]

Q. "The Buddha has wonderful ways and knows how to deliver all beings. If he had no mind, who would ever deliver all beings?"[14]

A. "To have no mind means to deliver all beings. If he sees

[12] So long as there are conscious strivings to accomplish a task, the very consciousness works against it, and no task is accomplished. It is only when all the traces of this consciousness are wiped out that Buddhahood is attained.

[13] The idea is that when every effort is put forward to achieve some task, and you are finally exhausted and have come to an end of your energy, you give yourself up so far as your consciousness is concerned. In fact, however, your unconscious mind is still intensely bent on the work, and before you realize it you find the work accomplished. "Man's extremity is God's opportunity." This is really what is meant by "to accomplish the task by no-mind". But there is also a philosophical construction of the idea of Buddha's having no-mind. For, according to Zen philosophy, we are all endowed with the Buddha-nature from which Prajna issues, illumining all our activities, mental and physical. The Buddha-nature does this in the same way as the sun radiates heat and light, or as the mirror reflects everything coming before it, that is to say, unconsciously, with "no-mind", *wu-hsin* (in its adverbial sense). Hence it is declared that *fo wu hsin,* "Buddha is unconscious", or "By Buddhahood is meant the unconscious". Philosophically speaking, therefore, no special conscious strivings are necessary; in fact they are a hindrance to the attainment of Buddhahood. We are already Buddhas. To talk about any sort of attainment is a desecration, and logically a tautology. "Having no-mind", of "cherishing the unconscious", therefore, means to be free from all these artificial, self-created, double-roofing efforts. Even this "having", this "cherishing", goes against *wu-hsin.*

[14] Philosophically stated, how could the Unconscious achieve anything? How would it ever take up the great religious work of carrying all being over to the other shore of Nirvana?

any being who is to be delivered, he has a mind (*yu-hsin*) and is surely subject to birth and death."[15]

Q. "No-mind-ness (*wu-hsin*) is then already here, and how was it that Sakyamuni appeared in the world and left behind ever so many sermons? Is this a fiction?"

A. "With all the teachings left by him, the Buddha is *wu-hsin* (no-mind, unconscious)."[16]

Q. "If all his teachings come from his no-mind-ness, they must be also no-teachings."

A. "To preach is not (to preach), and not (to preach) is to preach. (All the activities of the Buddha come from no-ness, i.e. Sunyata, Emptiness.)"

Q. "If his teachings come out of his no-mind-ness, is my working karma the outcome of cherishing the idea of a mind (*yu-hsin*)?"

A. "In no-mind-ness there is no karma. But (as long as you refer to working out your karma) karma is already here, and your mind is subjected to birth and death. How then can there be no-mind-ness (in you)?"

Q. "If no-mind-ness means Buddhahood, has your Reverence already attained Buddhahood, or not?"

A. "When mind is not (*wu*), who talks about attaining Buddhahood? To think that there is something called Buddhahood which is to be attained, this is cherishing the idea of a mind (*yu-hsin*); to cherish the idea of a mind is an attempt to accomplish something that flows out (*yu-lou=asvara* in Sanskrit); this being so, there is no no-mind-ness here."

---

[15] There are two planes of living: the one is the plane of consciousness (*yu-hsin*), and the other is that of unconsciousness (*wu-hsin*). Activities belonging to the first plane with a *yu-hsin* are governed by the laws of karma, while those of the second plane are of the Unconscious, of non-discriminating Prajna, and characterized with purposelessness and therefore meritlessness. The genuinely religious life takes its start from here, and bears its fruit on the plane of consciousness.

[16] That is, the Buddha with all his worldly activities among us lives on the plane of unconsciousness, in a world of effortlessness and meritlessness, where no teleological categories are applicable.

Q. "If there is no Buddhahood to be attained, has your Reverence the Buddha-function?"[17]

A. "Where mind itself is not, whence is its functioning?"[18]

Q. "One is then lost in outer no-ness (*wu*); may this not be an absolutely nihilistic view?"

A. "From the first there is (no viewer and) no viewing; and who says this to be nihilist?"

Q. "To say that from the first nothing is, is this not falling into emptiness?"

A. "Even emptiness is not, and where is the falling?"

Q. "Both subject and object are negated (*wu*). Suppose a man were all of a sudden to make his appearance here and cut your head off with a sword. Is this to be considered real (*yu*) or not real (*wu*)?"

A. "This is not real."

Q. "Pain or no pain?"

A. "Pain too is not real."

Q. "Pain not being real, in what path of existence would you be reborn after death?"

A. "No death, no birth, and no path."

Q. "Having already attained the state of absolute no-ness, one is perfect master of oneself; but how would you use the mind (*yung-hsin*), when hunger and cold assail you?"

[17] As I stated elsewhere, Buddhist philosophy makes use of two conceptions, Body and Use, in explaining reality. The two are inseparable; where there is any functioning there must be a Body behind it, and where there is a Body its Use will inevitably be recognized. But when it is declared that there is no Buddhahood, how can there be any functioning of it? How then can a Zen abbot have anything to do with Buddhism?

[18] All starts from the Unconscious, all is in the Unconscious, and all sinks down into the Unconscious. There is no Buddhahood, hence no functioning of it. If a thought is awakened and any form of functioning is recognized, there is a discrimination, an attachment, a deviation from the path of the Unconscious. The master stands firmly in the Unconscious and refuses to be transferred to the plane of consciousness. This puzzles the novitiate monk.

A. "When hungry, I eat, and when cold I put on more clothes."

Q. "If you are aware of hunger and cold, you have a mind (*yu-hsin*)."

A. "I have a question for you: Has the mind you speak of as a mind (*yu-hsin hsin*) a form?"

Q. "The mind has no form."

A. "If you already knew that the mind has no form, that means that from the first the mind is not, and how could you talk about having a mind?"

Q. "If you should happen to encounter a tiger or a wolf in the mountains, how would you use your mind (*yung-hsin*)?"

A. "When it is seen, it is as if it were not seen; when it approaches, it is as if it never approached; and the animal (reflects) no-mind-ness. Even a wild animal will not hurt you."

Q. "To be as if nothing were happening, to be in no-mindness, absolutely independent of all things, what is the name of such a being?"

A. "Its name is Vajra the Mahasattva (Vajra the Great Being)."

Q. "What form has he?"

A. "From the first he has no form."

Q. "Since he has no form, what is that which goes by the name of Vajra the Great Being?"

A. "It is called Vajra the Great Formless One."

Q. "What merits has he?"

A. "When your thoughts, just one of them, are in correspondence with Vajra, you are able to erase the grave offences which you have committed while going through cycles of birth and death during Kalpas numbering as many as the sands of the Ganga. The merits of this Vajra the Great One are immeasurable; no word of mouth can reckon them, no minds are capable of describing them; even if one lives for ages numbering as many as the sands of the Ganga, and talks about them, one cannot exhaust them."

Q. "What is meant by 'one being in one thought in correspondence with it'?"

A. "When one is forgetful of both memory and intelligence, one is in correspondence with it."[19]

Q. "When both memory and intelligence are forgotten, who is it that interviews the Buddhas?"

A. "To forget means no-ness (*wang chi wu*). No-ness means Buddhahood (*wu chi fo*)."

Q. "To designate no-ness as no-ness is all very well, but why call it the Buddha?"

A. "No-ness is emptiness, and the Buddha too is emptiness. Therefore, it is said that no-ness means Buddhahood and Buddhahood no-ness."

Q. "If there is not an iota of thing, what is it to be named?"

A. "No name whatever for it."

Q. "Is there anything resembling it?"

A. "Not a thing resembling it; the world knows no compeer."

III. SOME MONDO (QUESTIONS AND ANSWERS, DIALOGUE) ILLUSTRATING THE NO-MIND

1. A monk asked Chih of Yun-chu of the eighth century: "What is meant by seeing into one's Self-nature and becoming a Buddha?"

CHIH: "This Nature is from the first pure and undefiled, serene and undisturbed. It belongs to no categories of duality such as being and non-being, pure and defiled, long and short, taking-in and giving-up; the Body remains in its suchness. To have a clear insight into this is to see into one's Self-nature. Self-nature is the Buddha, and the Buddha is Self-nature. Therefore, seeing into one's Self-nature is becoming the Buddha."

[19] "To be forgetful of memory and intelligence" is an odd expression. "Forgetful", *wang*, is frequently used to express the idea of the unconscious. To forget both memory and intelligence, which constitute the essence of our empirical consciousness, is to return to the Unconscious, not to cherish any thought of a mind, to do away altogether with a *yung-hsin* or *yu-hsin*, which is the state of no-mind-ness. It is the repetition of the idea stated before, that to be back in the Unconscious is to attain Buddhahood.

MONK: "If Self-nature is pure, and belongs to no categories of duality such as being and non-being, etc., where does this seeing take place?"

CHIH: "There is a seeing, but nothing seen."

MONK: "If there is nothing seen, how can we say that there is any seeing at all?"

CHIH: "In fact there is no trace of seeing."

MONK: "In such a seeing, whose seeing is it?"

CHIH: "There is no seer, either."

2. A monk asked Ching-t'sen, of Chang-sha: "What is meant by 'one's everyday thought is the Tao'?"

CHING-T'SEN: "When I feel sleepy, I sleep; when I want to sit, I sit."

MONK: "I fail to follow you."

CHING-T'SEN: "In summer we seek a cool place; when cold we sit by a fire."

3. A Vinaya master called Yuan came to Tai-chu Hui-hai, and asked: "When disciplining oneself in the Tao, is there any special way of doing it?"

HUI-HAI: "Yes, there is."

YUAN: "What is that?"

HUI-HAI: "When hungry one eats; when tired, one sleeps."

YUAN: "That is what other people do; is their way the same as yours?"

HUI-HAI: "Not the same."

YUAN: "Why not?"

HUI-HAI: "When they eat, they do not just eat, they conjure up all kinds of imagination; when they sleep, they do not just sleep, they are given up to varieties of idle thoughts. That is why theirs is not my way."

4. Chen-lang came up to Shih-tou and asked: "What is the idea of Dharma's coming over here from the West?"

SHIH-TOU: "Ask the post over there."

CHEN-LANG: "I do not understand."

SHIH-TOU: "Neither do I."

This remark made Chen-lang realize the truth. Later, when a monk came to him asking for his instruction, he called out: "O reverend sir!" The monk answered, "Yes," whereupon Chen-lang said: "You are turning away from yourself." "If so, why do you not see to it that I behave properly?" This said, Chenlang wiped his eyes as if trying to see better. The monk had no words.

5. When Yao-shan Wei-yen was sitting cross-legged quietly, a monk came to him and said: "In this immovable position what are you thinking?"

YAO-SHAN: "Thinking of that which is beyond thinking."

MONK: "How do you go on with thinking that which is beyond thinking?"

YAO-SHAN: "By not-thinking."

6. A monk asked Yao-shan to enlighten him, as he was still groping in the dark as to the meaning of his own life. Yao-shan kept quiet for a while. This keeping quiet is pregnant with meaning, and if the monk were ready for it he could have comprehended what made Yao-shan remain silent. But in point of fact the monk failed, and Yao-shan continued: "It is not difficult for me to say a word to you on the matter before us. The point, however, is to grasp the meaning, as soon as it is uttered, without a moment of deliberation. When this is done there is an approach to the truth. On the other hand, there is a delay on your part, and you begin to reason things out, and the fault will be finally laid at my door. It is after all better to keep the mouth closed so that we both escape further complications."

7. Chung-i Hung-en, a disciple of Ma-tsu, was once asked by Yang-shan: "How can one see into one's self-nature?" Chung-i said: "It is like a cage with six windows, and there is in it a monkey. When someone calls at the east window, 'O monkey, O monkey!' he answers. At the other windows the same response is obtained." Yang-shan thanked him for the instruction, and said: "Your instructive simile is quite intelligible, but there is one thing on which I wish to be enlightened. If the inside monkey is asleep, tired out, what happens when the outside one comes to interview it?" Chung-i got down from his straw seat and taking Yang-shan's arm began to dance, saying: "O monkey, O monkey, my interview with you is finished. It is like an animalcule making its nest among the eyebrows of a mosquito: it comes out at the street crossing and makes a

loud cry: 'Wide is the land, few are the people, and one rarely meets friends!' "

8. Pai-chang asked: "What is the ultimate end of Buddhism?" Ma-tsu said: "This is just where you give up your life."

9. When Pai-chang was asked by Ma-tsu what way he would use in the demonstration of Zen thought, Pai-chang held up his *hossu*. Ma-tsu asked: "Is that all? Anything further?" Thereupon Pai-chang threw the *hossu* down.

10. When Pao-che of Ma-ku Shan one day accompanied his master, Ma-tsu, in his walk, he asked: "What is Great Nirvana?" The master said: "Hasten!" "What is to be hastened, O Master?" "Look at the stream!" was the answer.

11. A Buddhist scholar called on Yen-kuan Ch'i-an, who asked: "What is your special branch of study?"

SCHOLAR: "I discourse on the *Avatamsaka Sutra*."

MASTER: "How many Dharmadhatus does it teach?"

SCHOLAR: "From the broadest point of view, there are innumerable Dharmadhatus related to one another in the closest possible relationship; but summarily stated, four are reckoned."

The master then held up his *hossu*, saying, "To which of those Dharmadhatus does this belong?"

The scholar meditated for a while, trying to find the right answer. The master was impatient and gave out this statement: "Deliberate thinking and discursive understanding amount to nothing; they belong to the household of ghosts; they are like a lamp in the broad daylight; nothing shines out of them."

12. Another monk asked Wei-kuan: "Where is Tao?"

KUAN: "Right before us."

MONK: "Why don't I see it?"

KUAN: "Because of your egoism you cannot see it."

MONK: "If I cannot see it because of my egoism, does your Reverence see it?"

KUAN: "As long as there is 'I and thou', this complicates the situation and there is no seeing Tao."

MONK: "When there is neither 'I' nor 'thou' is it seen?"

KUAN: "When there is neither 'I' nor 'thou', who is here to see it?"

13. When Chih-chang of Kuei-sung Ssu had tea with Nan-

chuan P'u-yuan, Nan-chuan said: "We have been good friends, talked about many things and weighed them carefully, and we know where we are; now that we each go our own way, what would you say when someone comes up and asks you about ultimate things?"

CHIH-CHANG: "This ground where we sit now is a fine site for a hut."

NAN-CHUAN: "Let your hut alone; how about ultimate things?"

Chih-chang took the tea-set away, and rose from his seat. Whereupon Nan-chuan said: "You have finished your tea, but I have not."

CHIH-CHANG: "The fellow who talks like that cannot consume even a drop of water."

IV. AN INTERPRETATION OF THE ZEN UNCONSCIOUS

To understand the scheme of thought conceived by Hui-neng and his school, the following interpretation may be of use to readers who are not used to the oriental way of viewing the world.

What comes first in importance in the philosophy of Hui-neng is the idea of self-nature. But self-nature, I must warn the reader, is not to be conceived as something of substance. It is not the last residue left behind after all things relative and conditional have been extracted from the notion of an individual being. It is not the self,. or the soul, or the spirit, as ordinarily regarded. It is not something belonging to any categories of the understanding. It does not belong to this world of relativities. Nor is it the highest reality which is generally ascribed to God or to Atman or to Brahma. It cannot be described or defined in any possible way, but without it the world even as we see it and use it in our everyday life collapses. To say it is is to deny it. It is a strange thing, but as I go on my meaning will become clearer.

In the traditional terminology of Buddhism, self-nature is Buddha-nature, that which makes up Buddhahood; it is absolute Emptiness, *Sunyata,* it is absolute Suchness, *Tathata.*

May it be called Pure Being, the term used in Western philosophy? While it has nothing to do yet with a dualistic world of subject and object, I will for convenience' sake call it Mind, with the capital initial letter, and also the Unconscious. As Buddhist phraseology is saturated with psychological terms, and as religion is principally concerned with the philosophy of life, these terms, Mind and the Unconscious, are here used as synonymous with Self-nature, but the utmost care is to be taken not to confuse them with those of empirical psychology; for we have not yet come to this; we are speaking of a transcendental world where no such shadows are yet traceable.

In this self-nature there is a movement, an awakening, and the Unconscious becomes conscious of itself. This is not the region where the question "Why?" or "How?" can be asked. The awakening or movement or whatever it may be called is to be taken as a fact which goes beyond refutation. The bell rings, and I hear its vibrations as transmitted through the air. This is a plain fact of perception. In the same way, the rise of consciousness in the Unconscious is a matter of experience; no mystery is connected with it, but, logically stated, there is an apparent contradiction, which once started goes on contradicting itself eternally. Whatever this is, we have now a self-conscious Unconscious or a self-reflecting Mind. Thus transformed, Self-nature is known as Prajna.

Prajna, which is the awakening of consciousness in the Unconscious, functions in a twofold direction. The one is towards the Unconscious and the other towards the conscious. The Prajna which is orientated to the Unconscious is Prajna properly so called, while the Prajna of consciousness is now called mind with the small initial letter. From this mind a dualistic world takes its rise: subject and object, the inner self and the external world, and so on. In the Mind, therefore, two aspects are also distinguishable: Prajna-mind of non-discrimination and dualistic mind. The mind of the first aspect belongs to this world, but so long as it is linked with Prajna it is in direct communication with the Unconscious, it is the Mind; whereas the mind of the second aspect is wholly of this world, and delighted with it, and mixes itself with all its multiplicities.

The mind of the second aspect is called by Hui-neng "thought", *nen nien*. Here, mind is thought, and thought mind; *nien* (*nen*) is *hsin* (*shin*) and *hsin nien*. From the relative point of view, the mind of the first aspect may be designated "no-mind" in contradistinction to the mind of the second aspect. As the latter belongs to this side of our ordinary experience, so called, the former is a transcendental one and in terms of Zen philosophy is "that which is not the mind", or "no-mind", or "no-thought".

To repeat, Prajna is a double-edged sword, one side of which cuts the Unconscious and the other the conscious. The first is also called Mind, which corresponds to "no-mind". The "no-mind" is the unconscious phase of the mind which is the conscious side of Prajna. The diagram below will help to clear up this scheme of the Unconscious:

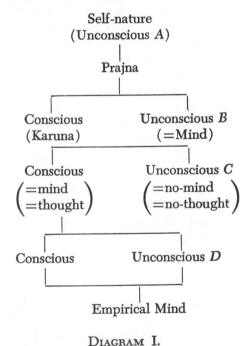

DIAGRAM I.

In this the Unconscious *A, B,* and *C* belong to the transcendental order, and are essentially of one and the same nature, whereas the unconscious *D* is of the empirical mind which is the subject of psychology.

With the above interpretation of Hui-neng's Zen thought, helped by the diagrammic analysis, read the following definitions of *munen* (*wu-nien*), "no-thought" or "no-mind" gathered from the *T'anching,* and I hope Hui-neng will become more intelligible, and with him all the rest of the Zen masters cited above in various connections:

Hui-neng defines *wu-nien,* "To have thoughts as not having them" (or would it better to translate: "To have thoughts and yet not to have them"?) This evidently means to be conscious of the Unconscious or "to find the Unconscious in consciousness", both of *C* grade above the empirical plane. A few lines below, Hui-neng has this for *wu-nien*: "Facing all environing objects the mind remains unstained"; that is, no thoughts are raised in the mind. By "environing objects" a world of consciousnesses is meant, and not to be stained in it pointed to the Unconscious, a state where no "thoughts", no consciousness, interfere with the functioning of the mind. Here we recognize again the Unconscious of *C* grade.

The following statements by Hui-neng are quite clear without comments:

"Turning thoughts on Self[-nature], they are kept away from the environing objects; thoughts are not raised on the environing objects."

"To raise thoughts towards the environing objects, and on these thoughts to cherish false views, this is the source of worries and imaginations."

"What is *wu-nien,* no-thought-ness? Seeing all things and yet to keep your mind free from stain and attachment, this is no-thought-ness."

"He who understands the idea of no-thought-ness has a perfect thoroughfare in the world of multiplicities. He who understands the idea of no-thought-ness sees the realm of all the Buddhas; he who understands the idea of no-thought-ness attains to the stage of Buddhahood."

What Hui-neng wishes to express by the idea of *munen* (*wu-nien,* no-thought-ness) may be gathered from these quotations, aided by Diagram I. But note, in regard to the diagram, that the Unconscious developing by degrees, as it were, down to the empirical mind has nothing to do with any form of grading. When it is analysed and shown in the form given above we are apt to imagine that there are grades in the Unconscious, in the sense that they are different in kind, and that in the lower ones there is nothing of the higher. This is not true, for all the Unconscious are merged in one another. When the one is thoroughly grasped all the rest will be comprehended. But at the same time we can say that the unconscious becomes purified, so to speak, as we rise from the Unconscious in the empirical mind, and that before we come to the unconscious Prajna we have most thoroughly to purge all the conscious defilements belonging to the empirical Unconscious. This is, however, one practical point of view of Zen discipline; theoretically stated, all the Unconscious are of one taste.

As to what the awakening of Prajna means in the system of Hui-neng, I have already repeatedly made references to it. But in order to avoid misunderstanding more quotations are here given:

"When one awakens genuine Prajna and reflects its light [on Self-nature], all false thoughts disappear instantaneously. When Self-nature is recognized, this understanding at once leads one to the Buddha-stage."

"When Prajna with its light reflects [within], and penetratingly illumines inside and outside, you recognize your own Mind. When your own Mind is recognized, there is emancipation for you. When you have emancipation, this means that you are in the Samadhi of Prajna, which is *munen* (no-thought-ness)."

"When used, it pervades everywhere, and yet shows no attachment anywhere. Only keep your original Mind pure and let the six senses run out of the six portals into the six dust[-worlds]. Free from stain, free from confusion, [the mind] in its coming and going is master of itself, in its functioning knows no pause. This is the Samadhi of Prajna, a masterly emancipation, and known as the deed of no-thought-ness."

The Samadhi of Prajna so called is the Unconscious itself. When Prajna is entirely directed towards Self-nature and its other direction is ignored, it extricates itself, if we can say so, from its own contradictory nature and is itself. This is a dialectical contradiction inherent in our experiences, and there is no escape from it; in fact all our experiences, which means our life itself, are possible because of this supreme contradiction. To escape it is the sign of a confused mind. Therefore, says Hui-neng:

"As to not making your mind move towards anything, this is extirpating thoughts, which means being bound up in the Dharma, and is known as a perverting view."

This citation may not be quite clear, as it has a historical significance. At the time of Hui-neng, indeed prior to him and even after him, there were some who endeavoured to escape the fundamental contradiction inherent in life itself by destroying all thought-activities, so that there was a state of absolute void, of utter nothingness, of negation imagined to be most thoroughgoing. Such are killing life itself, deceiving themselves thereby to gain it in its true form. They bind themselves by false ideas, taking the Dharma for annihilation. In point of fact, however, annihilation in any form is impossible; what one imagines to be such is simply another way of affirmation. However violently or boisterously one may protest, no shrimps can get out of the closed-up basket.

Hui-neng's idea of *wu-nien*, which constitutes the central thought of Zen teaching, is continued naturally in the *Sayings of Shen-hui*, and then more definitely explained, as already set out. Let us now quote Te-shan and Huang-po. One of Te-shan's sermons reads thus:

"When you have nothing disquieting within yourself, do not try to seek anything outside. Even when you gain what you seek, this is not real gain. See to it that you have nothing disquieting in your mind, and be 'unconscious' about your affairs. Then there will be Emptiness which functions mysteriously, vacuity which works wonders. When you start to talk about the beginning and the end of this [mystery], you deceive yourself. Cherish an iota of thought, and this will cause karma to work, which puts you on evil paths. Allow a flash of imagination to cross your mind, and you will put yourself in bondage for ten-thousand *kalpas*. Such words as holiness and ignorance are no more than idle names; excellent forms and inferior shapes are both mere illusions. If you hanker after them, how can you escape complications? But trying to shun them will also bring great calamities upon you. In either case all ends in utter futility."

Huang-po Hsi-yun, in the beginning of his book, to which reference has already been made, alludes to the Mind which is the Buddha, and outside which there is no way to realize Enlightenment. The Mind means "no-mind-ness", to attain which is the ultimate end of the Buddhist life. Read the following in the light of Diagram I, and also in connection with Hui-neng's idea of Buddhahood, and the central teaching of Zen will become more comprehensible.

"The Master (Huang-po Hsi-yun) said to P'ei-hsin: Both the Buddhas and all sentient beings are of one Mind only, and there are no other dharma (objects). This Mind has no beginning, was never born, and will never pass away; it is neither blue nor yellow; it has no shape, no form; it does not belong to [the category of] being and non-being; it is not to be reckoned as new or old; it is neither short nor long, neither large nor small; it transcends all measurements, nameability, marks of identification, and forms of antithesis. It is absolute thisness; the wavering of a thought at once misses it. It is like vacuity of space, it has no boundaries, it is altogether beyond calculation.

"There is just this One Mind, which constitutes Buddhahood, and in it are the Buddhas and all sentient beings, showing no distinction, only that the latter are attached to form and seek [the Mind] outside themselves. Thus the more they seek, the farther it is lost. Let the Buddha seek himself outside himself, let the Mind seek itself outside itself, and to the end of time there will be no finding. Stop your thoughts, forget your hankerings, and the Buddha reveals himself right before your eyes.

"This Mind is no other than the Buddha, and the Buddha is no other than sentient beings. When it is sentient beings, this Mind shows no decrease; when it is the Buddha, it shows no increase. It inherently holds within itself all the six virtues of perfection, all the ten-thousand deeds of goodness, and all the merits numbering as many as the Ganga sands; there is in it nothing added from outside. When conditions present themselves before it, it gives itself freely; but when conditions cease, it becomes quiet. Those who have no firm faith in this Mind, which is the Buddha, and seek merit by attaching themselves to form and going through various disciplinary measures, cherish false ideas which are not in accord with the Tao.

"This Mind is the Buddha, and there are no Buddhas besides this, nor are there any other minds [which are the Buddha]. The purity of the Mind is like the sky with not a speck of form in it. When a mind is raised, when a thought is stirred, you turn away from the Dharma itself, which is known as attaching to form. Since beginningless time there have never been Buddhas attached to form. If you wish to attain Buddhahood by practising the six virtues of perfection and all the ten-thousand deeds of goodness, this is prescribing a course, and since beginningless time there have never been Buddhas graduating from a prescribed course. Only have an insight into One Mind, and you find that there is not a thing which you can claim to be your own. This constitutes true Buddhahood.

"The Buddha and sentient beings, they are of One Mind and there are no distinctions. It is like space with no mixtures, with nothing destructible in it; and it is like the great sun illumining the four worlds. When the sun rises, brightness fills the world, but space itself is not bright; when the sun sets, darkness fills the world, but space itself is not dark. Brightness and darkness are conditions, replacing each other; as for the characteristic vast vacuity of space, it remains ever unchanged. The Mind which constitutes the Buddha and all sentient beings is like that; if you regard the Buddha as a form which is pure, bright, and emancipated, and sentient beings as a form which is soiled, murky, benighted, and subject to birth and death, you cannot, as long as you hold this view, attain enlightenment even after the lapse of *kalpas* equal to the Ganga sands, because you are attached to form. You should know that there is One Mind only, and besides this there is not an atom of anything you can claim to be your own.

"The Mind is no other than the Buddha himself. Truth-seekers of this day fail to understand what this Mind is, and, raising a mind on the Mind, seek the Buddha in a world outside it, and attaching themselves to form practice discipline. This is a bad way, and not at all the one leading to enlightenment.

"[It is said that] it is better to make offerings to one monk who has realized no-mind-ness (*wu-hsin*) than to make offerings to all the Buddhas of the ten quarters. Why? No-mindness means having no mind (or thoughts) whatever. The body of Suchness inwardly is like wood or stone; it is immovable, unshakable; outwardly, it is like space where one knows no obstructions, no stoppage. It transcends both subject and object, it recognizes no points of orientation, it has no form, it knows neither gain nor loss. Those who run [after things outside] do not venture to enter into this Dharma, for they imagine that they will fall into a state of nothingness where they are completely at a loss what to do. Therefore they just give it a glance and beat a retreat. Thus they are generally seekers of wide learning. Indeed, those seekers of wide learning are like hairs (i.e. too many), whereas those who understand the truth are like horns [i.e. too few]."

Chinese expressions, especially those used in connection with Zen thought, are full of significance which, when translated into such languages as English, loses altogether its original suggestiveness. The very vagueness so characteristic of the Chinese style of writing is in fact its strength: mere points of reference are given, and as to how to connect them, to yield a meaning, the knowledge and feeling of the reader are the real determinant.

Zen, being no believer in verbosity, uses, when pressed for expression, the fewest possible words, not only in its regular, formal *"mondo"* (dialogue), but in all ordinary discourse in which Zen thought is explained. In Huang-po's sermon, quoted above, and also in Te-shan's, we come across some highly significant phrases, one of which by Te-shan is *tan wu shih yu hsin, wu hsin yu shih,* and another by Huang-po, *chih hsia wu hsin.* Here is the gist of Zen teaching. Te-shan's is literally "only [have] nothing in the mind, have no-mind in things": while Huang-po's is "Immediately-down [have] no-mind".

Both in Te-shan and Huang-po, Zen is taught to be something in direct contact with our daily life; there are no speculations soaring heavenward, no abstractions making one's head reel, and no sentimental sweetness which turns religion into a love-drama. Facts of daily experience are taken as they come to us, and from them a state of no-mind-ness is extracted. Says Huang-po in the above citations: "The original Mind is to be recognized along with the working of the senses and thoughts; only it does not belong to them, nor is it independent of them." The Unconscious, the recognition of which makes up *mushin,* lines every experience which we have through the senses and thoughts. When we have an experience, for example, of seeing a tree, all that takes place at the time is the perceiving of something. We do not know whether this perception belongs to us, nor do we recognize the object which is perceived to be outside ourselves. The cognition of an external object already presupposes the distinction of outside and inside, subject and object, the perceiving and the perceived. When this separation takes place, and is recognized as such, and clung to, the primary nature of the experience is forgotten, and from this an endless series of entanglements, intellectual and emotional, takes its rise.

The state of no-mind-ness refers to the time prior to the separation of mind and world, when there is yet no mind standing against an external world and receiving its impressions through the various sense-channels. Not only a mind, but a world, has not yet come into existence. This we can say is a state of perfect emptiness, but as long as we stay here there is no development, no experience; it is mere doing-nothing, it is death itself, so to speak. But we are not so constituted. There rises a thought in the midst of Emptiness; this is the awakening of Prajna, the separation of unconsciousness and consciousness, or, logically stated, the rise of the fundamental dialectical antithesis. *Mushin* stands on the unconscious side of the awakened Prajna, while its conscious side unfolds itself into the perceiving subject and the external world. This is what Huang-po means when he says that the original Mind is neither dependent upon nor independent of what is seen (*drista*), heard (*sruta*), thought (*mata*) or known (*jnata*). The Unconscious and the world of consciousness are in direct opposition, yet they lie back to back and condition each other. The one negates the other, but this negation is really affirmation.

Whatever this may be, Zen is always close to our daily experience, which is the meaning of Nansen's (Nan-ch'uan's) and Baso's (Ma-tsu's) utterance: "Your everyday mind (thought) is the Tao." "When hungry, we eat, and when tired, we sleep." In this directness of action, where there are no mediating agencies such as the recognition of objects, consideration of time, deliberation on values, etc., the Unconscious asserts itself by negating itself. In what follows,[20] I give the practical workings of the Unconscious as experienced by the masters who try hard to teach it to their pupils.

1. Hsiang-nien of Shou-shan (925–992) was asked: "According to the Sutra, all the Buddhas issue out of this Sutra; what is this Sutra?" "Softly, softly!" said the master. "How do I take care of it?" "Be sure not to get it stained." To make this *mondo* more intelligible to the reader, "this Sutra" does not necessarily mean the *Prajnaparamita* where the phrase occurs: it may be taken to mean Hui-neng's Self-nature, Huang-po's Original Mind, or in fact anything which is generally considered the Ultimate Reality from which all things take their rise. The monk now asks what is this Great Source of all things. As I said before, this conception of Great Source as existing separately somewhere is the fundamental mistake we all make

[20] The examples are taken almost at random from the *Records of the Transmission of the Lamp* (*Chuan-ting Lu*). This is a mine of such records, chiefly of the T'ang, Five Dynasties, and early Sung periods, roughly A.D. 600–1000.

in our attempt intellectually to interpret our experience. It is in the nature of the intellect to set up a series of antitheses in the maze of which it loses itself. The monk was no doubt a victim to this fatal contradiction, and it is quite likely that he asked the question "What is this Sutra?" at the top of his voice. Hence the master's warning: "Softly, softly." The text does not say whether this warning was readily taken in by the source of all the Buddha himself, but the next question as to how to take care of it (or him) shows that he got some insight into the matter. "What?", "Why?", "Where?", and "How?"—all these are questions irrelevant to the fundamental understanding of life. But our minds are saturated with them, and this fact is a curse on us all. Hsiang-nien fully realized it, and does not attempt any intellectual solution. His most practical matter-of-fact answer, "Softly, softly!", was enough to settle the gravest question at one blow.

2. A monk asked Hsiang-nien: "What is the Body of space?" Space may here be translated as the sky or void; it was conceived by ancient people to be a kind of objective reality, and the monk asks now what supports this void, what is its Body around which this vast emptiness hangs. The real meaning of the question, however, does not concern the vacuity of space, but the monk's own state of mind, at which he arrived probably after a long meditation practised in the conventional manner; that is, by wiping thoughts and feelings off his consciousness. He naturally imagined, like so many Buddhists as well as lay-people, that there was a being, though altogether indefinable, still somehow graspable as supporter of the unsupported. The master's answer to this was: "Your old teacher is underneath your feet." "Why, Reverend Sir, are you underneath the feet of your own pupil?" The master decided: "O this blind fellow!" The monk's question sounds in a way abstruse enough, and if Hsiang-nien were a philosopher, he would have discoursed at great length. Being, however, a practical Zen master who deals with things of our daily experience, he simply refers to the spatial relation between himself and his pupil, and when this is not directly understood and

a further question is asked, he is disgusted, and despatches the questioner with a slighting remark.

3. Another time Hsiang-nien was approached with this request: "I, a humble pupil of yours, have been troubled for long with an unsolved problem. Will you be kind enough to give it your consideration?" The master brusquely answered: "I have no time for idle deliberation." The monk was naturally not satisfied with this answer, for he did not know what to make of it. "Why is it so with you, Reverend Sir?" "When I want to walk, I walk; when I want to sit, I sit." This was simple enough; he was perfect master of himself. He did not need any deliberation. Between his deed and his desire there was no moral or intellectual intermediary, no "mind" interfered, and consequently he had no problems which harassed his peace of mind. His answer could not be anything but practical and truly to the point.

4. A monk asked Hsiang-nien: "What is your eye that does not deceive others?" This is a liberal translation; the question really demands the expression of the master's genuine, undeceiving attitude of mind which controls all his experiences. Our eye is generally found covered with all kinds of dust, and the refraction of light thereby caused fails to give us the correct view of things. The master responded right away, saying: "Look, look, winter is approaching."

Probably this *mondo* took place in a mountain monastery surrounded with trees, now bare and trembling in the wind, and both were looking at the snow-bearing clouds. The approach of the winter was quite certain; there was no deception about it. But the monk wondered if there were not something more than that and said: "What is the ultimate meaning of it?" The master was perfectly natural and his answer was: "And then we have the gentle spring breeze." In this there is no allusion to deep metaphysical concepts, but a plain fact of observation is told in the most ordinary language. The monk's question may elicit in the hands of the philosopher or theologian quite a different form of treatment, but the Zen master's eye is always on facts of experience accessible to everybody, and verifiable by him whenever he wants. Whatever mysticism enveloped the master was not on his side, but on the side of him who looks for it because of his own blindness.

These passages are enough to show the Zen masters' attitude towards the so-called metaphysical or theological questions which torment so many people's religiously susceptible hearts, and also the method they use in handling the questions for the edification of their pupils. They never resort to discussions of a highly abstract nature, but respect their daily experiences, which are ordinarily grouped under the "seen, heard, thought, and known". Their idea is that in our "everyday thought" (*ping-chang hsin*) the Unconscious is to be comprehended, if at all; for there is no intermediary between it and what we term "the seen, heard, thought, and known". Every act of the latter is lined with the Unconscious. But to impress my readers to the point of tiresomeness, I will give a few more examples.

5. A monk asked Ta-tung of T'ou-tzu Shan: "When the Prince Nata returns all the bones of his body to his father, and all the flesh to his mother, what remains of his Original Body?"

Ta-tung threw down the staff which was in his hand.

The question is really a very serious one, when conceptually weighed, as it concerns the doctrine of *anatman* so called. When the five *skandhas* are broken up, where does the person go which was supposed to be behind the combination? To say that the five *skandhas* are by nature empty and their combination and illusion is not enough for those who have not actually experienced this fact. They want to see the problem solved according to the logic which they have learned since the awakening of consciousness. They forget that it is their own logic which entangles them in this intellectual *cul-de-sac,* from which they are at a loss how to get out. The teaching of *anatman* is the expression of an experience, and not at all a logical conclusion. However much they try to reach it by their logical subtleties they fail, or their reasoning lacks the force of a final conviction.

Since the Buddha, many are the masters of the Abhidharma who have exhausted their power of ratiocination to establish logically the theory of *anatman,* but how many Buddhists or outsiders are there who are really intellectually convinced of the theory? If they have a conviction about this teaching it comes from their experience and not from theorizing. With the Buddha, an actual personal conviction came first; then came a logical construction to back up the conviction. It did not matter very much indeed whether or not this construction was satisfactorily completed, for the conviction, that is the experience itself, was a *fait accompli.*

The position assumed by the Zen masters is this. They leave the logical side of the business to the philosopher, and are content with conclusions drawn from their own inner experiences. They will protest, if the logician attempts to deny the validity of their experience, on the ground that it is up to the logician to prove the fact by the instruments which he is allowed to use. If he fails to perform the work satisfactorily— that is, logically to confirm the experience—the failure is on the side of the logician, who has now to devise a more effective use of his tools. The great fault with us all is that we force logic on facts whereas it is facts themselves that create logic.

6. A monk asked Fu-ch'i: "When the conditions (such as the four elements, five *skandhas,* etc.) are dispersed, they all return to Emptiness, but where does Emptiness itself return?" This is a question of the same nature as the one cited concerning the original body of Prince Nata. We always seek something beyond or behind our experience, and forget that this seeking is an endless regression either way, inward or outward, upward or downward. The Zen master is well aware of this, and avoids the complications. Fu-ch'i called out, "O Brother!" and the monk answered: "Yes, Master." The master now asked: "Where is Emptiness?" The poor monk was still after conceptual images, and completely failed to realize the whereabouts of Emptiness. "Be pleased to tell me about it."

This was his second request. The master had no more to say, but quizzically added: "It is like a Persian tasting red pepper."

In his day—that is, in the T'ang period—the Chinese capital must have harboured people from the various strange countries of the West, and we find, as in the present case, references to Persians (*po-ssu*) in Zen literature. Even Bodhi-Dharma, the founder of Zen Buddhism in China, was regarded by some to be a Persian, perhaps by this no more than a man from a foreign country. Evidently some T'ang historians did not distinguish Persians from Indians. By a Persian tasting red pepper, the master means his inability to express the experience in the proper Chinese words, being a stranger to the country.

7. A monk came to T'ou-tzu and asked: "I have come from a distant place with the special intention of seeing you. Will you kindly give me one word of instruction?" To this, the master replied: "Growing old, my back aches today." Is this one word of instruction in Zen? To a pilgrim who has come a long way from the remotest part of the country to be specially instructed by the old master, "My back aches" seems to be giving the cold shoulder—altogether too cold. But it all depends how you look at the matter. Inasmuch as Zen deals with our everyday experience, this old master's expression of pain in his back must be regarded as directly pointing to the primary Unconscious itself. If the monk were one who had long pondered on the matter, he would at once see where T'ou-tzu is trying to make him look.

But here is a point on which to be on guard concerning the conception of the Unconscious. Although I have repeatedly given warnings on the subject, I here quote T'ou-tzu again. A monk asked him: "How about not a thought yet rising?" This refers to a state of consciousness in which all thoughts have been wiped out and there prevails an emptiness; and here the monk wants to know if this points to the Zen experience; probably he thinks he has come to the realization itself. But the master's reply was: "This is really nonsensical!" There was another monk who came to another master and asked the same question, and the master's answer was: "Of what use can it be?" Evidently the master had no use for the state of unconsciousness conceived by most Buddhists.

T'ou-tzu on another occasion was asked: "What about the time when the golden cock has not yet crowed?" This purports to cherish the same view as expressed by the two preceding monks. T'ou-tzu said: "There is no sound." "What after the crowing?" "Everybody knows the time." Both are matter-of-fact answers, and we may wonder where this mysterious, elusive, incomprehensible Zen may be.

To imagine that Zen is mysterious is the first grave mistake which many make about it. Just because of this mistake the Unconscious fails to act in its unconscious way, and the real issue is lost in conceptual entanglements. The mind is divided between two opposing concepts, and the result is unnecessary worry. The following illustrates the way to avoid the contradiction, or rather to live it, for life is in reality a series of contradictions. A monk asked T'ou-tzu: "Old Year is gone and New Year has arrived: is there one thing that has no relation whatever to either of the two, or not?"

As has already been seen, Zen is always practical, and lives with events of daily occurrence. The past is gone and the present is here, but this present will also soon be gone, indeed it is gone; time is a succession of these two contradicting ideas, and everything which takes place in this life of ours bestrides the past and present. It cannot be said to belong to either of the two, for it cannot be cut in pieces. How, then, does an event of the past go over to the present so that we have a complete conception of the event as complete? When thought is divided like this, we may come to no conclusion. It is thus for Zen to settle the matter in the most conclusive manner, which is in the most practical manner. Therefore, the master answered the monk's question: "Yes." When it was asked again "What is it?" the master said: "With the ushering of New Year, the entire world looks rejuvenated, and all things sing 'Happy New Year'."

VI. ZEN AND PHILOSOPHY

Chapter 8

The Role of Nature in
Zen Buddhism

I

At the outset it is advisable to know what we mean by Nature, for the term is ambiguous and has been used in various senses. Let me here just mention a few of the ideas associated in the Western mind with Nature.

The first thing is that Nature is contrasted with God; the natural stands on the one hand against the divine. Nature is something working against what is godly, and in this sense often means "creation" or "the earth". God created the world, but strangely the world goes against him, and God is found fighting against his own creation.

The adjective "natural", while in one sense standing in contrast to the divine, in another sense accords with it. When "naturalness" is used in contrast to artificiality it acquires something of the divine. Childlikeness is often compared to godliness. Child life has more in it of godliness than adult life, being much closer to Nature. God, then, is not altogether absent in Nature.

When we contrast Nature with Man, we emphasize the physical, material aspect of Nature rather than its moral or spiritual aspect, which is pre-eminently involved when we contrast it with God. Nature has thus two aspects as we humans view it. Inasmuch as it is "natural", it is godly; but when it is material it functions against human spirituality or godliness, whatever that may mean. As long as Nature is regarded as the material world, as our senses perceive it, it is something we want to conquer. Nature here faces us as a kind of power, and wherever there is the notion of power it is connected with

that of conquest. For Man, therefore, Nature is to be conquered and made use of for his own material welfare and
comfort. Nature affords him a variety of opportunities to
develop his powers, but at the same time there is always on
the part of Man the tendency to exploit and abuse it for his
selfish ends.

*   *   *   *   *

The Nature-Man dichotomy issues, as I think, from the
Biblical account in which the Creator is said to have given
mankind the power to dominate all creation. It is fundamentally due to this story that Western people talk so much about
conquering Nature. When they invent a flying machine they
say they have conquered the air; when they climb to the top
of Mt. Everest they loudly announce that they have succeeded
in conquering the mountain. This idea of conquest comes from
the relationship between Nature and Man being regarded as
that of power, and this relationship involves a state of mutual
opposition and destruction.

This power-relationship also brings out the problem of rationality. Man is rational, whereas Nature is brutal, and Man
strives to make Nature amenable to his idea of rationality. Rationality is born with the rising of consciousness out of the
primordial Unconscious. Consciousness makes it possible for
the human being to reflect upon his own doings and the events
around him. This reflection gives him the power to rise above
mere naturalness and to bring it under his control.

There is no discipline in Nature because it operates blindly.
Discipline, which is something human and artificial, and to
that extent works for bad as well as for good, belongs entirely
to humankind. As long as he is capable of it, Man trains himself for a definite purpose.

Nature, on the other hand, is purposeless, and it is because
of this purposelessness that Nature in one sense is "conquered"
by Man and in another sense conquers Man. For however
purposeful Man may be, he does not know ultimately whither
he is going, and his pride has after all no substance whatever.

In this paper, then, let us understand Nature as something

antithetical to what is ordinarily known as divine; as something irrational yet amenable to our mechanical, economic, utilitarian treatment; as something not human, not in possession of human feelings, and devoid of moral significance; as something which finally overpowers Man in spite of Man's partial and temporary success. In short, Nature is brutally factual, with no history objectively set before us and to be regarded as commercially exploitable, but finally swallowing us all in the purposelessness of the Unknown.

Concretely speaking, Nature consists of mountains and rivers, grass and trees, stones and earth, suns, moons and stars, birds and animals. Nature is all that constitutes what is commonly known as Man's objective world.

II

When Nature is seen in this light it may seem well defined, but Nature has a great deal more to say to us. Nature is indeed an eternal problem, and when it is solved, we know not only Nature but ourselves; the problem of Nature is the problem of human life.

From the human point of view, anything that is not of human origin may be said to be of Nature. But Man is, after all, part of Nature itself. First of all, Man himself is not Manmade but Nature-made, as much as anything we regard as of Nature. If so, what is Man-made? There is nothing in Man that does not belong in Nature. All things Man-made must be considered Nature-made and not Man-made. If God created the world, he created Man as part of it. God did not create Man as something separate from Nature so that Man can stand outside Nature as a controlling power and have things "Manmade" put against things "Nature-made".

But as far as the Biblical account is concerned, Man was made in God's image and Nature was to be dominated by Man.[1] And this idea is the real beginning of human tragedy. I wish to ask if it is the right way of thinking—this idea of domination. For when the idea of power, which is domina-

[1] Genesis i, 27–8.

tion, comes in, all kinds of struggles arise, and as this struggle is always ego-centred its outcome is tragic.

Nature, as we have seen, includes all "created" things. To think that these are all under human control is altogether illogical and cannot be consistently maintained. But Western people unconsciously follow this idea and their moral attitude towards Nature is thereby determined. Man, though made in God's image, has his own way of doing things, which is by no means God's way. For this reason he was expelled from Eden. He is now partly God's and partly Satan's child, and what he does quite frequently contradicts the divine commands and also sometimes his own self-interest. As to Nature, it also acts against God, though it cannot be anything else but God's creation.

Man is against God, Nature is against God, and Man and Nature are against each other. If so, God's own likeness (Man), God's own creation (Nature), and God himself—all three are at war. But with our human way of thinking, God did not create the world just to see it revolt against himself and make it fight within itself.

From another point of view, however, it is in the nature of things that as soon as there is a world of the many there is conflict. When the world is once out of God's hand, he cannot control it; it is sure to revolt and fight in every possible way. So we have now Nature against God and Man against Nature and God.

In Biblical terms Nature is the "flesh", "lust of the flesh", "sinful flesh", etc. This brings the fight between Nature and Man to a more concrete and sensuous level. The human body, which is a mixture of God and Nature, becomes a most bloody fighting arena for these two forces.

From these considerations we can summarize the Western attitude towards Nature thus:

(1) Nature is something hostile to Man and drags him down when he is struggling to reach God. The temptations of Nature symbolized as "the flesh" are often irresistible and make man exclaim: "The spirit is willing but the flesh is weak."[2]

[2] Matthew xxvi, 41.

(2) While Nature and God are warring against each other, Nature and Man are also at war. Or rather, as commanded by God, Man is always striving to exercise his dominating power over Nature.

(3) There is no way for Man to approach Nature in a conciliatory, friendly spirit. One works to destroy the other. There is nothing in Nature that will help Man in his spiritual advancement.

(4) Nature is a material world and the material world is meant for exploration and exploitation.

(5) In another sense the material world is brute fact, stands as the *pour-soi* against the *en-soi*. Intellect cannot do anything with it, but has to take it as it is and make the best of it.

(6) The dichotomy of Nature-and-Man implies hostility, even an utter irreconcilability, and is, therefore, mutually destructive.

(7) No idea seems to be present here which indicates or even suggests human participation in, or identification with, Nature. To the Western mind Nature and Man are separate.

III

Man relies on Nature for food and cannot help being influenced by Nature. He finds himself engaged in farming, hunting, fishing, etc., and each of these engagements contributes to his character, for Nature cannot be conceived as a merely passive substance upon which Man works. Nature is also power and energy; Nature reacts to human calls. When Man is agreeable and in conformity with Nature's way, it will cooperate with Man and reveal to him all its secrets and even help him to understand himself. Each of us as a farmer or hunter or carpenter gets from Nature what he looks for in it and assimilates it in his own field. To this extent, Nature remoulds human character.

To treat Nature as something irrational and in opposition to human "rationality" is a purely Western idea, and sometimes we feel the proposition ought to be reversed. It is irrational of Man to try to make Nature obey his will, because

Nature has its own way of carrying on its work which is not always Man's way, and Man has no right to impose his way upon Nature.

Nature, it is true, lacks consciousness. It is just the reed and not "a thinking reed". Because of this lack of consciousness it is regarded by Man as brute fact, as something with no will and intelligence of its own. It knows of nothing but an absolute "must", and permits no human interference except in its "must" way. It knows no favouritism and refuses to deviate from its course of inevitability. It is not accommodating; it is Man who must accommodate himself to Nature. Nature's "must" is absolute, and Man must accept it. In this respect Nature has something of the divine will.

This is the reason, I think, why being natural or spontaneous has an alluring quality in it. When a child performs deeds which polite society would condemn as undignified or improper or even immoral, the offences are not only condoned but accepted as acts of innocent childlikeness. There is something divine in being spontaneous and not being hampered by human conventionalities and their artificial hypocrisies. There is something direct and fresh in this lack of restraint by anything human, which suggests a divine freedom and creativity. Nature never deliberates; it acts directly out of its own heart, whatever this may mean. In this respect Nature is divine. Its "irrationality" transcends human doubts or ambiguities, and in our submitting to it, or rather accepting it, we transcend ourselves.

This acceptance or transcendence is a human prerogative. We accept Nature's "irrationality" or its "must" deliberately, quietly, and whole-heartedly. It is not a deed of blind and slavish submission to the inevitable. It is an active acceptance, a personal willingness with no thought of resistance. In this there is no force implied, no resignation, but rather participation, assimilation, and perhaps in some cases even identification.

IV

Nature is sometimes treated by Western people as something already "there" into which Man comes, and which he finds himself confronting, with hostility, because he feels he does not belong in it. He is conscious of a situation in which he is surrounded by all kinds of inert matter and brute fact. He does not know why he is there, nor does he realize what is coming to him. Endowed with consciousness, however, he thinks he can decide his future course, and he feels entirely responsible for his decision. He is lonely and helpless because Nature is threatening and ready to swallow him down into its own maw. He is overawed and trembles, not knowing what is best to do. This is the position, according to some modern thinkers, when Man encounters Nature. Here is no room for God to enter, but the dichotomy of Man and Nature is still maintained and in a more acutely oppressive relationship. Nature is brute fact and has nothing in common with Man. Man makes use of it economically with no sense of kinship with it, hence with no sense of gratitude or sympathetic affiliation.

Nature is here an unknown quantity, unfriendly and ready to frustrate Man's attempt to dominate it. Nature promises nothing but sheer emptiness. Whatever Man may build upon it is doomed to destruction. It is for this reason that modern men are constantly assailed with feelings of fear, insecurity, and anxiety.

There is, however, another way of considering Nature and Man. Inasmuch as Nature stands before Man as an unknown quantity and Man comes to it with his consciousness from somewhere else than Nature, Nature and Man cannot be friendly and sociable, for they have no way to communicate. They are strangers. But the very fact that Man finds himself encountering Nature demonstrates that the two are not unknown to each other. To this extent, then, Nature is already telling Man something of itself and Man is to that extent understanding Nature. Then Man cannot be said to be entirely an outsider but somehow stands in relation to Nature; perhaps comes out of Nature itself. Man must be after all an insider.

v

Here there is room for Zen Buddhism to enter, and to give its own views on the relationship of Nature and Man.

While separating himself from Nature, Man is still a part of Nature, for the fact of separation itself shows that Man is dependent on Nature. We can therefore say this: Nature produces Man out of itself; Man cannot be outside of Nature, he still has his being rooted in Nature. Therefore there cannot be any hostility between them. On the contrary, there must always be a friendly understanding between Man and Nature. Man came from Nature in order to see Nature in himself; that is, Nature came to itself in order to see itself in Man.

This is objective thinking, to say that Man comes from Nature and that Man sees himself through Nature, or that Nature sees itself through Man. There is another way of seeing into the situation, by shifting our position from objectivity to subjectivity. This probing into subjectivity is probing into the very basis of Nature as it is in itself.

To turn to subjectivity means to turn from Nature to Man himself. Instead of considering Man objectively in opposition to Nature, our task is now to make Man retreat, as it were, into himself and see what he finds in the depths of his being. The probing of Nature thus becomes the problem of Man: Who or what is Man?

.   .   .   .   .

A Zen master once asked a monk: "Do not think of good, do not think of evil; when no thoughts arise let me see your primary face."

The monk answered: "I have nothing shapely to show you."[3]

This kind of *mondo* ("question and answer") has taken

[3] *The Transmission of the Lamp* (*Dentoroku*), Fas. VIII, under "Nansen".

place in Zen from its start in the T'ang period—that is, in the eighth century. To those who have never been initiated into the Zen way of treating the problem of Nature or Man this "question and answer" will appear uncouth and not susceptible of rationalization. It is altogether out of the realm of discursive understanding.

"What does 'the primary face' mean?", you may ask. What has "the face" to do with the problem of Man and his situation? And then what has one to do with good and evil and "no thoughts rising"? A few words may be needed before we can come to Zen.

Generally speaking, Zen refuses to make use of abstract terms, to indulge in metaphysical speculations, or to involve itself in a series of questions and answers. Its discourse is always short, pithy, and right to the point. When words are found to be a round-about way of communication, the Zen master may utter "Katz!" without giving what is ordinarily considered a rational or an intelligible reply.

In the same way, when told that he looks like a dog, he will not get excited and make an angry retort. Instead, he may simply cry "Bow-wow", and pass on!

As to the use of a stick, there is one master noted for its liberal application. Tokusan (Teh-shan, 790–865) used to say: "When you say 'Yes', you get thirty blows of my stick; when you say 'No', you get thirty blows of my stick just the same." The Zen monks generally carry a long staff in travelling from one monastery to another along the mountain path. The stick in Zen has been a very expressive means of communication. Zen thus avoids as much as possible the use of a medium, especially intellectual and conceptual, known as "language".

In the above cited *mondo,* therefore, we have first of all a reference to good and evil. This has nothing to do with our sense of moral evaluation, and simply refers to our dualistic habit of thinking. "Good and evil" can be anything: black and white, yes and no, affirmation and negation, creator and the created, heaven and hell, etc. When we are told not to think of them, it means to transcend all forms of dichotomy and to enter into the realm of the absolute where "no thought" prevails. The question, therefore, proposed by the Zen master here concerns the absolute and is not one of morality or psychology.

What does Zen mean by asking a man to show his "primary face"? When I tell you that this is the innermost man or self in itself or Being-as-it-is, you will be surprised and declare: "What an odd language Zen people use!" But this oddity partly characterizes the Chinese language as well as Zen.

"The primary face" is possessed by every one of us. According to Zen, it is not only physical but at once physical and metaphysical, material and spiritual, gross and subtle, concrete and abstract. The Zen master wants to see this kind of "face" presented to him by his monk. In one important sense "this face" must go through the baptism of "Do not think of good, do not think of evil", and of "Have no thoughts whatever". For the face we have on the surface of our relative psychological way of thinking is not "the primary face" demanded by the master.

But here is another difficulty, the answer given by the monk: "I have nothing shapely to show you." This means: "I am sorry, master, that my primary face is not very presentable, and not worthy of your regard." The monk seems to be talking about his own face, which is recognizable by every Tom, Dick, and Harry. Is this face really the "primary face"? If so, Zen does not seem to have anything miraculous about it. What, then, is all this fuss about going beyond the duality of our thinking? The Zen master's answer to such questions will be: "This is on the plane of pure subjectivity and a matter of personal determination." In fact all Zen *mondo* come out of this subjectivity experience.

Here is another *mondo*.

Monk: "Before my parents gave birth to me, where is my nose [or face or self]?"

Master: "When you are already born of your parents, where are you?"[4]

Here the monk has "the nose" instead of "the face", but this does not mean any difference as far as Zen is concerned.

[4] *The Transmission of the Lamp*, Fas. VIII.

The Chinese masters always prefer to be concrete. Instead of talking about "Being" or "Reason" or "Reality", they talk about stones, flowers, clouds, or birds.

To give another example, when a Zen master was walking with his monk attendant he happened to notice a bird flying, and asked the monk: "What bird is that?" The monk answered: "It is gone already." The master turned toward the monk and taking hold of his nose gave it a twist. The monk cried in pain: "Oh! Oh!" The master remarked: "It is still there!" We notice here, too, the nose is playing an important role in the discussion of Being. No high-flown abstract terminology here, but ordinary plain talking on the plane of our daily experience. "The primary face", the painful "nose", the flying "bird", and, in fact, any sensuous object that is seen or heard turns into the subject of the deepest metaphysical significance in the hands of the Zen masters.

We have been digressing. In the *mondo* prior to the one just cited in regard to the flying bird, the monk wants to know where his nose is before he was born of his parents, or even before this earth or Nature came into being. This exactly corresponds to Christ's statement: "Before Abraham was, I am."[5] The "nose" is Christ and the monk is desirous of interviewing Christ himself who *is*, even before the birth of Abraham. Western people will never dare to ask such questions. They would think it sacrilegious to intrude on ground which is sacrosanct to all Christians or "God-fearing" minds. They are too dualistically minded and unable to think of going beyond tradition and history.

The master's answer is also significant. He ignores time-sequence in which birth-and-death takes place with all other events which make up human history. He pays no attention to the serialism of time. When the monk asks about his "nose" before his coming into this world of sense and intellect, the master retorts by referring to the monk's actual presence, to his "as-he-is-ness". From the relative point of view this answer is no answer; it does not locate the monk's "nose", but asks

[5] John viii, 58.

the counter-question regarding himself as he stands before the
master, perhaps in a shabby monkish robe and with a not
very smoothly shaven face and a not very shapely nose.

The point that I am trying to make is that Zen starts where
time has not come to itself; that is to say, where timelessness
has not negated itself so as to have a dichotomy of subject-
object, Man-Nature, God-world. This is the abode of what I
call "pure subjectivity". Zen is here and wants us to be here
too. In terms of Nature, Zen is where one of the masters remarked: "When I began to study Zen, mountains were mountains; when I thought I understood Zen, mountains were not
mountains; but when I came to full knowledge of Zen, mountains were again mountains."

When the mountains are seen as not standing against me,
when they are dissolved into the oneness of things, they are
not mountains, they cease to exist as objects of Nature. When
they are seen as standing against me, as separate from me, as
something unfriendly to me, they are not mountains either.
The mountains are really mountains when they are assimilated
into my being and I am absorbed in them. As long as Nature
is something differentiated from me and is displayed before
me as if it were an unknown quantity and a mere brute fact,
Nature cannot be said even to be unfriendly or actively hostile.

On the other hand, Nature becomes part of my being as
soon as it is recognized as Nature, as *pour-soi*. It can never
remain as something strange and altogether unrelated to me.
I am in Nature and Nature is in me. Not mere participation
in each other, but a fundamental identity between the two.
Hence, the mountains are mountains and the rivers are rivers;
they are there before me. The reason I can see the mountains
as mountains and the waters as waters is because I am in
them and they are in me; that is, *tat tvam asi*. If not for this
identity, there would be no Nature as *pour-soi*. "The primary
face" or "my nose" is to be taken hold of here and nowhere
else.

Identity belongs in spatial terminology. In terms of time, it
is timelessness. But mere timelessness does not mean anything.
When Nature is seen as confronting me there is already time,

and timelessness now turns itself into time. But time-serialism makes sense only when it goes on in the field of timelessness, which is the Buddhist conception of *sunyata* ("emptiness"). In this *sunyata* the mountains are mountains and I see them as such and they see me as such; my seeing them is their seeing me. It is then that *sunyata* becomes *tathata* ("suchness"); *tathata* is *sunyata* and *sunyata* is *tathata*.

When we come to this stage of thinking, pure subjectivity is pure objectivity, the *en-soi* is the *pour-soi*; there is perfect identity of Man and Nature, of God and Nature, of the one and the many. But the identity does not imply the annihilation of one at the cost of the other. The mountains do not vanish; they stand before me. I have not absorbed them, nor have they wiped me out of the scene. The dichotomy is there, which is suchness, and this suchness (*tathata*) in all its suchness is emptiness (*sunyata*) itself. The mountains are mountains and yet not mountains. I am I and you are you, and yet I am you and you are I. Nature as a world of manyness is not ignored, and Man as a subject facing the many remains conscious of himself.

VI

Zen avoids discoursing or arguing, for this leads us nowhere after much ado. Zen does not make light of philosophy and of all that drives us to philosophizing, but Zen's business is to make us realize that philosophizing does not exhaust the human urge to reach the ultimate. Hence the following *mondo:*

Yakusan (Yueh-shan Wei-yen, 750–834) asked Ungan (Yun-yen T'an-ch'eng, 781–841): "I understand you know how to play with the lion. Am I correct?"

Ungan: "Yes, you are right."

Yakusan: "How many lions can you play with?"

Ungan: "Six."

Yakusan: "I also know how to play with the lion."

Ungan: "How many?"

Yakusan: "Just one."

Ungan: "One is six and six is one."[6]

Ungan later came to Isan (Kwei-shan Ling-yu, 771–853) and Isan asked: "I am told that you knew how to play with the lion when you were at the Yakusan monastery. Is that right?"

Ungan said: "That is right."

Isan went on: "Do you play with it all the time? Or do you sometimes give it a rest?"

Ungan: "If I wish to play with it, I play; if I wish to give it a rest, I give it a rest."

Isan: "When it is at rest, where is it?"

Ungan: "At rest, at rest!"[7]

The lion which is the subject of the *mondo* here is Nature and the player is the self or "subjectum", as I would sometimes call the self. Nature is held at five points (six according to Buddhist psychology) by the self. When Isan says that he knows how to play with six lions, he refers to our five (or six) senses wherewith Nature is taken hold of. The senses are like the windows through which Nature is observed. Nature may, for all we know, be more than that, but we have no more than the five senses, beyond which we have no means to differentiate Nature. In a physical world of senses more than five (or six) we should perceive something more in Nature, and our life would be richer to that extent. Seven windows would surely give us more of Nature. This is, however, a mere possibility worked out by looking through the sense-windows as we have them, which are aided by the intellect or the *manovijnana,* according to Buddhist psychology. From this, we can think of a world of four or more dimensions, indeed of any number. Mathematicians have all kinds of numbers, imaginary, negative, complex, etc., which are of no sensuous demonstration. Our actual physical world is limited. We can think of an infinitely extending space, but specialists tell us that space is limited and that it is mathematically calculable.

What concerns Zen is the problem of the self which plays with the "six lions" or looks out through the "six windows"—

[6] *The Transmission of the Lamp,* Fas. XIV.
[7] Ibid.

the subjectum, or what I call pure subjectivity. This is what interests Zen and Zen wants us to get acquainted with it. But the Zen way of acquaintance is unique, for it does not proceed with the dichotomy of Man-Nature or subject-object. Zen takes us at once to the realm of non-dichotomy, which is the beginningless beginning of all things. Time has not yet come to its own consciousness. Zen is where this consciousness is about to rise. Or it may be better to say that consciousness is caught at the very moment of rising from the unconscious. This moment is an absolute present, the crossing point of time and timelessness, of the conscious and unconscious. This crossing moment, which is the rising moment of an *ekacittakshana,* that is, the moment of no-mind or no-thought, refuses to be expressed in language, in words of the mouth. It is a matter of personal determination.

While Ungan was sweeping the ground, Isan asked: "You are busily employed, are you not?"

Ungan: "There is one who is not at all busily employed."

Isan: "In that case you mean to say that there is a second moon?"

Ungan set up the broom and said: "What number is this moon?"

Isan nodded and went away.

Gensha (Hsuan-sha Shih-pei, 834–908), hearing of this, remarked: "This is no other than a second moon!"[8]

"A second moon" refers to a dualistic conception of the self. There is one who is busily engaged in work and there is another who is not working and quietly unmoved observes all that goes before him. This way of thinking is not Zen. In Zen there is no such separation between worker and observer, movement and mover, seer and the seen, subject and object. In the case of Ungan, the sweeping and the sweeper and the broom are all one, even including the ground which is being swept. There is no second moon, no third moon, no first moon either. This is beyond verbalism. But Man is no Man unless

[8] *The Transmission of the Lamp,* Fas. XIV.

he knows how to communicate. Hence Ungan's setting up the broom. The language of Zen has characteristics of its own.

To give another example: When Ungan was making tea, Dogo (Tao-wu Yuan-chih, 779–835) came in and asked: "To whom are you serving tea?"

Ungan: "There is one who wants it."

Dogo: "Why don't you make him serve himself?"

Ungan: "Fortunately, I am here."[9]

"I" is the one who wants tea and also the one who makes tea; "I" is the server and the served.

Ungan once asked a nun: "Is your father still alive?"

The nun answered: "Yes, master."

Ungan: "How old is he?"

Nun: "Eighty."

Ungan: "You have a father whose age is not eighty, do you know him?"

Nun: "Is he not the one who thus comes?"

Ungan: "He is still a child [of his]."[10]

The problem of the self evaporates into sheer abstraction when pursued analytically, leaving nothing behind. Zen realizes this; hence Ungan's setting up the broom, which is an eloquent demonstration. When appeal is made to verbalism, which takes place frequently, such references to "father" or to "I" point out where the Zen way of thinking tends as to the use of words.

VII

Pure subjectivity, as sometimes supposed, is not to be located where "not one *cittakshana* ('thought-instant' or *nien* or *nen*) has yet been awakened". This is condemned by Zen masters as "nonsensical" or "useless". Nor is pure subjectivity pure timelessness, for it works in time and is time. It is not Man facing Nature as an unfriendly stranger but Man thoroughly merged in Nature, coming out of Nature and going

9 Ibid.
10 Ibid.

into Nature, and yet conscious of himself as distinguishable in a unique way. But their distinguishability is not conceptual, and can be prehended as such in what I call *prajna*-intuition in timeless time, in an absolute present.

Daido of Tosu (Ta-tung of T'ou-tzu-shan, 819–914) was asked: "Who is Vairocana-Buddha?"[11]

Tosu answered: "He already has a name."

"Who is the master of Vairocana-Buddha?"

"Prehend (*hui-ch'u*) him when Vairocana has not yet come to existence."

The highest being is to be comprehended or intuited even prior to time. It is the Godhead who *is*, even before it became God and created the world. The Godhead is the one in whom there was yet neither Man nor Nature. "The master of Vairocana" is the Godhead. When he came to have "a name", he is no more the Master. To have "a name" for Vairocana is to make him negate himself. The Godhead negates himself by becoming God, the creator, for he then has "a name". In the beginning there is "the word", but in the beginningless beginning there is the Godhead who is nameless and no-word.

Zen calls this "mind of no-mind", "the unconscious conscious", "original enlightenment", "the originally pure", and very frequently just "this" (*che-ko*). But as soon as a name is given the Godhead ceases to be Godhead, Man and Nature spring up and we are caught in the maze of an abstract, conceptual vocabulary. Zen avoids all this, as we have seen. Some may say that Zen is rich in suggestions but that philosophy needs more, that we must go further into the field of analysis and speculation and verbalization. But the truth is that Zen never suggests; it directly points at "this", or produces "this" before you in order that you may see it for yourself. It is then for you to build up your own philosophical system to your intellectual satisfaction, for Zen does not despise intellection merely as such.

In point of fact Zen constantly uses words against its own

[11] *The Transmission of the Lamp*, Fas. XV. This may be regarded as corresponding to the Christian God, though not as creator.

declaration that it stands outside all words. So long as Zen is of Man while yet not of Man it cannot help it. Take up the following *mondo* and see how Zen makes use of words, and communicates what cannot be communicated.

A monk asked a master: "I am told that even when the sky is devoid of clouds it is not the original sky. What is the original sky, O master?"

The master said: "It is a fine day today for airing the wheat, young man."[12]

This is no answer from the relative point of view. For when we are asked such questions we generally try to define "the original sky" itself. The master mentions wheat because they lived very close to the field and were much dependent on the harvests. The wheat might easily be rice or hay. And if the master felt at the time like taking a walk, he might have said: "Let us saunter out for relaxation. We have lately been confined too much to the study."

On another occasion, the master was more educationally disposed and appealed to the following method. One day, Sekiso (Ch'ing-chu of Shih-shuang shan, 807–888), one of his chief disciples, asked: "When you pass away, O master, how should I answer if people come and ask me about the deepest secrets of reality?"

The master, Dogo, called to his boy attendant, who answered: "Yes, master." Dogo told him to fill the pitcher with clean water, and remained silent for a little while. He then asked Sekiso: "What did you ask me about just now?" Sekiso naturally repeated the question. But the master apparently paid no attention to his disciple and left the room.

Was this not a most curious way of treating a most fundamental question of life? Sekiso was serious, but the master treated him as if he were not concerned with the question or the questioner. From our usual way of thinking, Dogo was highly enigmatic in his behaviour and bizarre in his pedagogic methodology. What should we make of him and his way of handling Zen?

[12] *Transmission of the Lamp,* Fas. XIV, under "Dogo".

This "calling and responding" (*hu-ying*) is one of the methods frequently used by Zen masters in order to make us come to a Zen awakening. The awakening itself is a simple psychological event, but its significance goes deep down to the basic make-up of human and cosmic consciousness. For we humans thereby penetrate into the structure of reality which is behind the dichotomy of subject and object, of Man and Nature, of God and Man. In terms of time we are back at the point where there is yet no consciousness or mind or intellectualization; therefore, it is a moment of timelessness, a moment of no-*ekacittakshana* rising in the breast of the Godhead. A *satori*-event takes place at this moment, and there is for the first time a possibility of communication—a wonderful event, biologically speaking, in the evolution of consciousness, in which Nature comes to itself and becomes Man, known in Zen as "the original face" or "the nose" or "the primary man". In fact various other concrete names are given to "Man". This, however, is not symbolization.

There is a story told of a great Chinese Buddhist thinker called Dosho (Tao-sheng, died 434) who, when he found his intuition not acceptable to his contemporaries, talked to rocks in the desert. Before the introduction in China of a complete text of the *Mahaparinirvana Sutra,* scholars were in doubt as to the possibility of the Buddha-nature being present in all beings regardless of their sentiency or consciousness. But the philosopher in question was convinced that every being, man or no-man, was in possession of the Buddha-nature. Later, when a complete *Nirvana Sutra* was translated into Chinese, this was found to have been actually told by Buddha. In the meantime the philosopher was expelled as a heretic from the Buddhist community of the time. But being absolutely sure of his intuition, he is said to have discoursed on the topic to a mass of rocks in the field. They were found to be nodding, showing that they were in perfect agreement with the speaker.

The allusion in the following *mondo* to the rocks is based on this incident, recorded in the history of Chinese Buddhism during the period of Six Dynasties (317–589 A.D.).

Ungan once asked a monk: "Where have you been?"

The monk answered: "We have been talking together on the rock."

The master asked: "Did the rock nod, or not?"

The monk did not reply, whereupon the master remarked: "The rock had been nodding even before you began to talk."

In the case of Dosho, the rocks nodded in response to his talk on the omnipresence of the Buddha-nature, but in this *mondo* Ungan remarks that the rock had been nodding even prior to Dosho's eloquent discourse. Nature is already Man, or otherwise no Man could come out of it. It is ourselves who fail to be conscious of the fact.

VIII

Hiju Yesho (P'ai-shu Hui-hsing), a disciple of Yueh-shan Wei-yen, was asked by a monk: "What is Buddha?"

Yesho answered: "The cat is climbing up the post."

The monk confessed his inability to understand the master. The latter said: "You ask the post."[13]

To those who for the first time come across such a *mondo* as this, the Zen master will appear as one who has lost his head. In the first place, what has Buddha to do with the cat, the post, and her climbing it? And then how can the post explain to the monk what the master means by these strange references?

However far we go with our usual reasoning, we cannot make anything out of this *mondo*. Either we are out of our human faculties or the master is moving somewhere where our customary walk does not take us. No doubt, there is a realm of transcendence where all the Zen masters have their exclusive abode, and Nature must be hiding this from our world of sense-and-intellect.

Juten (Pao-fu Ts'ung-chan, died 928), seeing a monk come to him, struck the post with his staff and then struck the monk. The monk felt the pain and exclaimed: "It hurts!" The master remarked: "How is it that 'that' does not cry out in pain?"

[13] *The Transmission of the Lamp*, Fas. XIV.

The monk failed to answer.

Here is another reference to the post. The post is an object in Nature. As long as it stands against Man, it is unintelligent and shows in it no sign of friendliness. But let Man see it or hear it, and it immediately becomes a part of Man and feels him in every ingredient of its being. It will surely nod its head when Man questions it. Therefore, when a master heard a monk striking the board in front of the Meditation Hall, it is said that he cried: "It hurts!"

This is the reason why Zen masters are frequently approached with the question: "What is your 'environment' (*kyogai*)?" The reference is to Nature, and the question is to find out how it affects them, or, more exactly, how the masters inwardly respond to Nature. Even this does not quite accurately interpret what the term "*kyogai*" (here rendered as "environment") signifies. It may not be out of place to say a few words in regard to this term, for it has a weighty bearing on our understanding Zen in its relation to Nature.

I do not think there is any English word which truly corresponds to this Chinese and Japanese word. *Kyogai* (*ching-ai*) originally comes from the Sanskrit *gocara* or *vishaya* or *gati*, which mean more or less the same thing. They are a "realm" or "field" where any action may take place. *Gocara* is especially significant; it means "the pasture" where cows graze and walk about. As the cattle have their grazing field, man has a field or realm for his inner life. The wise man has his *Weltanschauung* whereby he views the whole world, and this enters into the content of his *kyogai*. The *kyogai* is his mode or frame or tone of consciousness from which all his reactions come and wherein all outside stimulations are absorbed. We generally imagine that we all live in the same objective world and behave in the same way. But the truth is that none of us has the same *kyogai*. For each of us lives in his inner sanctum, which is his subjectivity and which cannot be shared by any other individual. This strictly individual inner structure or frame of consciousness, utterly unique, is one's *kyogai*. When a monk asks a master what his *kyogai* is, the monk wishes to know his inner life, his "spiritual" environment. The question, therefore, is equivalent to asking what is one's Zen understanding. And it goes without saying that this Zen understanding is Zen's response to Nature, including Nature's role in Zen.

From the several *mondo* already quoted, we can see that the masters are totally identified with Nature. To them there is no distinction between the *en-soi* and the *pour-soi*, nor is there any attempt on their part to identify themselves with Nature or to make Nature participate in their life. The masters simply express themselves at the point where time has not yet cut, as it were, into timelessness. It may be, however, better to say that they are at the crossing or cutting point itself and that it is this point that makes the masters the instruments of communication in order that Nature may become conscious of itself. Pure Being descends from its seat of absolute identity and, becoming dichotomous, speaks to itself. This is what Zen calls the master's *kyogai* or his "frame of consciousness", or his inner life, which is his Zen way of behaving.

Let me quote a few more examples in which the masters make constant reference to Nature as if the latter were other than themselves. Here are some of the answers the masters gave to their inquisitive monks:[14]

1. "The full moon in the autumnal sky shines on the ten thousand houses."

2. "The mountains and rivers, in full extension, lie before you, and there is nothing to hinder your surveying glance."

3. "The white clouds are rising as far as one's eyes can survey from every peak of the mountain range; while a fine drizzling rain falls silently outside the bamboo screens."

4. "The green bamboos are swaying in the winds; the cold pine trees are shivering in the moonlight."

5. When a monk asked if anything of Buddhism could be formed in the desert, the master answered: "The larger rocks and the smaller rocks."

6. A master took a monk, who was eager to know the secrets

[14] The following are culled haphazard from *The Transmission of the Lamp*.

of Zen teaching, into a bamboo grove and told the monk: "You see that some of these bamboos are crooked while others are growing up straight."

7. When a master wanted to tell a monk what the mind of Buddha was, he said: "The white cow is lying by the cool stream in the open field."

8. When a Confucian scholar visited a Zen master, he asked: "What is the ultimate secret of Zen?" The master answered: "You have a fine saying in your *Analects:* 'I have nothing to hide from you.' So has Zen nothing hidden from you."

"I cannot understand," said the scholar.

Later, they had a walk together along the mountain path. The wild laurel happened to be blooming. The master said: "Do you smell the fragrance of the flowering tree?" The scholar responded: "Yes, I do." "Then," declared the master, "I have hidden nothing from you."

9. A monk was anxious to learn Zen and said: "I have been newly initiated into the Brotherhood. Will you be gracious enough to show me the way to Zen?" The master said: "Do you hear the murmuring sound of the mountain stream?" The monk answered: "Yes, I do." The master said: "Here is the entrance."

10. To a monk's question about the ultimate meaning of Buddhism, a master answered: "A stream of water is flowing out of the mountains, and there are no obstacles that would ever stop its course." Then he added:

"The mountain-flowers are spread out like gold brocades. Here is Manjusri striking right into your eyes.

"The birds in the secluded depths of the woodland are singing their melodies each in their own way. Here is Avalokiteshvara filling up your ears.

"O monk! What is there that makes you go on reflecting and cogitating?"

11. A master once gave the following verse in appreciation of his relationship to his mountain retreat:

"Peak over peak of mountains endlessly above the bridge;

One long stream below the bridge flowing on mile
 after mile;
There is one lonely white heron
That is my constant visitor at this retreat."

IX

These quotations from *The Transmission of the Lamp,*
which is a store-house of Zen *mondo,* Zen stories, and Zen
sermons, abundantly illustrate the relationship in which Zen
stands to Nature and the role which Nature plays in the make-
up of Zen. Indeed, Zen cannot be separated from Nature, for
Zen knows no polarization. Pure subjectivity from which Zen
starts absorbs all that constitutes Nature or the objective world
so called.

Karl Jaspers distinguishes three realms of Being: Being-
there, Being-oneself, and Being-in-itself, and then proceeds to
state that these three realms "are in no sense reducible to one
another". Blackham in his *Six Existentialist Thinkers* (p. 58)
speaks for Jaspers:

"The person who is made aware of them may participate
in all three; Transcendence embraces the world of objects and
subjects: but the logical understanding, founded upon the objects of empirical existence, being-there, is unable without fal-
sification to describe the other realms of existence or to bring
them into a common system; their discontinuity is invincible,
only to be reconciled in the *life* of a person and *by faith* in
Transcendence."[15]

Now, the ways of the philosopher are to talk about a "system", "continuity", "reconciliation", "logical understanding",
etc. But the philosopher starts with "logicism" and then tries
to come to "life" instead of reversing the process. In "life" itself there is no reconciling, no systematizing, no understanding;
we just live it and all is well with us. "To awaken philosophic
faith in Transcendence" is also unnecessary, for this is something added to life by the so-called logical understanding. Nor

[15] The italics are mine.

is there in life itself any such distinction as the "three realms of being". All these things are piling so many heads over the one which is there from the very first. The original one is buried deeper and deeper as we go on philosophizing, and finally we lose sight of it.

Seppo (Hsueh-feng I-ts'un, 822–908) once gave this sermon to his monks: "You are all like those who, while immersed in the ocean, extend their hands crying for water." This is really the human situation in which we who call ourselves rational and thinking find ourselves.

But human life is not like that of other living beings. We do not want to live just an animal life; we like to know the worth of life and to appreciate it consciously. This is, however, the very moment wherein we negate ourselves by deviating from life itself. It is for this reason that we philosophize and become "thinkers". But it is not by thinking that we come back to life, nor is it by "philosophic faith" or by "divine revelation" that we are brought to the presence and the silence of "transcendence". Zen, however, does not like the odour of abstraction which oozes out from even such terms as "Transcendence". For, in fact, as soon as appeal is made to words, we leave life itself and involve ourselves in every kind of "logical" controversy. We construct our own traps and then struggle to escape from them, and as long as we are what we are, we cannot get away from this dilemma. It is only for those who have attained *prajna*-intuition that an escape is provided from the almost hopeless intricacies of intellection.

In the meantime, every one of us feels an inward urge to effect such an escape in one way or another. The philosophic way is to appeal to Reason, in whatever sense the term may be interpreted, whereas the "religiously" inclined resort to "faith" or "revelation". The Zen way of escape—or, better, of solution—is direct apprehension or grasping "it" or "this".

"This" is pure subjectivity, or being-in-itself, or absolute self. It is also called "the one passage to the highest" or "the one solitary way of escape". There are many names given to this way of Zen, for almost every master had his own terminology. In spite of these endless complexities, all Zen masters strive to express that something in our life as we live it which gives us the key to the difficulties raised by the intellect and also stills the anxieties produced by our attachment to a world of relativities.

We can have a glimpse into this truth in a few extracts from Zen masters' discourses on the use of words:

1. Question: "Whenever appeal is made to words, there is a taint. What is the truth of the highest order (*hiang-shang shih*)?"

Answer: "Whenever appeal is made to words, there is a taint."

2. Question: "Where is one solitary road to being oneself?"

Answer: "Why trouble yourself to ask about it?"

3. Question: "Fine words and wonderful meanings make up the contents of the Doctrine. Can you show me a direct way without resorting to a triple treatment?"

Answer: "Fare thee well."[16]

4. Question: "Whenever appeal is made to words, we are sure to fall into every form of snare. Please, O master, tell me how to deal directly with it."

Answer: "You come to me after doing away with every kind of measuring instrument."[17]

I should like to add a few words here on escapism, with which some writers on Buddhism try to connect Zen.

"To escape", or "to be emancipated", or "to be disengaged", or any word or phrase implying the idea of keeping oneself away from a world of becoming, is altogether inadequate to express the Zen way of achieving "salvation". Even "salvation" is a bad term, because Zen recognizes nothing from which we are to be saved. We are from the first already "saved" in all reality, and it is due to our ignorance of the fact that we talk about being saved or delivered or freed. So with "escape", etc., Zen knows no traps or complexities from which we are to escape. The traps or complexities are our own creation. We

[16] Or, "Take good care of yourself."
[17] All these four *mondo* are quoted from *The Transmission of the Lamp*, Fas. XVIII.

find ourselves, and when we realize this, we are what we have been from the very beginning of things.

For example, we create the three realms, to use Jaspers' terms, of "being-there", "being-oneself", and "being-in-itself"; or the two modes according to Sartre of *en-soi* and *pour-soi*, or the two categories in Western thinking of God and the created, or of God and Nature, or of Man and Nature. These are all of human creation, and we cling to them as if they were absolutely determined, binding us as something inextricably, fatalistically unescapable. We are our own prisoners. We defeat ourselves, believing in defeatism, which is itself our own creation. This is our ignorance, known as *avidya* in Buddhism. When this is recognized we realize that we are free, "men of no-business" (*Wu-shih chih jen*).

Zen, therefore, does not try to disengage us from the world, to make us mere spectators of the hurly-burly which we see around us. Zen is not mysticism, if the latter is to be understood in the sense of escapism. Zen is right in the midst of the ocean of becoming. It shows no desire to escape from its tossing waves. It does not antagonize Nature; it does not treat Nature as if it were an enemy to be conquered, nor does it stand away from Nature. It is indeed Nature itself.

Buddhism is often regarded as pessimistic and as urging us to escape from the bondage of birth and death. Dr. Rhys Davids, for instance, states that "the ultimate goal of Buddhism is to untie the knots of Existence and find a way to escape".[18] This way of interpreting Buddhism has been going on among Buddhist scholars as well as Buddhist devotees, but it is not in conformity with the spirit of Buddha as one who experienced Enlightenment and declared himself as the all-conqueror, the all-knower, the all-seer.

x

We have now come to the point where our discourse on "pure subjectivity" finally leads us. For "pure subjectivity" is

[18] Quoted by H. S. Wadia in *The Message of Buddha*, p. 170, London, J. M. Dent, 1938.

no other than "pure objectivity". Our inner life is complete when it merges into Nature and becomes one with it. There is nothing, after all, in the Zen master's *kyogai* (*gocara, ching-ai*), which differentiates itself as something wondrous or extraordinary. It consists, as in all other cases, in scenting the fragrance of the laurel in bloom and in listening to a bird singing on a spring day to its heart's content. What, however, makes a difference in the case of a Zen master is that he sees the flowers as they really are and not in a dreamy sort of way in which the flowers are not real flowers and the rivers are not really flowing rivers. Pure subjectivity, instead of vaporizing realities, as one might imagine, consolidates everything with which it comes in touch. More than that, it gives a soul to even non-sentient beings and makes them readily react to human approach. The whole universe which means Nature ceases to be "hostile" to us as we had hitherto regarded it from our selfish point of view. Nature, indeed, is no more something to be conquered and subdued. It is the bosom whence we come and whither we go.

There is, then, in the teaching of Zen no escapism, no mysticism, no denial of existence, no conquering Nature, no frustrations, no mere utopianism, no naturalism. Here is a world of the given. Becoming is going on in all its infinitely varied forms, and yet there is the realm of transcendence within all these changing scenes. Emptiness is Suchness and Suchness is Emptiness. A world of *rupa* is no other than *sunyata,* and *sunyata* is no other than this *rupaloka,* which is a Buddhist term for Nature.

Dokai of Fuyo (Fu-jung Tao-k'ai, died 1118),[19] of the Sung dynasty, writes in one of his poems on the relationship between Emptiness and Suchness:

From the very first, not one dharma[20] is in existence; all is Emptiness;
And where in this is there room for talk about being enlightened in the Perfect Way?

[19] Supplementary volumes to *The Transmission of the Lamp,* Fas. X.
[20] A thing, an object, that which subsists.

Thus I thought no intelligence has ever come to us from
the Shorin,[21]
But, lo! the peach blossoms as of old are smiling in the
spring breeze.

Seccho (Hsueh-tou), of the eleventh century, has the following stanza in which he finds himself musing surrounded
by the trees and looking at the stream filled with the illusive
shadows of the mountains. Is he musing? Is he lost in a dream?
What philosophy has he here?

The spring mountains are covered with greens, layer
after layer, in utter confusion;
The shadows are seen serenely reflected in the spring
waters below.
Between the heavens and the earth in a lonely field
I stand all by myself before a vista whose end nobody
knows.[22]

We must now come to the conclusion. I have not so far
been able to be even tentatively complete in my treatment of
the subject. There are many other matters left out, among
which I would mention the problem of necessity and freedom.
We think Nature is brute fact, entirely governed by the laws
of absolute necessity; and there is no room for freedom to
enter here. But Zen would say that Nature's necessity and
Man's freedom are not such divergent ideas as we imagine, but
that necessity is freedom and freedom is necessity.

A second important problem in Zen's treatment of Nature
is that of teleology. Has Zen any purposefulness when it declares that the sun rises in the morning and that I eat when
hungry? To discuss the matter fully requires time and space,
more than we can afford at this session.

A third problem is that of good and evil. What has Zen to
say about morality? What relationship is there between Zen

[21] The Shorin (Shao-lin) is the temple where Bodhi-
Dharma is said to have retreated after his unsuccessful interview with Wu, the Emperor of the Liang, and spent nine years
absorbed in meditation.
[22] *The Hekigah Shu* (*Pi-yen Chi*).

and the Western idea of the divine commands which imply fear and obedience? To this Zen would say that Zen is on the other shore of good and evil, but this does not mean that Zen is unconcerned with ethics.

A fourth problem is the fact of human depravity. In other words, what has Zen to say about demonology? Nature has no demons; they are human creations. It is Man who peoples Nature with all kinds of demons and permits them to do him all kinds of evil. It is an interesting subject, especially seeing that Man with all his boast of his rationality keeps on committing deeds of irrationality—that is, of demonology.

CHAPTER 9

Existentialism, Pragmatism and Zen

I

It is significant that the first number of *Philosophy East and West* contains two articles referring to Zen thought. They come from the learned pens of university professors: Dr. H. E. McCarthy of Honolulu and Dr. Van Meter Ames of Cincinnati.[1] The former interprets Goethe's *Faust* in the spirit of Zen, whereas the latter discusses Zen in reference to pragmatism and existentialism.

Dr. McCarthy's article is illuminating and brings out quite fully and clearly the poetical spirit of Zen which is embodied in *Faust*. When I first read *Faust*, I was deeply impressed with the ideas pervading the work, thinking how strongly they reminded me of Zen. The spirit of Zen is really universal, as Dr. McCarthy states; it knows no distinction of East and West.

In fact, Zen, being life itself, contains everything that goes into the make-up of life: Zen is poetry, Zen is philosophy, Zen is morality. Wherever there is life-activity, there is Zen. As long as we cannot imagine life to be limited in any way, Zen is present in every one of our experiences, but this ought not to be understood as a kind of obscure immanentism. There is nothing hidden in Zen: all is manifest, and only the dim-eyed ones are barred from seeing it.

When I say that Zen is life, I mean that Zen is not to be confined within conceptualization, that Zen is what makes conceptualization possible, and therefore that Zen is not to be identified with any particular brand of "ism." In this respect,

[1] Harold E. McCarthy, "Poetry, Metaphysics, and Zen," and Van Meter Ames, "America, Existentialism, and Zen," *Philosophy East and West*, I, No. 1 (April, 1951).

Dr. Ames's comparison of Zen with pragmatism or existentialism may be said to be not quite to the point. It goes without
saying that Zen has its own way of expressing itself, and also
a theory to rationalize itself. But this ought not to be interpreted to mean that this theory is Zen.

There is something in the theory of Zen that may pass into
a form of pragmatism or existentialism, and I think Dr. Ames
has taken up this point for discussion in his article on "America,
Existentialism, and Zen." Therefore, it is evident that his Zen
does not cover the entirety of Zen as such. It is with this reservation, then, that I subscribe to most of what he states in his
interesting and thought-provoking thesis.

II

Availing myself of this opportunity, I wish to describe Zen
from various points of view in order to bring the moon of Zen
nearer to us for our closer observation. As I said before, Zen is
life; and since life, as our intellect conceives it, is made up of
various elements, let us elucidate Zen briefly under the following headings: metaphysics, including ontology and epistemol-
ogy, psychology, ethics, aesthetics, and religion.

Zen is not to be conceptualized, let me repeat, if it is to be
experientially grasped; but inasmuch as we are all human in
the sense that we cannot remain dumb, but have to express
ourselves in one way or another, indeed, we cannot have even
an experience if we cease to give expression to it. Zen would
not be Zen if it were deprived of all means of communication.
Even silence is a means of communication; the Zen masters
often resort to this method. This is because human silence is
not to be subsumed under the same category as animal silence
or the silence of heavenly bodies; even these silences, from the
human point of view, are full of eloquence. Man is man because he is forever striving to express himself. The saying that
man is a rational being means no more than this.

The conceptualization of Zen is inevitable: Zen must have
its philosophy. The only caution is not to identify Zen with

a system of philosophy, for Zen is infinitely more than that. What, then, is the philosophy of Zen?

Zen is a school of Buddhism and has developed from the enlightenment-experience of Śākyamuni. This experience is best expressed by the doctrine of *śūnyatā*, which means "emptiness." *Śūnyatā* is a most difficult term for which to find an equivalent in English, and I think it is best to leave the original untranslated, trying in the meantime to make its significance as clear as possible.

First, I must state that *śūnyatā* is not a negative term, as might be suggested, when it is translated as "emptiness" or "void." It is a positive concept with a definite connotation, but it ought not to be considered an outcome of abstraction or generalization, for it is not a postulated idea. It is what makes the existence of anything possible, but it is not to be conceived immanently, as if it lay hidden in or under every existence as an independent entity. A world of relativities is set on and in *śūnyatā; śūnyatā* envelops, as it were, the whole world, and yet is in every object existing in the world. The doctrine of *śūnyatā* is neither an immanentism nor a transcendentalism; if we can say so, it is both. If it is declared that immanentism and transcendentalism contradict each other, *śūnyatā* is this contradiction itself. A contradiction implies two terms which are set against each other. *Śūnyatā* is absolutely one; hence, there is no contradiction in it.

A contradiction is felt only when we are out of *śūnyatā*. As long as we live in it, there is no contradiction, and this is where Zen wants us to be. With Zen, therefore, *śūnyatā* is to be experienced and not conceptualized. To experience means to become aware of, but not in the way in which we become aware of the world of sense-and-intellect. In the latter case, we always have a subject that is aware of something and an object of which the subject is aware, for the world of sense-and-intellect is a dichotomous world of subject and object. To be aware of *śūnyatā*, according to Zen, we have to transcend this dichotomous world in such a way as not to be outside it. *Śūnyatā* is to be experienced in a unique way.

This unique way consists in *śūnyatā's* remaining in itself and yet making itself an object of experience to itself. This means dividing itself and yet holding itself together. In the case of an ordinary experience, this is impossible, because in the world of ordinary experience every experience is conceptualized, since this world is really our intellectual reconstruction and not reality as it is in itself, not in its "suchness," as Buddhist philosophers would say. *Śūnyatā* is experienced only when it is both subject and object.

The philosopher's way is to start first from the experience and logic of a reconstructed world, and, failing to recognize this fact, he proceeds to apply his "logic" to the experience of *śūnyatā*. This necessitates that *śūnyatā* step out into this world, which means destroying *śūnyatā*. The more thoroughly "logicized," the more thoroughly is *śūnyatā* destroyed. The proper way to study *śūnyatā* is to experience it, to become aware of it, in the only way *śūnyatā* can be approached. That is to say, the philosopher has to purge every residue of what the mind has accumulated by assiduously applying himself to the work of intellection. He has to reverse his process of reasoning, realizing that this is a weapon that is quite efficient in dealing with things of this world of relativities, but that, when we want to get down into the very bedrock of reality, which is *śūnyatā*, we must appeal to another method; and there is no other method than that of casting away this intellectual weapon and in all nakedness plunging right into *śūnyatā* itself. As I said before, *śūnyatā* is what makes this world possible. This being so, when we apply the method to the realization of *śūnyatā*, which we use to know this world, to know things of and in this world, we are trying to force the method to work where it is not useful and where it does not yield fruit.

"Knowing and seeing" *śūnyatā* is *śūnyatā* knowing and seeing itself; there is no outside knower or spectator; it is its own knower and seer. In this respect, *śūnyatā* is *ātman*, master of itself, is not at all conditioned by anything outside. Here is the question: If it is *śūnyatā* itself that sees and knows itself, how can we humans talk about it? We are relatively determined—all our knowledge is conditioned—and so, how can this relatively conditioned being come to the experience of *śūnyatā?*

The answer is: We are *śūnyatā*. We can talk of *śūnyatā* only because we are it. If this were not the case, there would be no philosophy in this world. It is entirely due to *śūnyatā* that we can reason, although reasoning itself cannot lead us to *śūnyatā*. Reasoning comes out of *śūnyatā; śūnyatā* is in it; every step of reasoning leaves the mark of *śūnyatā*. It is *śūnyatā* that urges us to go beyond reasoning while we are all the time engaged in reasoning. *Śūnyatā* wants to see itself, to know itself, and it is this want on the part of *śūnyatā* that leads to reasoning, and reason, not knowing this cause of its own activity, defeats itself in spite of its ambitious claim for omniscience. Reasoning defeats itself, finds itself altogether futile, in its attempt to reach *śūnyatā*, because reasoning, instead of trying to see *śūnyatā* itself in the process of reasoning, strives to reach *śūnyatā* as the goal of reasoning, that is, when all the reasoning comes to an end. When we the reasoners realize that *śūnyatā* is working, in reasoning itself, that reasoning is no other than *śūnyatā* in disguise, we know *śūnyatā*, we see *śūnyatā*, and this is *śūnyatā* knowing and seeing itself; and so, we can say that when *śūnyatā* knows itself it is not *śūnyatā* but we ourselves as *śūnyatā*. *Śūnyatā* knows itself through us, because we are *śūnyatā*.

When *śūnyatā* is awakened to itself or becomes aware of itself, which is "knowing and seeing" itself, we have another name for it: *śūnyatā* is *tathatā*, "suchness." *Tathatā* is a concept that is characteristic of Buddhist philosophy. Let us take it up for consideration now.

III

While *śūnyatā* may erroneously appear to be negativistic, there is nothing in the concept of *tathatā* that would suggest the idea of negativity. *Tathatā* is the viewing of things as they are: it is an affirmation through and through. I see a tree, and I state that it is a tree; I hear a bird sing and I say that a bird sings; a spade is a spade, and a mountain is a mountain; the fowls of the air fly and the flowers of the field bloom: these are statements of *tathatā*. When a Zen master was asked,

"What is everyday thought (*hsin*)?" he said, "I sleep when I am tired, I eat when I am hungry." This "everyday thought" is declared to be the ultimate Tao, the highest teaching of Buddhist philosophy.

If *śūnyatā* denies or rejects everything, *tathatā* accepts and upholds everything; the two concepts may be considered as opposing each other, but it is the Buddhist idea that they are not contradictory, that it is from our relativistic point of view that they seem so. In truth, *tathatā* is *śūnyatā*, and *śūnyatā* is *tathatā*; things are *tathatā* because of their being *śūnyatā*. A Buddhist philosopher declares: A mountain is a mountain and water is water before a *śūnyatā*-experience takes place; but after it a mountain is not a mountain and water is not water; but again when the experience deepens, a mountain is a mountain and water is water. This requires a supplementary remark. When the philosopher says that with the experience of *śūnyatā* a mountain ceases to be a mountain and water to be water, this experience must be regarded as not quite reaching its deepest depths: it is still on the level of intellection; there is something of conceptualization; it is not thoroughly purged of all the dregs. When *śūnyatā* is really *śūnyatā* it becomes identical with *tathatā*.

The *tathatā*-concept is what makes Zen approach pragmatism and existentialism: they all accept experience as the basis of their theorization, and this experience is closely attached to the world of relativities. Zen, however, is different in a most significant way from pragmatism: Whereas pragmatism appeals to the practical usefulness of truth, that is, the purposefulness of our action, Zen emphasizes the purposelessness of work or being detached from teleological consciousness, or, as Zen characteristically expresses it, not leaving any trace behind as one lives one's life. It is in this spirit that Hui-nêng (Yeno in Japanese), the sixth patriarch and the originator of Chinese Zen, strongly insisted on the identity or simultaneity of *dhyāna* and *prajñā*. When Hui-neng is said to have had his insight into the truth of Zen while listening to *The Diamond Sūtra*, we can trace the same idea lurking in the phrase which contributed to his enlightenment, namely, "to awaken the mind while abiding nowhere," and this means nothing less or more than a non-teleological interpretation of life.

Teleology is a term belonging to a world of time, relativity, causality, morality, and so on, while Zen lives beyond all these limitations. As long as the lilies of the field and the fowls of the air live just to demonstrate the glory of the divine life, they are living a purposeless life. So are human beings: When we live not trying to add one cubit to our stature, or without worrying about the morrow as to what to wear or what to eat, but letting the evil of the day take care of itself, is not this kind of life just as glorious as that of the fowls or of the lilies? Will not this kind of life be the life God wanted us to live, that is, free from all teleological vexations and humanly intentional complexities? Time and teleology are interwoven, and Zen transcends time and, therefore, teleology also. So, we read in the *Dhammapada*, verse 385:

> For whom there exists neither the hither nor the farther
> shore, nor both the hither and the farther shore,
> He who is undistressed and unbound—him I call a Brahman.[2]

Zen diverges from existentialism in this: There are various brands of existentialism but they seem to agree in holding that finite man is infinitely removed from God, that "the sea of possibilities opening ahead is frightening. They mean freedom, and unlimited freedom means unbearable responsibility."[3] To these thoughts Zen is a stranger, because for Zen the finite is infinite, time is eternity, man is not separated from God, "before Abraham was I am." Furthermore, Zen does not find anything frightening in infinite possibilities, unlimited freedom, never-ending responsibilities. Zen moves along with infinite possibilities; Zen enjoys unlimited freedom because Zen is freedom itself; however unending and unbearable responsibility may be, Zen bears it as if not bearing it at all. In Christian terminology, this means that my responsibility is shifted to

[2] *The Dhammapada*. Translation by Narada Thera with a foreword by Dr. Cassius A. Pereira (rev. 2d ed.; Colombo: Daily News Press, 1946), p. 63.

[3] *Philosophy East and West*, I, No. 1 (April, 1951), p. 44.

God's shoulder, that "not my will, but thy will be done," and this is Zen's attitude toward moral responsibility. This is not shunning it, of course. Zen is ready to bear it to its full extent, if necessary, to sacrifice life itself; but the point is that Zen practices the virtue of *dāna,* "giving," the first of the six *pāramitās,* on the plane of *tathatā,* as if "cutting the spring breeze in the midst of a lightning flash."

Kierkegaard was somewhat neurotic and morbid when he dilated on fear: He was obsessed with the feeling because he had an abnormal sense of his separation from God, which prevented a full understanding of the meaning of the freedom which issues from the experience of *tathatā.* The existentialist generally interprets freedom on the plane of relativity where there is no freedom in its highest sense. Freedom can be predicated only of *tathatā* and its experience. The existentialist looks into the abyss of *tathatā* and trembles, and is seized with inexpressible fear. Zen would tell him: Why not plunge right into the abyss and see what is there? The idea of individualism fatally holds him back from throwing himself into the devil's maw.

IV

To Zen, time and eternity are one. This is open to misinterpretation, as most people interpret Zen as annihilating time and putting in its place eternity, which to them means a state of absolute quietness or doing-nothing-ness. They forget that if time is eternity, eternity is time, according to Zen. Zen has never espoused the cause of doing-nothing-ness; eternity is our everyday experience in this world of sense-and-intellect, for there is no eternity outside this time-conditionedness. Eternity is possible only in the midst of birth and death, in the midst of time-process. I raise a finger, this is in time, and eternity is seen dancing at the tip of it. When this is translated into terms of space, the one finger contains in it the three thousand chiliocosms. This is not symbolism. To Zen it is an actual experience.

In one sense Zen may be regarded as momentalistic, but not

as this is commonly understood. Zen has eternity in momentarism, whereas momentarism is devoid of eternity. With momentalists each fleeting moment is only fleeting and does not carry eternity along with it. Momentalists are therefore irresponsible in a bad sense, they are anti-moral, they are not at all free, not masters of themselves, for they are controlled by the consciousness of momentariness. Zen designates this state of mind as "abiding," as having "a fixed abiding place." One who has an "abiding place" is a prisoner, just like a man tied to a post or hedged around with fences. A free Zen-man has no such abode anywhere; he lives in a circle whose circumference has no limits;[4] therefore, wherever he is he is always at the centre of reality, he is reality itself. A momentalist life has no meaning whatever: it is like animal life or plant life—life is there, to be sure, but there is no meaning to it. Why? Because the momentalist is not conscious of eternity while living in time; each moment is to him just that and no more; and like the dog romping about in the yard, he enjoys it; his joy is animalistic and has no value whatsoever.

Momentarism does not know what is meant by the absolute present. Zen lives in this, and therefore is *tathatā*-conscious. In *The Diamond Sūtra* we read: "The past mind is unattainable, the future mind is unattainable, the present mind is unattainable."[5] This is a significant statement. The idea is that consciousness is in time, it operates in time, it is time itself, and that consciousness is a locus of what is known in Buddhist philosophy as *kṣaṇa* (*nien* in Chinese, and *nen* in Japanese). I venture to translate *kṣaṇa* as consciousness-unit, for consciousness is serially tracing these units. In terms of time, a consciousness-unit is the shortest possible division of time. But

---

[4] In the *Dhammapada,* 179 and 180, we read about "the trackless Buddha of infinite range," which exactly corresponds to the Mahāyāna idea of "not leaving any trace" and of "a tub with its hoops all broken off."

[5] Cf. *Dhammapada,* 348. "Let go the front, let go the back, let go the middle. Crossing to the farther shore of existence, with mind released from everything, do not again undergo birth and death." The front, the back, and the middle correspond to the future, the past, and the present.

as we cannot fix any limit to time-division, we can say that a consciousness-unit is only theoretically assumed. *Ekakṣaṇa*,[6] that is, the idea of such an ultimate unit, is, to all intents and purposes, unattainable—and this is what is meant by the statement above quoted from *The Diamond Sūtra*. An *ekakṣaṇa* is unattainable, and so is the absolute present, and an *ekakṣaṇa* is an absolute present, eternal Now. Zen is thus said to be realized in an *ekakṣaṇa*.

Every moment of consciousness is an *ekakṣaṇa*, and yet no *ekakṣaṇa* is to be picked out of it and pointed out as such. An *ekakṣaṇa* means the bursting of time out of eternity; it is the awakening of consciousness out of the darkest recesses of the unconscious. At the awakening of an *ekakṣaṇa* the unconscious comes to itself, or we can say that eternity then cuts into time. Therefore, the unconscious is known only through consciousness, and eternity through time. There is no eternity as such: it is always to be in time-process; there is no so-called unconscious which does not come along with consciousness. *Ekakṣaṇa* is often designated as *akṣaṇa*,[7] and the two terms are used synonymously. *Akṣaṇa* means no-*kṣaṇa*. No-*kṣaṇa*, however, does not mean the effacement of consciousness; it is in and with consciousness, it is an *ekakṣaṇa*, and yet unattainable as such. No-*kṣaṇa* has a positive connotation as eternity.

We can make the same assertion about such ideas as no-acting (*akarma*), no-thinking or no-mind (*acitta*), or no-abiding (*aprasthita*). They are all positive ideas, though negatively expressed. As each *ekakṣaṇa* is *akṣaṇa*, each act is no-act, each thought is no-thought, and each locus of consciousness is no-locus. A mind is said to be awakened to self-awareness, and yet there is no awakening of mind to be so specifically designable: this is the way Zen is to be understood and the way Zen expresses itself.

One may ask, Why these contradictions? The answer is, They are so because of *tathatā*. They are so just because they are so, and for no other reason. Hence, no logic, no analysis,

[6] *Eka* is "one," *ekakṣaṇa* is "one thought-instant."
[7] Literally, "no-thought-instant." In Chinese, *wu-mien;* in Japanese, *mu-nen.*

and no contradictions. Things, including all possible forms of contradiction, are eternally of *tathatā*. "A" cannot be itself unless it stands against what is not "A"; "not-A" is needed to make "A" "A," which means that "not-A" is in "A." When "A" wants to be itself, it is already outside itself, that is, "not-A." If "A" did not contain in itself what is not itself, "not-A" could not come out of "A" so as to make "A" what it is. "A" is "A" because of this contradiction, and this contradiction comes out only when we logicize. As long as we are in *tathatā*, there is no contradiction whatever. Zen knows no contradictions; it is the logician who encounters them, forgetting that they are of his own making. Zen takes everything in as it is, and contradictions resolve themselves without much ado. It is not Zen's way to annihilate the whole world or to reduce it to an abstract nonentity in order to experience the dissolution of contradictions.

The main trouble with the human mind is that while it is capable of creating concepts in order to interpret reality it hypostatizes them and treats them as if they were real things. Not only that, the mind regards its self-constructed concepts as laws externally imposed upon reality, which has to obey them in order to unfold itself. This attitude or assumption on the part of the intellect helps the mind to handle nature for its own purposes, but the mind altogether misses the inner workings of life and consequently is utterly unable to understand it. This is the reason we have to halt at contradictions and are at a loss as to how to proceed.

In the *Dhammapada*, 369, we have:

Empty this boat, O Bhikkhu! Emptied by you it will move swiftly,
Cutting out lust and hatred, to *Nibbāna* you will thereby go.

"Emptying this boat" means emptying our mind of all the concepts we have constructed to handle reality intellectually and to make it yield the best results for our practical life. The sciences have thus developed, mechanical appliances have achieved wonderful results, and our so-called standard of living has attained unprecedented heights. But as to the spiritualization of life or a deeper insight into its significance, I am afraid we have not made much advance: we are not making our life-boat move more swiftly than we did in the past. "Lust and hatred," which are also contents of the boat, are increasing and amassing, and are not cut at all, for intellectualization is helpless to get the boat rid of lust, hatred, and the like.

The doctrine of *śūnyatā,* it is to be remembered, does not mean emptying the boat-of-reality, for reality itself is *śūnyatā,* and there is nothing to empty. *Śūnyatā* is a positive conception, and it is in this positiveness that *śūnyatā* is identified with *tathatā.* Zen views reality as *tathatā,* and because of this *tathatā*-view of reality Zen is said to be radical empiricism. Zen is empiric, because it appeals to *prajñā*-intuition as the means of taking hold of reality itself without any round-about methodology. Zen empiricism is radical because *prajñā*-intuition lies underneath all forms of intuition and intellection, and beyond *prajñā*-intuition there is nothing which makes us come into direct contact with reality. Compared with *prajñā*-intuition, sense experience is not at all direct, for it is an intellectual or conceptual reconstruction. When we see a tree and call it a tree, we think this sense experience is final; but in point of fact this sense experience is possible only when it is conceptualized. A tree is not a tree until it is subsumed under the concept "tree." *Tathatā* is what precedes this conceptualization; it is where we are even before we say it is or it is not; it is when God was still in a state of absolute self-contentment, when He had not yet conceived the idea or will to create, when He had not yet uttered his fiat, "Let there be light." But here I have already said too much, and *tathatā* is far away at an infinite distance.

v

In a way we can say that in the Zen conception of *tathatā* there is something reminding us of an aesthetic appreciation of works of art or of beauties of nature. Let me cite a Japanese *haiku* (a poem of seventeen syllables) to illustrate what I mean. *Haiku* is the shortest form of poetical expression, and because of this we can more readily analyze its content. Toward the end of the Tokugawa regime there was a poetess named Chiyo, and as she was native of Kaga province she is well known as "Kaga no Chiyo." One of her noted *haikus* is:

> *Asagao ya!*
> *Tsurube   torarete,*
> *Morai midzu.*

Literally it means: "Oh, the morning-glory.[8] The bucket made captive, [I] beg for water."

The *haiku* requires explanation. Early one morning in June, Chiyo went to get water from the outside well. The bucket, which was placed at the edge, was found to be entwined by the morning glory in bloom. Those who have visited Japan must have noticed how beautifully the morning glory opens in bloom before sunrise—the flower looks so fresh, wet with dew. The beauty must have struck Chiyo very deeply indeed that particular morning when she came out for water. She was moved so much by its ethereal beauty that she remained speechless for a little while, until finally she could just say, "Oh, the morning glory!"

This "Oh, the morning glory!" contains everything that any poetic spirit could say about the flower; anything he could add would be but a commentary, which after all does not add much to the original utterance. So it is with Chiyo's "The bucket made captive, I beg for water." She put these two lines just in the way of contrast between the beautiful thing not belonging in this world of defilements and the practical affairs of daily life where utilitarianism rules. The poetess was so absorbed in her contemplation of beauty that it took her a little time to recover from it.

How deeply, how thoroughly she was impressed with the beauty of the flower which was not of this earth is understood from the fact that she did not try to unwind the vine from the bucket, which she could have done readily without hurting the plant. But her sense of identification with the beauty was

---

[8] Would it be better to translate this, "Behold the morning glory!"?

so possessing that the idea did not suggest itself to her; she had no desire to pollute things celestial with anything savouring of workaday business. The poetess was, however, also a woman, a country-woman taking care of her house; she could not help thinking about her business: the only thing she could do would be to go to her neighbour and ask for the water she needed for her morning work. Such a reminder of relative life in this world, such an awakening from an undifferentiated absorption in the beauty, marks our human situation, in which we all are inescapably involved.

We cannot remain forever in a state of undifferentiation; we are so mad as to give expression to every experience we go through, and by thus expressing ourselves we realize that the experience grows deeper and clearer. A dumb experience is no experience at all; it is human to express, that is, to appeal to differentiation and analysis; and so, we can say that animals have no experience whatever. *Tathatā* cannot remain expressionless and undifferentiated; it has to that extent to be conceptualized. While to utter, "Oh, the morning glory!" is to come out of the identification, and, hence, to be no more of *tathatā*, this coming out of itself, this negating itself in order to be itself, is the way in which we all are constituted. And this conceptualization inevitably leads to contradictions which can only be dissolved in the synthesis of *prajñā*-intuition.

Psychologically, Chiyo the poetess required time to be awakened from her contemplation of beauty; but, metaphysically speaking, her absorbing identification and her awakening to differentiation are simultaneous; and this simultaneity takes place in an absolute present—it is an *ekakṣaṇa* of *tathatā*. This is the philosophy of Zen.

There is a noetic element in *tathatā*. *Tathatā* is not just a poetic contemplation of, or an absorbing identification with, reality; there is an awareness in it and this awareness is *prajñā*-intuition. *Prajñā*-intuition may thus be defined as differentiation undifferentiated; here the whole is intuited together with its parts; here the undifferentiated whole comes along with its infinitely differentiated, individualized parts. The whole is seen here differentiating itself in its parts, not in a pantheistic or immanentist way. The whole is not lost in its parts, nor does individuation lose sight of the whole. The One is the all without going out of itself, and each one of the infinitely varied and variable objects surrounding us embodies the One, while retaining each its individuality.

VI

Zen is often charged with aloofness, solitariness, and being detached from the masses. To a certain extent this is true. The Zen-man is sometimes found to be living in the rarefied atmosphere of "intellectual" superiority; he is apt to be standing aloof from society and from being useful to the community where he belongs. But the fact is that Zen has its conative or affective aspect along with its noeticism. The enlightenment-experience is not devoid of the great compassionate heart (*mahākarunā*), but, so far, historical circumstances have prevented its asserting itself in this direction. Zen is socially-minded as much as any other religion, but this has been manifested or demonstrated more individualistically, owing to its emphasis upon individual experience. As to serving others in social ways, Zen has had its own way of doing it. The following examples will illustrate what I mean.

Since Adam was ordered in the beginning of things, "In the sweat of thy face shalt thou eat bread till thou return unto the ground," we are all to work hard to remove "thorns and thistles" from the cursed ground in order to raise our staff of life and "be fruitful and multiply and replenish the earth and subdue [!] it." This was especially the case in China, where Zen first developed in the form we have it now. The Chinese are great agricultural people and work hard at it. So it was natural for the Zen masters to refer constantly to farming and things connected with farming.

Hui-neng, the sixth patriarch, worked in the backyard pounding rice and chopping wood all the time he was under Hung-jen, the fifth patriarch. Ma-tso hurt his legs while working on the farm with his disciples, one of whom happened to push his wheelbarrow over them. Isan and Hsing-san did not forget to discuss problems of reality while picking tea leaves. When Pai-chang was asked what would become of him after death, he immediately answered, "I am going to be born as a donkey at one of my villagers'." This meant that the master was willing to do anything to compensate for all that the villagers did for him and his monasteries.

Zen literature abounds with such phrases as "in the market place," "in the middle of the crossroads," meaning busily engaged in all kinds of work, or "the face smeared with dirt and the head covered with ashes," also describing a man who toils and is heavy laden. It is a well-known fact that Zen does not despise manual labor, refusing to be "an idle man in the daylight." Pai-chang made this his motto: "A day passed by doing nothing is a day of no-eating"; he was prepared to eat his daily bread in the sweat of his face. In "The Ten Cow-herding Pictures" the last scene shows a happy-looking man entering the market place. The market place contrasts with the mountain retreat: the former is the place where a man serves society, while the latter is where he trains himself to be qualified for public work. The monastery is not meant just to be a hiding place from the worries of the world; on the contrary, it is a training station where a man equips himself for life's battlefield, that is, to do all that can possibly be done for his community. All Buddhists talk about "helping all people to cross the stream of birth and death."

The only thing that makes Buddhists look rather idle or backward in so-called "social service" work is the fact that Eastern people, among whom Buddhism flourishes, are not very good at organization; they are just as charitably disposed as any religious people and ready to put their teachings into practice. But they are not accustomed to carry on their philanthropic undertakings in a systematic way; rather, they have been encouraged to go on with their work quietly, privately, individually, and without letting others know what they are doing. When we read the history of Buddhism in regard to this phase of its activities, we notice how Buddhists labored for the welfare and edification of the masses.

The saddest thing is that most of us are ignorant, benighted, and utterly egocentric in spite of all the churches, temples, synagogues, mosques, and other institutions of education secular and spiritual. This is what makes the enlightened ones feel sometimes despondent and cheerless, traces of which we can detect in all our saintly figures. Dr. Ames writes: "In utter poverty and desperate circumstances insensibility may be the best, but to think it is the best that human life can offer is a sad delusion."[9] He is quite right. As long as man is what he is, he cannot remain insensible to any happenings that may take place in his surroundings. His nerves are racked to the utmost when he observes all the human pains, tortures, and miseries unspeakable after an atomic bomb bursts in the midst of a thickly populated city. And the worst thing is that one is utterly helpless in the face of these sufferings. The only remedy one can have, if it is granted, is the gospel of insensibility! How inhuman! But when I reflect that all such things are desperately beyond our individual control, although I am inclined to think that all our group activities are the accumulations of individual thought and action, I cannot help being in deep sympathy with the Biblical writer who makes God soliloquize in this wise:

And God saw that the wickedness of man was great in the earth, and that every imagination of the thoughts of his heart was only evil continually. And it repented the Lord that he had made man on the earth, and it grieved him at his heart. And the Lord said, I will destroy man whom I have created from the face of the earth; both man, and beast, and the creeping things, and the fowls of the air; for it repenteth me that I have made them.[10]

Is God now in earnest engaged in the gigantic task of effacing man from the earth? Apparently he is. If so, inasmuch as man is man, he must have a philosophy to cope with the situation. Can Zen offer this?

[9] *Op. cit.*, p. 39.
[10] *Genesis* 6:5–7.

VII. ZEN AND JAPANESE CULTURE

CHAPTER 10

Painting, Swordsmanship, Tea Ceremony

I. PAINTING

Zen came to Japan in the twelfth century and during the eight hundred years of its history it has influenced Japanese life in various ways, not only in the spiritual life of the Samurai but in the artistic expressions of it by the learned and cultured classes. The Sumiye, which is one of such expressions, is not painting in the proper sense of the word; it is a kind of sketch in black and white. The ink is made of soot and glue, and the brush of sheep's or badger's hair, and the latter is so made as to absorb or contain much of the fluid. The paper used is rather thin and will absorb much ink, standing in great contrast to the canvas used by oil-painters, and this contrast means a great deal to the Sumiye artist.

The reason why such a frail material has been chosen for the vehicle of transferring an artistic inspiration is that the inspiration is to be transferred on to it in the quickest possible time. If the brush lingers too long, the paper will be torn through. The lines are to be drawn as swiftly as possible and the fewest in number, only the absolutely necessary ones being indicated. No deliberation is allowed, no erasing, no repetition, no retouching, no remodelling, no "doctoring", no building-up. Once executed, the strokes are indelible, irrevocable, not subject to future corrections or improvements. Anything done afterwards is plainly and painfully visible in the result, as the paper is of such a nature. The artist must follow his inspiration as spontaneously and absolutely and instantly as it moves; he just lets his arm, his fingers, his brush be guided by it as if they were all mere instruments, together with his whole being, in the hands of somebody else who has temporarily taken possession of him. Or we may say that the brush by itself executes the work quite outside the artist, who just lets it move on without his conscious efforts. If any logic or reflection comes between brush and paper, the whole effect is spoiled. In this way Sumiye is produced.

It is easily conceivable that the lines of Sumiye must show an infinite variety. There is no chiaroscuro, no perspective in it. Indeed, they are not needed in Sumiye, which makes no pretentions to realism. It attempts to make the spirit of an object move on the paper. Thus each brush-stroke must beat with the pulsation of a living being. It must be living too. Evidently, Sumiye is governed by a set of principles quite different from those of an oil-painting. The canvas being of such strong material and oil colours permitting repeated wipings and overlayings, a picture is built up systematically after a deliberately designed plan. Grandeur of conception and strength of execution, to say nothing of its realism, are the characteristics of an oil-painting, which can be compared to a well-thought-out system of philosophy, each thread of whose logic is closely knitted; or it may be likened unto a grand cathedral, whose walls, pillars, and foundations are composed of solid blocks of stone. Compared with this, a Sumiye sketch is poverty itself, poor in form, poor in contents, poor in execution, poor in material, yet we Oriental people feel the presence in it of a certain moving spirit that mysteriously hovers around the lines, dots, and shades of various formations; the rhythm of its living breath vibrates in them. A single stem of a blooming lily apparently so carelessly executed on a piece of coarse paper—yet here is vividly revealed the tender innocent spirit of a maiden sheltered from the storm of a worldly life. Again, as far as a superficial critic can see, there is not much of artistic skill and inspiration—a little insignificant boat of a fisherman at the centre of a broad expanse of waters; but as we look we cannot help being deeply impressed with the immensity of the ocean which knows no boundaries, and with the presence of a mysterious spirit breathing a life of eternity undisturbed in the midst of the undulating waves. And all these wonders are achieved with such ease and effortlessness.

If Sumiye attempts to copy an objective reality it is an utter failure; it never does that, it is rather a creation. A dot in a Sumiye sketch does not represent a hawk, nor does a curved line symbolize Mount Fuji. The dot is the bird and the line is the mountain. If resemblance is everything with a picture, the two dimensional canvas cannot represent anything of objectivity; the colours fall far too short of giving the original, and however faithfully a painter may try with his brushes to remind us of an object of nature as it is, the result can never do justice to it; for as far as it is an imitation, or a representation, it is a poor imitation, it is a mockery. The Sumiye artist thus reasons: why not altogether abandon such an attempt? Let us instead create living objects out of our own imagination. As long as we all belong to the same universe, our creations may show some correspondence to what we call objects of nature. But this is not an essential element of our work. The work has its own merit apart from resemblance. In each brush-stroke is there not something distinctly individual? The spirit of each artist is moving there. His birds are his own creation. This is the attitude of a Sumiye painter towards his art, and I wish to state that this attitude is that of Zen towards life, and that what Zen attempts with his life the artist does with his paper, brush, and ink. The creative spirit moves everywhere, and there is a work of creation whether in life or in art.

A line drawn by the Sumiye artist is final, nothing can go beyond it, nothing can retrieve it; it is just inevitable as a flash of lightning; the artist himself cannot undo it; from this issues the beauty of the line. Things are beautiful where they are inevitable, that is, when they are free exhibitions of a spirit. There is no violence here, no murdering, no twisting-about, no copying-after, but a free, unrestrained, yet self-governing display of movement—which constitutes the principle of beauty. The muscles are conscious of drawing a line, making a dot, but behind them there is an unconsciousness. By this unconsciousness nature writes out her destiny: by this unconsciousness the artist creates his work of art. A baby smiles and the whole crowd is transported, because it is genuinely inevitable, coming out of the Unconscious. The "Wu-hsin" and "Wu-nien"[1] of which the Zen master makes so much, as we have already seen elsewhere, is also eminently the spirit of the Sumiye artist.

Another feature that distinguishes Sumiye is its attempt to catch spirit as it moves. Everything becomes, nothing is stationary in nature; when you think you have safely taken hold of it, it slips off your hands. Because the moment you have it is no more alive; it is dead. But Sumiye tries to catch things alive, which seems to be something impossible to achieve. Yes, it would indeed be an impossibility if the artist's endeavour were to represent living things on paper, but he can succeed to a certain extent when every brush-stroke he makes is directly connected with his inner spirit, unhampered by extraneous matters such as concepts, etc. In this case, his brush is his own arm extended; more than that, it is his spirit, and in its every movement as it is traced on paper this spirit is felt. When this is accomplished, a Sumiye picture is a reality itself, complete in itself, and no copy of anything else. The mountains here are real in the same sense as Mount Fuji is real; so are the clouds, the stream, the trees, the waves, the figures. For the spirit of the artist is articulating through all these masses, lines, dots, and "daubs".

It is thus natural that Sumiye avoids colouring of any kind, for it reminds us of an object of nature, and Sumiye makes no claim to be a reproduction, perfect or imperfect. In this respect Sumiye is like calligraphy. In calligraphy each character, composed of strokes horizontal, vertical, slanting, flowing, turning upward and downward, does not necessarily indicate any definite idea, though it does not altogether ignore it, for a character is primarily supposed to mean something. But as an art peculiar to the Far East where a long, pointed, soft hair-brush is used for writing, each stroke made with it has a meaning apart from its functioning as a composite element of a character symbolizing an idea. The brush is a yielding instrument and obeys readily every conative movement of the writer

[1] *Mu-shin* and *mu-nen* in Japanese. See p. 17 et seq. of the present book.

or the artist. In the strokes executed by him we can discern his spirit. This is the reason why Sumiye and calligraphy are regarded in the East as belonging to the same class of art.

The development of the soft-haired brush is a study in itself. No doubt it had a great deal to do with the accidents of the Chinese character and writing. It was a fortunate event that such a soft, yielding, pliable instrument was put into the hand of the artist. The lines and strokes produced by it have something of the freshness, tenderness, and gracefulness which are perceivable in animated objects of nature, especially in the human body. If the instrument used were a piece of steel, rigid and unyielding, the result would be quite contrary, and no Sumiye of Liang-kai, Mu-ch'i, and other masters would have come down to us.

That the paper is of such a fragile nature as not to allow the brush to linger too long over it is also of great advantage for the artist to express himself with it. If the paper were too strong and tough, deliberate designing and correction would be possible, which is, however, quite injurious to the spirit of Sumiye. The brush must run over the paper swiftly, boldly, fully, and irrevocably just like the work of creation when the universe came into being. As soon as a word comes from the mouth of the creator, it must be executed. Delay may mean alteration, which is frustration; or the will has been checked in its forward movement; it halts, it hesitates, it reflects, it reasons, and finally it changes its course—this faltering and wavering interferes with the freedom of the artistic mind.

While artificiality does not mean regularity or a symmetrical treatment of the subject, and freedom mean irregularity, there is always an element of unexpectedness or abruptness in Sumiye. Where one expects to see a line or a mass this is lacking, and this vacancy instead of disappointing suggests something beyond and is altogether satisfactory. A small piece of paper, generally oblong, less than two feet and a half by six feet, will now include the whole universe. The horizontal stroke suggests immensity of space and a circle eternity of time —not only their mere unlimitedness but filled with life and movement. It is strange that the absence of a single point where it is conventionally expected should achieve this mystery, but the Sumiye artist is a past master in this trick. He does it so skilfully that no artificiality or explicit purpose is at all discernible in his work. This life of purposelessness comes directly from Zen.

II. LITERATURE: THE HAIKU

Having seen something of the connection Sumiye has with Zen, let me proceed to make my remarks on the spirit of "Eternal Loneliness". So far we can say, Zen's influence in Far Eastern painting has been general, as it is not limited to the Japanese, and what I have described may apply equally to the Chinese. What follows, however, can be regarded as specifically Japanese, for this spirit of "Eternal Loneliness" is something known pre-eminently in Japan. By this spirit, or this artistic principle, if it can be so designated, I mean what is popularly known in Japan as "Sabi" or "Wabi" (or "Shibumi"). Let me say a few words about it now, using the term "Sabi" for the concept of this group of feelings.

"Sabi" appears in landscape gardening and the tea-ceremony as well as in literature. I shall confine myself to literature, especially to that form of literature known as "Haiku", that is, the seventeen syllable poem. This shortest possible form of poetical expression is a special product of the Japanese genius. This made a great development in the Tokugawa era, more particularly after Basho (1643–1694).

He was a great travelling poet, a most passionate lover of nature—a kind of nature troubadour. His life was spent in travelling from one end of Japan to another. It was fortunate that there were in those days no railways. Modern conveniences do not seem to go very well with poetry. The modern spirit of scientific analysis leaves no mystery unravelled, and poetry and Haiku do not seem to thrive where there are no mysteries. The trouble with science is that it leaves no room for suggestion, everything is laid bare, and anything there is to be seen is exposed. Where science rules the imagination beats a retreat.

We are all made to face so-called hard facts whereby our minds are ossified; where there is no softness left with us, poetry departs; where there is a vast expanse of sand no verdant vegetation is made possible. In Basho's day, life was not yet so prosaic and hard-pressed. One bamboo hat, one cane stick, and one cotton bag were perhaps enough for the poet to wander about with, stopping for a while in any hamlet which struck his fancy and enjoying all the experiences, which were mostly the hardships of primitive travelling. When travelling is made too easy and comfortable, its spiritual meaning is lost. This may be called sentimentalism, but a certain sense of loneliness engendered by travelling leads one to reflect upon the meaning of life, for life is after all a travelling from one unknown to another unknown. In the period of sixty, seventy, or eighty years allotted to us we are meant to uncover if we can the veil of mystery. A too smooth running over this period, however short it may be, robs us of this sense of Eternal Loneliness.

The predecessor of Basho was Saigyo of the Kamakura period (1186–1334). He was also a traveller-monk. After quitting his official cares as a warrior attached to the court his life was devoted to travelling and poetry. He was a Buddhist monk. You must have seen the picture somewhere in your trip through Japan of a monk in his travelling suit, all alone, looking at Mount Fuji. I forget who the painter was, but the picture suggests many thoughts, especially in the mysterious loneliness of human life, which is, however, not the feeling of forlornness, nor the depressive sense of solitariness, but a sort of appreciation of the mystery of the absolute. The poem composed by Saigyo on that occasion runs:

> The wind-blown
> Smoke of Mt. Fuji
> Disappearing far beyond!
> Who knows the destiny
> Of my thought wandering away with it?

Basho was not a Buddhist monk but was a devotee of Zen. In the beginning of autumn, when it begins to rain occasionally, nature is the embodiment of Eternal Loneliness. The trees become bare, the mountains begin to assume an austere appearance, the streams are more transparent, and in the evening when the birds, weary of the day's work, wend their homeward way, a lone traveller grows pensive over the destiny of human life. His mood moves with that of nature. Sings Basho:

> "A traveller—
> Let my name be thus known—
> This autumnal shower."

We are not necessarily all ascetics, but I do not know if there is not in every one of us an eternal longing for a world beyond this of empirical relativity, where the soul can quietly contemplate its own destiny.

When Basho was still studying Zen under his master Buccho, the latter one day paid him a visit and asked, "How are you getting along these days?"

Basho: "After a recent rain the moss has grown greener than ever."

Buccho: "What Buddhism is there prior to the greenness of moss?"

Basho: "A frog jumps into the water, hear the sound!"

This is said to be the beginning of a new epoch in the history of Haiku. Haiku before Basho was a mere word-play, and lost its contact with life. Basho, questioned by his master about the ultimate truth of things which existed even prior to this world of particulars, saw a frog leaping into an old pond, its sound making a break into the serenity of the whole situation. The source of life has been grasped, and the artist sitting here watches every mood of his mind as it comes in contact with a world of constant becoming, and the result is so many seventeen syllables bequeathed to us. Basho was a poet of Eternal Loneliness.

Another of his Haiku is:

> A branch shorn of leaves,
> A crow perching on it—
> This autumn eve.

Simplicity of form does not always mean triviality of content. There is a great Beyond in the lonely raven perching on the dead branch of a tree. All things come out of an unknown abyss of mystery, and through every one of them we can have a peep into the abyss. You do not have to compose a grand poem of many hundred lines to give vent to the feeling thus awakened by looking into the abyss. When a feeling reaches its highest pitch we remain silent, because no words are adequate. Even seventeen syllables may be too many. In any event Japanese artists more or less influenced by the way of Zen tend to use the fewest words or strokes of brush to express their feelings. When they are too fully expressed, no room for suggestion is possible, and suggestibility is the secret of the Japanese arts.

Some artists go even so far as this, that whatever way their strokes of the brush are taken by the viewer is immaterial; in fact the more they are misunderstood the better. The strokes or masses may mean any object of nature; they may be birds, or hills, or human figures, or flowers, or what not; it is perfectly indifferent to them, they declare. This is an extreme view indeed. For if their lines, masses, and dots are judged differently by different minds, sometimes altogether unlike what they were originally intended for by the artist, what is the use at all of attempting such a picture? Perhaps the artist here wanted to add this: "If only the spirit pervading his product were perfectly perceived and appreciated." From this it is evident that the Far Eastern artists are perfectly indifferent to form. They want to indicate by their brush-work something that has strongly moved them innerly. They themselves may not have known how to give expression to their inner movement. They only utter a cry or flourish the brush. This may not be art, because there is no art in their doing this. Or if there is any art, that may be a very primitive one. Is this really so? However advanced we may be in "civilization", which means artificiality, we always strive for artlessness; for it seems to be the goal and foundation of all artistic endeavours. How much art is concealed behind the apparent artlessness of Japanese art! Full of meaning and suggestibility, and yet perfect in artlessness—when in this way the spirit of eternal loneliness is expressed, we have the essence of Sumiye and Haiku.

III. FENCING

That the Zen form of Buddhism has influenced Japanese life, especially in its aesthetic aspect, to such an extent as has never been attained by the other forms, is due to the fact that Zen directly appeals to the facts of life instead of to concepts. The intellect is always indirect in its relation to life, it is a generalizing agency, and what is general lacks in instinctive force, that is, in will-power. Zen is not solely the will, it contains a certain amount of intellection too, inasmuch as it is an intuition. Standing in contrast to the conceptualizing tendency of the other schools of Buddhism, Zen's appeal to life is always more fundamental. This is the chief reason why Zen takes hold so strongly of Japanese life.

The art of fencing, to master which was one of the most absorbing occupations of the governing classes of Japan since the Kamakura era, achieved a wonderful development, and many different schools of it have been prospering until quite recently. The Kamakura era is closely related to Zen, for it was then that as an independent school of Buddhism Zen was first introduced to Japan. Many great masters of Zen ruled the spiritual world of the time, and in spite of their contempt of learning, learning was preserved in their hands. At the same time the soldiers thronged about them, eager to be taught and disciplined by them. The method of their teaching was simple and direct; not much learning in the abstruse philosophy of Buddhism was needed. The soldiers were naturally not very scholarly; what they wanted was to be not timid before death, which they had constantly to face. This was a most practical problem on their part, and Zen was ready to grapple with it, probably because the masters dealt with the facts of life, and not with concepts. They would probably say to a soldier who came to be enlightened on the question of birth and death that "There is no birth and death here; get out of my room as quick as you can." So saying they would chase him away with a stick they generally carried. Or if a soldier came to a master saying, "I have to go through at present with the most critical event of life; what shall I do?" the master would roar, "Go straight ahead, and no looking backward!" This was how in feudal Japan the soldiers were trained by Zen masters.

Since the soldiers were constantly threatened as regards their lives, and since their swords were the only weapons that turned their fate either way to life or to death, the art of fencing developed to a wonderful degree of perfection. It is not strange, then, that Zen had much to do with this profession. Takuan (1573–1645), one of the greatest figures in the Zen world of the Tokugawa period, gave full instruction in Zen to his disciple, Yagiu Tajima-no-kami (died 1646), who was fencing teacher to the Shogun of the day. The instructions are not of course concerned with the technique of the art itself, but with the mental attitude of the fencer. To follow them intelligently must have cost a great deal of spiritual training on the part of his illustrious disciple. Another great fencing master of the Tokugawa period was Miyamoto Musashi (1582–1645), who was the founder of the school called Nitoryu. He was not only a fencer but a Sumiye artist, and as such he was equally great. His pictures are very highly valued and have "Zen flavour", so to speak. One of his famous sayings on fencing is:

> Under the sword lifted high
> There is hell making you tremble;
> But go ahead,
> And you have the land of bliss.

Not mere recklessness, but self-abandonment, which is known in Buddhism as a state of egolessness. Here is the religious significance of the art of fencing. This was the way that Zen got deeply into the life of the Japanese people—their life in its various aspects, moral, practical, aesthetic, and, to a certain extent, intellectual.

As was stated somewhere else, it may be better to regard the Buddhist teaching of Non-ego as the practical method of expounding the philosophy of the Unconscious. The Unconscious evolves silently through our empirical individual consciousnesses, and as it thus works the latter takes it for an ego-soul free, unconditioned, and permanent. But when this concept takes hold of our consciousness, the really free activities of the Unconscious meet obstructions on all sides. Emotionally, this is the source of torments, and life becomes impossible. To restore peace in the most practical manner, Buddhism now teaches us to abandon the thought of an ego-soul, to be free from this clinging, to dry up this main spring of constant annoyance; for it is thus that the Unconscious regains its original creativity. Great things so called seem to be achieved always by our direct appeal to the Unconscious. Not only great spiritual events but great moral, social, and practical affairs are the results of the immediate working of the Unconscious. Egolessness is meant to direct our attention to this fact.

To the Japanese mind, "Muga" and "Mushin"[2] signify the same thing. When one attains the state of "Muga", the state of "Mushin", the Unconscious, is realized. "Muga" is something identified with a state of ecstasy in which there is no sense of "I am doing it". The feeling of "self" is a great hindrance to the execution of a work. Although absence of self-consciousness does not guarantee the greatness of an achievement, to be conscious of it, especially in the sense of self-pride or self-conceit, at once depreciates from the spiritual point of view the value of the accomplishment. Not only that, the accomplishment itself is doubted as to its final success. There is always a taint of self attached to it. We instinctively turn away from it as not directly coming from the Unconscious. Anything from the latter seems to go beyond moral judgments; it has a peculiar charm of its own as being a first work of the Unconscious. That we can feel this charm bears testimony to the Unconscious. The aim of all the artistic discipline in Japan gathers around the self-appreciation of it, which is at once its own realization. "Muga" or "Mushin" or effortlessness is thus the consummation of art.

[2] In Chinese, *wu-wo* (non-ego) and *wu-hsin* (no-mind); in Sanskrit, *anatmya* and *acitta*. See p. 281–82, and p. 17 of the present work.

This is the gist of Takuan's Zen instruction given to Yagiu Tajima-no-kami on fencing:

"What is most important in the art of fencing is to acquire a certain mental attitude known as 'immovable wisdom'. This wisdom is intuitively acquired after a great deal of practical training. 'Immovable' does not mean to be stiff and heavy and lifeless as a rock or a piece of wood. It means the highest degree of motility with a centre which remains immovable. The mind then reaches the highest point of alacrity ready to direct its attention anywhere it is needed—to the left, to the right, to all the directions as required. When your attention is engaged and arrested by the striking sword of the enemy, you lose the first opportunity of making the next move by yourself. You tarry, you think, and while this deliberation goes on, your opponent is ready to strike you down. The thing is not to give him such a chance. You must follow the movement of the sword in the hands of the enemy, leaving your mind free to make its own counter-movement without your interfering deliberation. You move as the opponent moves, and it will result in his own defeat.

"This—what may be termed the 'non-interfering' attitude of mind—constitutes the most vital element in the art of fencing as well as in Zen. If there is any room left even for the breadth of a hair between two actions, this is interruption. When the hands are clapped, the sound issues without a moment's deliberation. The sound does not wait and think before it issues. There is no mediacy here, one movement follows another without being interrupted by one's conscious mind. If you are troubled and cogitate what to do, seeing the opponent about to strike you down, you give him room, that is, a happy chance for his deadly blow. Let your defence follow the attack without a moment's interruption, and there will be no two separate movements to be known as attack and defence. This immediateness of action on your part will inevitably end in the opponent's self-defeat. It is like a boat smoothly gliding down the rapids; in Zen, and in fencing as well, a mind of no-hesitation, no-interruption, no-mediacy, is highly valued.

"So much reference is made in Zen to a flash of lightning

or to sparks issuing from the impact of two flint-stones. If this is understood in the sense of quickness, a grievous mistake is committed. The idea is to show immediateness of action, an uninterrupted movement of life-energy. Whenever room is left for interruption from a quarter not in vital relation with the occasion, you are sure to lose your own position. This of course does not mean to desire to do things rashly or in the quickest possible time. If there were this desire in you its very presence would be an interruption. When it is asked, 'What is the ultimate reality of Buddhism?' the master answers without a moment's delay, 'A branch of plum-blossom', or 'The cypress tree in the courtyard'. There is something immovable within, which, however, moves along spontaneously with things presenting themselves before it. The mirror of wisdom reflects them instantaneously one after another, keeping itself intact and undisturbed. The fencer must cultivate this."

A life of non-interruption here described as necessary to the mastery of fencing is the life of effortlessness (*anabhogacarya*) or of desirelessness (*apranihita*), which is the essence of Bodhisattvahood. Artistically, this is the art of artlessness. The Confucians would say: "What does heaven say? What does the earth say? But the seasons come and go and all things grow." The followers of Lao-tsu would paradoxically declare, "Benevolence and righteousness are products of human artificiality when the highest truth no more prevails in its own way." Or, "It is the principle of non-action that makes all things move." Or, "Just because the axle moves not, the spokes revolve." All these remarks tend to show that the centre of life-gravity remains immovable, and that when this has successfully taken hold of all the life activities, whether artistic or poetic or religious or dramatic, whether in a life of quietude and learning or in one of intense action, a state of self-realization obtains, which expresses itself in a most exquisite manner in the life and acts of the person.

IV. TEA CEREMONY

To conclude: the spirit of Eternal Loneliness (*vivikta-dharma*) which is the spirit of Zen expresses itself under the name of "Sabi" in the various artistic departments of life such as landscape gardening, the tea-ceremony, painting, flower arrangement, dressing, furniture, in the mode of living, in no-dancing, poetry, etc. The spirit comprises such elements as simplicity, naturalness, unconventionality, refinement, freedom, familiarity singularly tinged with aloofness, and everyday commonness which is veiled exquisitely with the mist of transcendental inwardness.

For illustration, let me describe a tea-room in one of the temples attached to Daitokuji, the Zen temple which is the headquarters of the tea-ceremony. Where a series of flagstones irregularly arranged comes to a stop, there stands a most insignificant-looking straw-thatched hut, low and unpretentious to the last degree. The entrance is not by a door but a sort of aperture; to enter through it a visitor has to be shorn of all his encumbrances, that is to say, to take off both his swords, long and short, which in the feudal days a samurai used to carry all the time. The inside is a small semi-lighted room about ten feet square; the ceiling is low and of uneven height and structure. The posts are not smoothly planed, they are mostly of natural wood. After a little while, however, the room grows gradually lighter as our eyes begin to adjust themselves to the new situation. We notice an ancient-looking kakemono in the alcove with some handwriting or a picture of Sumiye type. An incense-burner emits a fragrance which has the effect of soothing one's nerves. The flower-vase contains no more than a single stem of flowers, neither gorgeous nor ostentatious; but like a little white lily blooming under a rock surrounded by in no way sombre pines, the humble flower is enhanced in beauty and attracts the attention of the gathering of four or five visitors especially invited to sip a cup of tea in order to forget the worldly cares that may be oppressing them.

Now we listen to the sound of boiling water in the kettle

as it rests on a tripod frame over a fire in the square hole cut in the floor. The sound is not that of actually boiling water but comes from the heavy iron kettle, and it is most appropriately likened by the connoisseur to a breeze that passes through the pine grove. It greatly adds to the serenity of the room, for a man here feels as if he were sitting alone in a mountain-hut where a white cloud and the pine music are his only consoling companions.

To take a cup of tea with friends in this environment, talking probably about the Sumiye sketch in the alcove or some art topic suggested by the tea-utensils in the room, wonderfully lifts the mind above the perplexities of life. The warrior is saved from his daily occupation of fighting, and the businessman from his ever-present idea of money-making. Is it not something, indeed, to find in this world of struggles and vanities a corner, however humble, where one can rise above the limits of relativity and even have a glimpse of eternity?